Daring to DREAM

Love & Peace
Diane '06

Beyond
Blacklight

Daring to DREAM

DIANE DUPUY

**Beyond
Blacklight**

Canadian Cataloguing in Publication Data

Dupuy, Diane
Daring to Dream

ISBN 0-9730736-1-6

1. Famous PEOPLE Players
2. Puppets
3. Black-light theatre
4. Liberace
I. Dupuy, Diane II. Title

Editor: Fina Scroppo
Art Director: Judith Hancock, Saatchi & Saatchi
Illustrations: Ed Stockelbach
Proofreading: Suzanne Moutis
Electronic Page Layout & Print Production:
    Beth Crane, Heidy Lawrance Associates

All inquiries should be addressed to:
Beyond Blacklight Inc.
33 Lisgar St.
Toronto, ON M6J 3T3
416-532-1137; fax 416-532-6945
Toll-free: 1-888-453-3385
website: www.fpp.org
E-mail: famouspeopleplayers@bellnet.ca

Printed in Canada by Transcontinental

TABLE OF CONTENTS

This book is dedicated to my mother,
Mary Christine Thornton,
and my father, Robert Stanley Thornton,
who encouraged me to let my dreams take flight.

ACKNOWLEDGEMENTS

This book was beautifully edited by Fina Scroppo,
who, as always, gives her time and talent
with passion and perfection. Despite being
a devoted new mother to her son, Daniel, she is able
to find the time to leave no stone unturned
in helping me make my deadlines
to complete this book.

The illustrations throughout the book were done
by my wonderfully nutty and crazy friend
Edward Stockelbach, whom I have known since
we were 18, when we both shared our dreams
together with laughter and excitement.

The Die is Cast

Did you know that when you were born, an angel
flew through the window carrying your special dream,
locked it in your heart and flew away?
Now it's up to you to unlock your dream, discover
it and dedicate the rest of your life to developing it.

Dreams do come true when you believe in yourself.
This is the story of how I unlocked my dream.

I felt old, tired and worn to a frazzle. I sat down at the dressing room table and looked in the mirror. I was shocked to see my mother's face staring back at me. I've changed. I've gotten older and I don't know how that happened.

October 26, 1986. I could hear the rain pounding hard above me on the roof of Broadway's famous Lyceum Theater. When is that rain going to stop?

I looked up at the cracks in the ceiling. Whoopi Goldberg must have noticed them too. I wondered if she had been nervous, sitting in this same chair, applying her make-up, on opening night.

Okay, Dupuy, you're looking better, but SMILE. I imagined the interviews that lay ahead of me.

"It's a pleasure meeting you, Mrs. Dupuy. Is that spelled D-U-P-U-I-S?"

"No, it's D-U-P-U-Y."

"I'm curious—how did you get here?"

"I flew Air Canada."

"No, no! I mean to Broadway."

I looked into the mirror again and saw a petrified face staring back at me. I was waiting for her answer. I was suddenly taken by surprise when a hand clapped in front of my face. The imaginary interviewer disappeared.

"Hey, Dupuy." It was Renato, one of my dearest performers. He was wearing the black velvet jumpsuit that would disguise him on stage as he waved his props. "The glue, I'm looking for the glue." He sounded panicky. "My fish needs to be glued; the tail is coming off."

"It's in wardrobe, in the basement, three flights down. Here," I said, getting up, "I'll help you find your way."

We walked out to the top of the stairs; the sound of the rainstorm outside followed us. Renato was so excited he was skipping. "We're gonna be GREAT!" he said.

"I hope so," I said faintly.

"What do you mean you *hope* so? You're not losing faith in us after all we've been through?" He stopped and faced me, stretching out his strong leg in front so I couldn't get past him.

"No." I forced my way around him. "I'm just...well I'm..." I was trying to find the right words to give myself confidence. "I'm just nervous, that's all."

The steps led to the main floor of the theatre, and I stopped to watch the performers rushing around the stage, checking and rechecking their props. "I need the glue," Renato said anxiously.

"I'm hurrying." I started to move toward the steps to take the next flight down. A crash of thunder boomed through the walls.

"There it is," I said. A can of glue sat on an old table. Water from the pipes in the ceiling dripped slowly onto the brush next to the bottle of glue. Renato grabbed the brush, dipped it into the can of glue, and meticulously brushed it over the torn part of the fish tail. Then he blew over it to dry it before sticking the pieces together. He waved the brightly painted foam goldfish, making it swim in the air like it would on stage.

"Perfect." He smiled.

You're right, I thought to myself. We had to take Broadway by storm to lift up the barrier and let ourselves through. All these years, we had felt caged in because of who we are. I worried that the show could flop. Those tough New York critics could say: "You gotta be kidding! Puppets under black light on Broadway! What was the director thinking?"

I looked around. Renato had disappeared. I started to climb back up the stairs, assuming he went to pre-set his props on backstage. All of a sudden, an imaginary critic stood before me with microphone in hand.

"So, Mrs. Dupuy, just who do you think you are, bringing a group of retarded people to perform on the most historic stage on Broadway? How could you do such a thing?"

"HOW DARE YOU!" I screamed in my head. *"That's why, that's exactly why I did it—to change the attitudes of people like you. We're tired of being reminded of what we*

can or cannot do because of an unfair label. We're good, real good, and we'll show you! If we can make it here, we can make it anywhere!" I pushed my arm past my imaginary critic and dismissed him. He disappeared from my mind.

It was these exact comments that we were always dodging. That's exactly why nowhere in the playbill was there a single word that suggested who we were. It was our secret. We were sneaking up on the enemy, disguising ourselves with the black light that hides us. We would mesmerize the audience with our illusions. Our confidence was getting stronger.

I walked into the large dressing room, and started gathering the performers together to go over some last-minute notes. Suddenly the imaginary critic appeared before me again.

"You can't just tell me you're good," he sneered. *"I'll decide who's good, because I'm the critic."*

"That's the unfairness of it!" I yelled in my mind. *"If we win, it's because we're good. If we fail, then you'll say it's because we're retarded."*

He laughed. *"You did this to yourself, remember?"*

"If Famous PEOPLE Players wins, then I win too."

"But if it fails. I will say you used those people to satisfy your own selfish ambition."

Oh my God, would the players hate me? I couldn't handle that. I love them so much.

"Hi there, Dearie."

It was Greg, who was getting ready for his performance. His tiny body was dressed in the black velvet jumpsuit. He looked like a mischievous little elf. He grabbed my hand and pulled me toward the director's chair that was waiting in front of the cast. I looked back to see if that critic of mine was still there, but the enemy had faded away.

The performers all stood in front of me, in their black jumpsuits, with their hoods dangling behind their backs. My Magicateers—that's what they were.

"Tonight, we're going to make magic. The magic of the human spirit—that's what's going to take on Broadway. The human spirit," I told them.

"We're gonna be great, Diane!" shouted Darlene.

"Sure, Dearie. The Mets will take it at Shea Stadium and the Famous PEOPLE Players will take it at the Lyceum Theater," said Greg.

"Now look here, Dupuy." Renato was waving his arms like an Italian maestro. "We're gonna do it! We've *gotta* do it!"

They left me speechless. Their passion filled the room.

"No kiddin'," said Greg, as everyone walked out of the dressing room and into the future—the future that would lift the barrier that would accept us as professionals for good.

Please, dear God, I prayed, *take care of them. Guide them with your spirit. Lift them up high—so high the world can see them.*

"Remember what I told you?" I turned to see Sam Ellis, our New York production supervisor, standing behind me. "If it's raining, you're gonna have a hit."

We stood there, staring out the dressing room window, watching the rain come down in buckets. Lightning flashed across the sky.

"They're all on stage now," said Sam.

I turned to follow him out of the dressing room. "I'd better give them one last hug," I said. I turned and raced back to the stage, with just minutes before the curtain rose. We huddled together, holding each other's hands— one on top of the other, crushed together. "Good show, good show, GOOD SHOW!" we chanted. The huddle broke apart, almost in slow motion, it seemed, and the performers took their positions on stage.

"Five minutes to curtain!"

I could hear them breathing under their hoods. I started to move toward the front of the house. As I passed Mickey Fox, the house property man, I thought how he'd seen it all—the hits, the flops. "Mickey, everybody keeps saying that it's going to go well. I'm so scared. What do you think is going to happen?"

Mickey looked at me as Sam's voice boomed over the microphone, "Two minutes to curtain!"

"I wish I could tell you, but I'm afraid I can't." He opened the door, so I could get to my seat.

"The die is cast, my dear, the die is cast."

CHAPTER ONE

Hi Ho Silver

His cane thumped across the hardwood floor as he went around and around, from the living room to the dining room to the kitchen to the front hall, then back to the living room. Thump, thump. I sat on the living room sofa, watching my *nonno* (grandfather in Italian). My *nonna* (grandmother) was in the kitchen making the *sugo* (sauce), for the polenta we were about to eat.

Opera music played loudly and, from time to time, Nonno would stop to listen. Tears would fill his eyes. He loved opera music.

My mother's parents, Guido and Zena Gioberti, came from Ascoli Piceno, a small town in the Italian region of Le Marche, famous for its olives, and its exquisite hand-painted ceramics and textiles. My nonno was a professional woodcarver, who could play just about any instrument. He would sometimes sit in his kitchen on Stirton Street, in Hamilton, Ontario, conducting an imaginary orchestra with his cane. The music on the radio filled the kitchen, along with the aroma of my nonna's spaghetti sauce. When Nonna wasn't cooking, she was sewing something—she was a gifted seamstress.

The Giobertis had immigrated to Canada when Guido was 19 and Zena was 15. Life wasn't easy as they struggled every day to make ends meet. Nonna's strong belief that dreams can come true helped them get through the days. She was labeled "DP" for Displaced Persons after immigrating to Canada, a term I constantly heard as a child.

Woodworking jobs were hard to find, so Guido drove a jitney—a cross between a taxi and a bus—to make some extra money. For a short ride of a few blocks passengers paid five cents, while a trip across town might cost a whole quarter, quite expensive at the time.

Eventually, after moving from one job to another, Guido and Zena ended up working together in a tailor shop. Except for the few years when my nonna was raising my mother and her sisters while running a private dress-making business from her house, Guido and Zena worked together all their lives.

Music was the passion that kept the fire burning in nonno and nonna's hearts. My nonno played all musical instruments except the violin, but the French horn was his favourite. He became an important member of the local Italian-Canadian band. Later he helped form what was to become the first Boy Scout band in Canada.

In their home, opera music was playing constantly. Whenever he could afford it, Nonno brought home a new record and played it over and over again. Once Nonno bought a record of a young baritone and was astounded at the singer's glorious voice. Who was this magnificent baritone? His name was not on the record label, but Nonno was determined to find out. He spent weeks searching and searching until he finally found the name of the mysterious singer, Leonard Warren.

Shortly afterward, when Leonard was about to make his debut at the Metropolitan Opera House in New York, he received a congratulatory telegram from my nonno: "This is just the beginning of a brilliant musical career," it read. Leonard was so moved that he wrote back, beginning a correspondence that lasted for years.

I was a little girl when we got word: "Leonard Warren's coming to visit!" He was touring with an opera company that was going to be premiering in Toronto, not far from Hamilton.

Everyone in the family bustled around, getting ready. My mother made homemade spaghetti, and it seemed that every piece of furniture in the house was draped with long strands of pasta. Broomsticks were positioned between chairs. As the strands came out of the pasta machine, my mother draped them over each of my arms. I had to walk carefully and hang them over the broomsticks. I would sneak a bite of the pasta.

"Don't," she'd warn. "They're not cooked, you'll get worms!"

How did she know? I thought.

"I have eyes in the back of my head, Diane," she said, and I believed her.

"Leonard Warren's coming and I have eyes in the back of my head," she would sing. Her fine soprano voice echoed throughout the house.

When Leonard Warren arrived, everyone sat around the dining room table eating Mom's homemade spaghetti and singing. After hearing my mother's voice, Warren insisted on arranging vocal lessons for her in New York with his singing coach.

My mother went on to sing with the Hamilton Opera Company in "La Bohème," with the great June Kowalchuk. June played Mimi, the lead, while my mother played the mischievous Musetta.

(Today, if you visit the Famous PEOPLE Players prop room, you'll often hear an aria from "Madame Butterfly," sung to the accompaniment of the air compressor while my mother is painting.)

Everyone on my mother's side of the family was strong and determined. Making pasta and music were as important as saying your prayers at night.

After prayers, Mom used to tell me the story of how she met Dad. She had taken her first job as a saleswoman in the drapery department of Robinson's department store in Hamilton. With her charm, she soon caught the eye of a young display artist. He fell in love with her from a distance as he watched her waiting on customers, and often left her little notes on the sales counter: "Good morning, Mary sunshine. An admirer, Stanley Thornton."

The two families couldn't have been more different. She came from a proud Italian Catholic family, and he was an English-Irish Protestant whose family often drank and sang to pass the time. They married in 1943 and I was born on September 8, 1948.

Our house on 42 Kingsway Drive was like a fairytale castle. It stood on the hill that rises above the city of

Hamilton. My mother's rock garden was beautiful, and flowering trees grew in the front and back yards.

My bedroom had a walk-in closet, where I often hid for fun and explored the imaginary world. I would scoot right to the back and hide behind the clothes. It was like a cave—the deeper you went, the further you'd be from the outside world. I scribbled different shapes and colours on the closet walls with my crayons. My mom had no idea about the art gallery that existed behind all the clothes.

Just before I started school, I visited my dad at his shop called Stanley Signs. I thought it was the neatest place in the world. As soon as you entered, you were surrounded by the smell and sight of a million paint colours. I loved to watch my dad work, the way he'd dip his brush carefully in the paint, then cautiously wipe it on his palette and lift his hand to start painting his creation. He was so talented. Others thought so too. Lots of people came to hang out in his shop, sitting on stools, watching my dad paint.

"Stanley Signs is the crossroads of life," Dad would say to me. "Sooner or later, everybody comes through here, right, Pumpkin?"

He'd give me a brush and paint and let me create my own pictures. He loved my splatters, and I was in heaven.

But I didn't feel like I was in heaven when he made me clean all the brushes and wipe the paint off the floor. He wouldn't let me leave until everything was clean. The man who laughed and joked with me would suddenly become serious and start to lose his temper when the job I had been assigned wasn't done to perfection. I didn't under-stand the hot-and-cold relationship we had.

Sometimes, when he disapproved of my table manners, he'd send me to sit in a dark basement for punishment. There'd be no warning when his mood would suddenly change, as if the Good Witch of the North, with her beautiful deep blue eyes, had become the Wicked Witch of the West with her ugly green face. One minute he was my very best friend, chasing me around the dining room table, and the next he'd say sternly, "Diane, go," as he opened the door, and I'd make my way down that flight of steps and retreat to the basement.

I wasn't scared of the dark basement. Instead I'd walk around the furnace, pretending to be a storybook character. I loved pretending—I would be Robin Hood or Cinderella or Sleeping Beauty. Sometimes I think I behaved 'badly' on purpose, so Dad would send me to the basement and I could let my imagination drift. At the bottom of those steps I discovered a world of my own—a world of magic and dreams, all in my imagination. Everything seemed to come to life before my eyes. It was my creative training ground.

When I was six, I remember the anticipation on the night before I started Grade 1. My mother was sitting at the sewing machine, putting the finishing touches on the new dress that I was going to wear on my first day.

"School is going to be great," she said, looking up at the kitchen clock. *Where's Dad?* I could hear her thoughts. *Why isn't he home?* I wondered.

School was far from great. In fact, it was awful. My teacher, a nun, slapped me across the face on my first day. I don't remember why, but I remember all the kids in the classroom staring at me. I wanted to cry, but I didn't. Instead

I reached for that strength I'd found when I was in my dark basement, pretending. *I'll be the Lone Ranger*, I thought. *The Lone Ranger doesn't cry.*

Each day presented another challenge. One day, the sister at the Sacred Heart School went around the classroom with a box of crayons and asked each one of us to choose one. I must have tried to take the whole box because she said, "One Diane, only one." I picked black. Then she handed out a piece of paper with circles on it and told us to colour it by following the lines.

Follow the line? What's that? I thought, and I scribbled and drew all over the page. That's what I was used to doing at my dad's shop and I knew that I was certain to impress the veil right off her head with my picture. Unfortunately, sister didn't share my approach to creativity. "I said follow the lines, Diane," she scolded.

At recess, the kids made fun of me. They'd often chant "She's got eyes as big as the world, she's got eyes as big as the world. Skinny, skinny. She's got eyes as big as the world. Retard, retard. She's got eyes as big as the world."

I was stunned. I wanted to cry, but I was too scared. So I ran to the church across the street to do my crying. I used a Kleenex to cover my head before entering, since I left my hat at home. Covering up was expected in those days.

I looked forward to the end of the day when school was over and I could go home. I felt ashamed. I walked up the hill to my house, opened the door, and flopped down on the couch. I curled up in the corner with my head buried between the pillows.

After awhile, Mom came over to me and asked, "What's the matter, Diane?" She hugged me as she knelt in front of the couch.

"Nothing."

"How was school?"

"It was fine, Mommy."

I was too ashamed to tell her what had happened... maybe she wouldn't love me anymore. I felt alone. I was different from the other children. First of all, I wore my hair in a "doorknob," as my mother called it—a big bun on top of my head. All the other girls wore their hair in pigtails down their backs. But I was a doorknob.

The other children used words like "freak," "retard," "bug eyes." They didn't know the effect those words had on me. To them, it was just a game, teasing anyone who was different, who didn't fit in with the rest of them. Being different wasn't good. If I chose a black crayon and didn't draw within the lines, then I was different. Everyone else drew within the lines with their pink, blue and red crayons.

It wasn't just the other kids who made me feel different. "Diane Thornton!" Sister bellowed. "There are three houses on the blackboard. I want you to put number one in this house, number two in this house, and number three in this house."

I took the chalk and put all three numbers in one house. Sister screamed, the kids laughed, and I thought to myself, *now why would I want to put numbers in a house in the first place?*

At the parent-teacher meetings, everyone's work was displayed on the blackboard, ornamented with gold stars, silver stars and rainbows. My work wasn't there. The sister brought out my arithmetic test to show my mom and dad. It was marked with black Xs all down the page. I had other academic problems too.

"What's wrong, Diane?" my parents asked me. "What's the matter? Please tell us what the problem is. We can't help you if you don't tell us what's wrong or what you don't understand."

All I could think of was why they didn't notice the two I got right. And why were those two check marks so much smaller than the Xs?

I was a failure and that was bad. But in the inner world I'd created, I could be anything I wanted to be! If I failed a test or the kids called me a retard, I could just shut them off and go into my imaginary world. Then I'd climb on my horse and I was Hi Ho Silver, away! I imagined going after bank robbers and saving the people of Hamilton from the bad guys. In my imaginary world, I was the hero.

I knew I was special—that there were times when I need to live inside my imagination. Thank God, so did my parents. Although they knew that my schoolwork was way below average, they also knew that my daydreams were a great gift and they encouraged me to explore them. "You're just like your dad," my mom would say, "a dreamer!"

In the shop, Dad created magic with his paints. I remember how he took his brush and dabbed it in the ugliest shades of green and brown on his palette, yet he took his brush and drew a beautiful picture of a tree. I knew then that I wanted to create pictures like him.

At Christmas, Mom gave me the greatest gift ever—a puppet theatre made from cardboard. Punch and Judy came to life in that theatre, and I began to write creative scripts to act out. Behind the curtain, the world of imagination began to seem real.

I could hear my mom and dad laughing at the silly things I said and the way my voice changed from one character to another. I didn't need any rehearsals to learn the parts because they were all part of me. And there were no limits on any character. I even took Elsie, a little cow, and made her dance with Sleeping Beauty.

My theatre helped me express my love for music too. My parents were amazed at my ability to select a musical number for each puppet. I was amazed at how good it felt to be unique in front of an audience. The more different I was, the more the audience loved me, yet at school, being different was taboo.

I put on shows in my backyard for the kids on the street. I'd organize plays using a bed sheet as the curtain and hang it from the clothesline. The puppet theatre came to life. I jumped out and became Sleeping Beauty. Nicky and Horst from down the street were all the other characters in the show. One of my puppets would sing the words of the Disney song, "When you wish upon a star, it makes no difference who you are."

Mom helped me a lot to encourage my creativity and help me better integrate into school. When she joined the parent-teacher association at school, she became the president and threw the greatest Halloween parties. It also helped that everyone thought Mom was a knockout and really cool, especially when she made unique costumes.

At one dance, Mom and Dad came dressed up as buttons and bows—he was covered in buttons and she in bows.

Eventually the kids stopped teasing me, but I still didn't make any friends at school. The only friends I had were the kids who lived on Kingsway Drive, Nicky and Horst.

But that changed the day Mom went to the hospital. I remember my Aunt Ann taking me to see her when I was six. I wasn't allowed inside, so I stood outside on the front lawn while Mom waved to me and blew me a kiss from the window of her room.

"You have a big surprise coming soon," said my aunt, and she was right. Mom brought home my baby brother, Robert. Back home, the family was very excited and we were back to making homemade spaghetti and hanging it on broomsticks. Dad was hugging Robert and Mom was fussing over him, but I wasn't jealous because I could feel he would be the best friend I never had.

When Robert could talk and was old enough to play, we became inseparable. We'd sit in the back of my closet to talk or make houses out of leaves in the backyard. Robert even helped me negotiate on someone else's behalf, actually on his behalf. One day when we went to Mass at St. Joseph's Chapel near our house (I loved going to church then, and still do), we sat in the front pew and I watched the altar boy assisting the priest, Father Beaudry. "Look, he gets to carry the big cross!" Robert observed.

"You can do that," I whispered to him. "Just look at him—who does he think he is? Showing off, ringing those bells?" Immediately after Mass, I convinced Robert to approach Father. "I'll do the talking, follow me."

We went back to the vestry, where the altar boy was polishing the chalice. What a great job, I thought. I wish I could be an altar boy so I could do that!

"Father, my name is Diane, and this is my brother, Robert Thornton. He would like to be an altar boy at St. Charles, where you also say Mass. Can you teach him?"

Father Beaudry smiled at us and patted Robert gently on the head.

"Robert, can you be here after school?"

"Yes I can, Father."

"Then you start tomorrow."

We were so thrilled that we both ran all the way home, up to the top of the hill, into the house and screamed for Mom to tell her the good news. Every day Robert went for training.

"I'm the altar boy on Sundays at St. Charles," he'd say to anyone who'd listen.

Everybody heard about it on Kingsway Drive. Horst was the first to be invited. Sunday came, and we got all dressed up. I wore my white gloves, hat and black patent shoes and, carried a purse. Mom looked stunning in her royal blue velvet suit that clung to her hourglass figure and topped off with her fancy hatpin and brooch. Then she bent down, spit on her fingers and slicked Robert's hair back, almost strangling him as she tightened the knot on his tie. Dad never went to church, but he came that Sunday just to view Robert's big debut.

I sat in the front pew—the proud sister. The out-of-tune organ started to play and we all stood up to watch Robert coming down the aisle, carrying the heavy crucifix. He looked petrified, and his tongue was sticking out to the side. It was my proudest moment. The Mass began and Robert moved across the sanctuary, following the priest from right to left. Then, as Father Beaudry knelt in prayer, Robert started to play with his fingernails.

Oh my goodness! He'll miss his cue, I thought. *I've got to get his attention.*

I tried to wave to him and coughed out loud, but nothing worked. He continued to play with his fingers. Then Father Beaudry noticed that the giant book on the altar hadn't been moved from the right to the left. Father, still bent over in prayer with his hands covering his face, tilted his head, lifted his fingers and said, "Pssst…pssst… pssst, Robert." Robert looked up and went to lift the huge book.

I watched in horror. *Oh my God, it's too heavy for him…Oh no! He's going to drop it…He's going to…* CRASH!

Unlike stage audiences, Father Beaudry was forgiving. Robert eventually overcame his stage fright and became a wonderful altar boy.

I found out that I was good at organizing other people. I remember the day in grade school when we were taking our first confession. All the kids were lined up waiting to face the priest inside the confession box. We all knew we were supposed to tell the priest what we had done wrong, but nobody knew what to say, so I got everyone organized. "You go in and tell Father Beaudry you stole seven pencils from Sister. You say you took her box of chalk." I pointed to each kid. "And you took all the paper in the classroom. As for me, I'll say I took the brushes from the blackboard."

By the time I got into the confession booth, Father Beaudry said, "Poor Sister, she has nothing left in the classroom to teach all you young children."

Just the same, I didn't have any close friends in school. I guess my mind always wandered and I never really got to know the other kids. I got bored easily. Perhaps boredom was also to blame for the time I failed Grade 3. Mom and Dad were furious and I was ashamed.

"How could you fail?" my mom and dad would continuously repeat. "What is it that you're just not getting?" My father spanked me. Even my cousins who were over at the time were shocked. "How could you do that, Diane?" I cried myself to sleep that night.

The following September, I was sent to a private school called Loretto Academy. I felt I had been sent to prison. On the first day, I was too afraid to go inside at the bell and waited instead in the schoolyard. Because I was nervous, I started talking to my imaginary horse, Silver. One of the nuns walked up to me and said, "Who are you talking to?"

"My horse, Silver."

"My, what a fine-looking horse you have there. You must be the Lone Ranger. I'm Mother Bertillo. Let's tie him up to this tree. He'll be waiting for you after school while we go in and learn how to read."

As we walked toward the school, she held my hand and said, "Why don't you tell me your other name?"

I looked up at her and said, "Diane Thornton, Mother."

I loved her from the first moment I saw her. She understood me, and she had my full attention. She appreciated the importance of imagination and she used her imagination to bring to life the stories about Jesus and the saints. I loved the story about St. Francis talking to the animals— I remember feeling that he was just like me. Then there was St. Patrick chasing the snakes out of Ireland. She described Jesus breaking the bread and making all the fish appear to feed hundreds of people as if she had been there herself. Even the sad stories, like Joan of Arc or Jesus suffering on the cross, helped us to understand the sacrifices you sometimes have to make to get what you want.

Loretto was a better place for me. The classes were smaller than at Sacred Heart School and the kids were nicer, especially the twins, Susan and Kitty. They didn't look like twins. Susan, who was tall and lanky, with bright red hair, looked more like Anne of Green Gables. Kitty was short and sloppy, with brown hair. She always spilled food all over her uniform and got into trouble for her clumsiness. We had lots of fun after school, too. Susan and I often ran home after school to sing and dance to one of our favourite records, *South Pacific*. "I'm gonna wash that man right out of my hair," we sang.

Everything was going so well that I didn't even notice the troubles at home. But just before Christmas 1958, Robert and I began to notice that Dad was not coming home at night. He'd be gone for days at a time. One terrible night, I woke up from a frightening dream. I ran downstairs to search for Mom. When I opened the front door, I saw my dad in a car kissing a strange woman while my mother cried on the veranda. I was devastated. For months, Mom and Dad pretended nothing happened, as if it had all been a bad dream.

Sometimes, I would wake up in the middle of the night and hear my mother crying alone in her room. Then, in September 1959, just after I started Grade 4, they separated. My mom became both mom and dad to us.

She was never home—holding down two, sometimes three, jobs. She worked as a seamstress, a salesperson at an exclusive sportswear store, and a cleaning lady after hours. Somehow, she still managed to keep the house spotless, put meals on the table, and throw the most magical birthday parties any kid could ever dream of.

Robert and I celebrate our birthdays just two days apart—he was born on September 10—so we always shared the same birthday parties. The best was one year when my mother gave us a surprise party. She invited all our friends on the street. Even Susan, my friend from school, was there. When we walked into the house, she was standing on my dad's La-Z-boy chair screaming, "SURPRISE," louder than anyone else. Mom had arranged for all of us to go to a farm with a hayride and foot-long hotdogs. We sang around the campfire and opened our presents. I got Nancy Drew books from Susan and Kitty. Robert got a Roy Rogers lunch pail and cowboy hat from the boys on the street.

Mom made everything feel like a game, even though she worked tirelessly, day after day. There were many nights when she stayed up way past our bedtimes sewing away, doing alterations for neighbours and friends. She never once reminded us that she was working hard to make ends meet because Dad had left us. Instead, she would say, "No matter what, he is your father—and no matter what happened between us, he must be respected."

We didn't always make it easy for Mom, either. In typical kid fashion, we would answer her back and even once burned a hole in the living room rug when playing cowboys and Indians. She'd chase us around the house and tell us how angry she was, but that would only last a couple of minutes and then we would go to bed.

Being with Dad was another matter—it was either up or down, depending on his mood or our behaviour. We'd go to his shop every day after school so he could supervise us while we did our homework. Even though I was improving at school, thanks to Mother Bertillo, spelling was my weakest area. Robert was smart and got good grades. I don't ever remember him making a mistake. So Dad always seemed to be disciplining me.

Over and over, he'd make me correctly spell out the words I had gotten wrong. With a smack from his metal ruler on my hand, he would emphasize the sound of each letter. "R," *whack!* "E," *whack!* "C," *whack!* "E," *whack! whack!* And so on, until I had spelled 'received.'

Although I hated being hit, I loved Dad. He could be hard on me, and then suddenly, with his Jekyll-and-Hyde personality, he could be comforting. He'd say, "Pumpkin, you're going to be a winner." Sometimes he would treat Robert and me to milkshakes at the TH&B Railroad Station, which was right next to his shop.

"Do you know what TH&B stands for, Pumpkin? Tramps, hobos and bums."

We laughed as we sat on the stools, sipping huge sodas and devouring the best burgers in town. One time he built us a super railroad set at the back of his shop to play with when we came to visit. It was complete with hills, bridges and a huge sign that read: "Tramps, Hobos and Bums Railway Station."

Every Saturday night Dad took us swimming at the YMCA. It was Family Night—but without Mom. We swam and swam, jumping in and out of the pool, till our eyes were bloodshot from the chlorine. Afterwards, he would buy us hot peanuts and walk us home, but he never came inside. It really hurt to watch him leave and head down the hill to meet the other woman. I hated her.

Robert and I were determined to get Daddy to come home for Christmas. I had an idea.

"Here's what we're going to do, Robert," I said.

Robert was immediately suspicious. "I'm not Ethel in *I Love Lucy* who comes up with crazy ideas that get her into a whole lot of trouble."

"You want Dad to come home, don't you?"

"Yes."

"Then we have to do something special."

I reached into the china cabinet and took out a bronze mug. "We're going Christmas caroling. The whole thing will work better if I knock on the door and say, 'My little brother wants to sing for you.'"

"ME! What about you?"

35

"Robert, when they see your cute little face, with your ears sticking out and singing your little heart out, it's going to break their hearts! Before you know it, we'll have the money to buy Dad a nice gift that we'll leave under the tree for him to come home to."

Reluctantly, Robert trudged through the deep snow to the neighbours' house. My little fundraising campaign was going through my mind as I knocked on the door. When the first neighbour opened it, she looked out and said, "Not now, I have guests for dinner."

"Oh please," I begged, "my brother really wants to sing for you and it will be nice music for your guests. It will only take a minute."

She took a deep breath and ushered us into her living room. There were four adults sitting there, sipping tea. Robert clutched the mug. Everyone went silent and for some reason I thought this was incredibly funny—watching my little brother standing there with the mug in his hands, his ears sticking out and his toque nearly falling off his head made me start to giggle.

He opened his mouth to sing. Silence.

I couldn't help myself. "*Tee hee*…." Silence.

Now Robert began to laugh too. "Oh, Holy…tee hee… Night." He laughed all the way through the first verse. Then he accidentally burped.

There wasn't a second verse. The lady turned us around and marched us out of the living room, sticking a two-dollar bill in the mug to get rid of us. When the door slammed behind us I threw myself into a snow bank, rolling around making angels and laughing hysterically. Robert was embarrassed, but I was shouting, "We got the money!"

The next day, we bought a beautiful tie. Then we wrapped it up and put it under the tree…but Dad never came home to get it. Our hearts sank. No gift in the world could bring Dad back home where he belonged. I couldn't get rid of the awful emptiness or block out the betrayal I felt because of the other woman in Dad's life.

My schoolwork was slipping and Dad became more and more abusive in his tutoring sessions. Slap after slap. Insult after insult. "You'll never amount to anything," he would say. I began to believe him, so why bother trying? I thought. I was a loser. My dad was right.

Mom, on the other hand, was so busy with her part-time dressmaking business that she decided to quit her job at the sportswear shop and start her own business. She got a bank loan and opened up a store on John Street called Fashion Court. We were happy for her, but we were saddened that Mom decided to sell the house. We moved from our pretty house on the escarpment to the back of a store. The landlord gave Mom six months of free rent just after Christmas in 1959.

It didn't take Mom long to turn Fashion Court into a sort of haute couture salon. People from all over Hamilton came to have Mom make them a dress. She worked 10 to 14 hours a day, seven days a week. Even on Sundays, after singing in the choir and watching Robert serve at Mass, she'd be back at the store cleaning and getting ready for Monday morning.

One thing about my mother is that when she makes up her mind to do something, she does it. Today, at Famous PEOPLE Players, she sews, paints, designs props for the show and still finds the time to make dresses for my two daughters. Nothing—absolutely nothing—stands in her way. The more it can't be done, the more she shows us it can be done. Even though she doesn't realize it, she continues to be my inspiration.

I missed our house on Kingsway. My secret hiding places in the basement and at the back of the closet now belonged to some stranger. I missed those dark places where my imagination flourished. But I was learning to put the painful memories at Kingsway behind me.

Mom made our new home look stunning, with black and gold wallpaper in the living room and a black, high-gloss floor covered with a white carpet. It wasn't like my friend Susan's traditional home. It was different—wild and fun—and it made me feel special. Father Beaudry even came for dinner one day and blessed our new home.

I would often help out Mom at the store after school and during the summer. When I wasn't working in the store, Susan and I would go to the movies. We loved the Palace Theatre in Hamilton, which was like a giant castle with its balconies decorated in red and gold plush, angels and cherubs on the ceiling, and heavy black velvet curtains on stage. We used to sit up in the balcony, and as we waited for the movie to begin, we would wave our arms shouting, "Let the show begin!" We were the King and Queen of Hamilton.

The biblical movies were wonderful. *The Ten Commandments* and *The Robe* kept me spellbound. And I loved the Westerns and movies with Doris Day with her peaches-and-cream complexion. But one of my favourite actresses was Audrey Hepburn. I wanted to go away to finishing school in Paris and then come back to be with Humphrey Bogart, as she did in *Sabrina*. Sometimes, I would imagine myself in Hepburn's role as Holly Golightly in *Breakfast at Tiffany's* with her cat, falling in love with George Peppard (little did I know that one day I would actually meet him). I was so in love with Audrey Hepburn that I even tried stretching my neck to look like her.

Susan and I continued our after-school musical performances. We sang our hearts out during our renditions of the songs "Bells are Ringing" and "Oklahoma." Mom was so impressed with my vocal abilities that she took me to audition for the *Flower Drum Song* at a local theatre. There were hundreds of kids there from Hamilton with their mothers. I sang "Honey Bun" from *South Pacific* for my audition, which earned me a spot in the finals, but it wasn't enough to get me the part. I was so disappointed. Mom assured me there would be other parts, but I never auditioned again because it brought back feelings of failure. I could hear my dad's voice echoing, "You will never amount to anything."

To make myself feel better, I would delve into my Nancy Drew mysteries. I think I read every book in the series. In fact, I read whatever mystery and adventure books I could get—one of my favourites was Robert Louis Stevenson's *Treasure Island*. Then, as I grew older, romance replaced adventure. I was now running to the theatre to see movies like *Gidget* and falling head over heels in love with Cliff Robertson. When I met him years later as a guest at Famous PEOPLE Players, he was even better-looking in person than on the screen—he made my knees wobble!

My love for the movies and music didn't carry over to school. During Grade 6, school was especially hard for me, particularly math. I just didn't understand the rules of division no matter how much I tried. I could remember the lines from *Breakfast at Tiffany's* a lot easier, like when Paul tells Holly in the pouring rain, that no matter where she goes, she will always bump into herself. That made more sense to me than 10,000 divided by three. As my grades became worse, so did my dad's temper.

Dad was drinking heavily. He often drank, but I wondered why I was just noticing it now? I could smell alcohol on his breath as he breathed in my face: "Can't you understand? Think, Diane, *think*."

I was afraid to see him, but Robert and I had to report to him every morning at Stanley Signs so he could check our homework before we went to school. It was frightening and I often threw up because I was so scared to face him. He would often fly into a rage about my appearance. "Your shoes are dirty!" he would scream.

One day, just to avoid being the one who always got into trouble, I told on Robert. I told Dad that Robert had punched Susan (omitting the fact that we had provoked him by not letting him play in our game). Dad flew into a rage, grabbing Robert by his arm and dragging him around the shop yelling, "I'll show you how to be a gentleman!"

I begged him to stop, as he pulled Robert's arm almost out of its socket while he cried hysterically. He finally let go and I took Robert home to change his clothes. I was distraught about putting my little brother in that position. Mom wasn't home and we never told her about what happened because we were both too scared. I was so upset when I got to school that I turned to Mother Bertillo for support. She took me to the chapel to pray and told me, "Your father is troubled and needs prayer, Diane. Pray hard for him."

There were brighter moments during that year. On the final week of school, Mother Bertillo choose a poem called "Beautiful Things" that she asked me to recite in front of the whole school in the auditorium. I was so proud to have been selected by my favourite teacher. To make her proud, I rehearsed the poem over and over, until I could recite it by heart. I even added my own hand gestures to accentuate the dramatics of the poem. There I stood before 600 students in the middle of the stage and poured my heart out. I was a hit—and I had the magnificent applause to prove it. I stepped down from the stage to see Mother Bertillo facing me. As she hugged me, she said, "I was saying to the other sisters: 'What is ever going to happen to our Diane?' Now I know. You are destined for the stage!" Then she broke the news: "Diane, I don't know how to tell you this, but you have to repeat another year of school." I was stunned and hurt—my favourite teacher in the whole world was failing me and I let her down.

My mom couldn't afford to send me back to Loretto Academy, so she sent me to St. Patrick's, the neighbourhood elementary school. It was like Sacred Heart all over again, with its own collection of bullies. They chased after me every day, tripping and hitting me. The problem escalated and I became a bed wetter; a problem that lasted for years.

When I finally got to Grade 7, I performed puppet shows for the class. The bullies loved the shows; perhaps it was the violence of Punch hitting Judy they enjoyed most. Maybe I should have told Judy to pray for Punch— that's what Mother Bertillo would have said. That was the last time I performed at school. I stored my puppets in a box under my bed because I felt they were now too childish.

Just when things seemed to improve, I hit another roadblock. One day, during Mass at school, I suddenly realized that I couldn't hear the priest. It was as if the speaker system suddenly broke down. I felt sick and dizzy, like I was sinking into the ground. My symptoms continued when we returned to class. I tried to get the teacher's attention, but when that failed I stood up and said, "Something is wrong with the floor—I'm sinking." I could see the other children's faces laughing, but I could barely hear anything.

I walked home at lunchtime, trying to follow the 'sinking' sidewalk and all its ripples. The last thing I remembered was that I was sick from eating some lunch and then I was lying in bed with a doctor examining me. I could hardly make out what he was saying—something about a virus in my inner ear. I was deaf and it affected my balance. For two weeks I lay in bed trying not to move because the slightest movement made me feel sick. One day I heard a pop in my right ear and I could hear again on one side, but I never recovered the use of my left ear. The virus caused permanent nerve damage. Today, I deal with the loss by turning my right ear toward people when they speak.

About the same time, Mom told us that we wouldn't be seeing Dad again because he was moving to Arizona. He sometimes frightened me, but I still loved him and I knew I would miss him.

I was now in Grade 8, and it was a time when something clicked, and brought out the fighter in me. A new girl in the neighbourhood came to join our class. She had epilepsy and sometimes suffered from seizures. During one of her seizures, she fell down and her skirt lifted above her waist, revealing her underwear. Many of my classmates thought it was funny, but I was so furious at their laughter that I yelled at them to leave her alone.

It was hard for me to defend myself, but when I saw someone else being bullied, I wasn't scared of anyone. I couldn't stand on the sidelines and I didn't care what they called me for jumping in. I learned an important lesson that day: Don't be afraid of what you've done, but be afraid of what you haven't done. It was a turning point in my personality.

It was also pivotal in the way I approached my short-lived high-school years at Central Tech. By this time, I had already made up my mind that I would never graduate. It was better to be tough—showing off and standing up to people—because then I'd be labeled as 'cool.'

I remember one teacher taking me out into the hallway and saying, "You know, Diane, you're going to fail if you persist with this attitude." I shrugged because I didn't care. I didn't like school. Instead, I was more interested in organizing parties and helping to choose the music for all the social functions at Central.

My lack of effort wasn't hard to spot by my teachers, either. One day, while I daydreamed in history class, my teacher, Mr. Wong, called me to the front of the class to read my report on Ponce de Leon and the Fountain of Youth. Everyone stared at me, but unshaken, I picked up my binder and walked boldly to the front of the classroom. Then, holding the binder in my arms, I stared down at the blank page and read. It was a great story; even Mr. Wong was truly impressed. "Very good, Diane," he said. "Now class, I want you to take notes because Diane is going to read it again."

I was lost. How could I repeat what I had just ad-libbed? Another detention, another failing grade and another failed grade. After my first attempt at Grade 9, I vowed I would never go back to school.

I took my first paying job at Eaton's lingerie department for $49 a week. I was happy to be out of school and working. I was earning money and that, for me, meant I was in control of my own life and I was finally taking some responsibility. But something was missing in my life—my dad. It had been five years since we'd last seen each other and I wanted to find him.

I was thrilled when I received a Christmas card from Dad. It was even more special that it had a picture on it with him holding his brush and palette and a sign he had made that said Merry Christmas Diane. I wrote him back right away and said I wanted to come and visit him. Within a week he called to make arrangements. My mother was obviously hurt to hear that I was cashing in my first paycheque to vacation in Arizona with Dad.

When the plane touched down, I got off and walked into a wall of hot air. I had never felt such heat. Dad was waiting in a roped-off area, wearing a cowboy hat. I dropped everything—my suitcase, and a package of Canadian pea-meal bacon that I had tucked under my arm—and ran past two elderly women into Dad's arms. Dad bent down to pick everything up and said to the ladies, "This is my daughter who came all the way from Canada to see her old man."

"How wonderful," they said. Dad was his old self. Perhaps a little bigger, sunburned, thicker glasses—but it was Dad and I was glad to see him after all these years.

"Let's take a good look at you, Pumpkin. Wait, I can't call you Pumpkin, you're too beautiful. I'll call you Miss Priss, 'cause you've turned into a princess."

I was so happy to see him. Tears rolled down my face.

"None of this bawling, 'cause us cow folks are going to the Wild West. This is going to be the best weekend ever."

And it was. When we visited Tombstone, it reminded me of every great Western movie I'd ever seen. I was walking the same streets as Wyatt Earp and Doc Holliday. There were women in long dresses and the cowboys, who were wearing six-shooters, broke into a 'gunfight' to dazzle the tourists. I felt transported to the O.K. Corral or to the set of *High Noon*. We rode horses in the desert and watched tumbleweed blow across the path of Dad's old station wagon.

During our travels, we would frequently drop in at a bar. On one occasion, we went into an old tavern on the side of the road near Sedona. Dad put one foot up on the rail, spat into the spittoon, and the bartender poured him a beer and slid it down the long mahogany bar. "Drinks are on the house," Dad announced. "Miss Priss is here all the way from Canada and we're off to see the world together." Everyone cheered.

I fell head over heels in love with Arizona—the red rocks, the cacti, the sunsets. It was as if I really was the Lone Ranger and my dad was Tonto. We drove in the car for more than a week to see some of the touristy sights, such as the Grand Canyon, before the sun went down.

It was hard for Dad to admit how much he really missed Robert and me. With tears in his eyes, he said, "Now you know how much I love you, Miss Priss. I don't know if you know how much. I miss you. You and Robert are the most important people in my life. I want you to believe me. I never meant for the trouble between me and your mother to hurt you." He was now married to that other woman. It did hurt me, but nothing was going to spoil our week of adventure. It was just the two of us—Hi Ho Silver! Up at the crack of dawn and we were off to our next attraction.

The week went by so fast. And when I returned home, I couldn't get Arizona or my dad out of my system. Bored with my life in Hamilton, I lost interest in my job and my sales dropped. Eventually I received my two weeks' notice. My mother was devastated.

"How could you lose your job? You were doing so well at it. You could work your way up to the top. They're looking for young people to make a career as buyers."

My mother's heart was even more crushed when I announced that I was leaving home to go live with Dad.

I set out for Phoenix in 1967. Mom was crying from the time I told her about my plans to the time she drove me to the airport in her Volkswagen Beetle. I felt guilty for what I was doing to her, but at the same time I really wanted to explore my relationship with my dad. And maybe, in the back of my mind, I always thought that we could all be a family together again. Robert was so furious I was leaving him behind that he didn't even come to the airport to say goodbye.

When I arrived in Phoenix, my dad looked different. He was quieter and more interested in how many pieces of luggage I had than in picking me up off the floor and swinging me around like the first time I had visited. Perhaps it had to do with the other woman in his life, who had just left him. I was thrilled.

But nothing was the same as the last time. There was no Wild West, no horse to ride, no desert mountain to climb. Instead, he had frequent visits from the bottles— Johnny Walker, Captain Morgan and Jack Daniels. Dad was drinking again and it got so bad that we had to move from his comfortable house in Phoenix and into a small, rundown apartment behind his sign shop in a tough part of town. The more he drank, the more customers he lost. And now he was taking out his frustrations on me. The verbal abuse began—I was frequently on the receiving end of his curses and threats. He said that he'd find me if I left him, and I believed him.

When his abuse became too much, I found a job in Phoenix and moved into an apartment with a new girl-friend I had met at work. Soon after I started my new job working in the bra section of a department store, I told Dad where I worked and he called me to demand $50. He said that if I didn't pay, he would report me to the immigration department for working in the country illegally. With that threat hanging over my head, I scraped together enough money—money I knew would be spent on booze.

The next week he wanted $60, my entire paycheque. I would have no money for food and I wouldn't be able to pay my share of the rent, but I was too terrified to argue with him—I thought he would kill me. My roommate was so frightened for my safety that she arranged for me to live with a group of her friends. They graciously let me sleep on their couch and share their food until I could get back on my feet and escape this nightmare.

When I felt that I had worn out my welcome, I would move on to another set of roommates. Everywhere I went people helped me, giving me food to eat and a place to sleep. It was the 1960s and everybody helped each other.

But no one could help me from a situation on the job. I was called to the security room of the department store where I worked. There was money missing from the till and I was being questioned about it. Even though I told my supervisor that I hadn't taken the money, I was told I had to take a lie detector test. Besides, she explained, if I was telling the truth, it would prove my innocence. I quickly agreed because I had nothing to hide.

I was escorted to a room with a polygraph operator who hooked me up to some wires and started asking me questions. It was the most humiliating experience of my life. When the questioning was over, I leapt to my feet.

"See? I told you I didn't take the money!" I said, pointing to the scribbles that the needle made on the paper. He shook his head and showed me. "The wiggly lines on the polygraph suggest that you did do it."

"But I would never steal from anyone!" I cried. Suddenly, my story tumbled out. I explained how I had been giving my dad money and never had anything left for myself, but no matter how bad it got for me, "I never stole," I kept repeating. So many people had helped me, given me a place to stay. I could never repay that kind of trust by stealing.

Tears streamed down my face, "Don't you believe me?" The elderly gentleman looked up at me, took his glasses off, put them down on the table and said, "Yes, I do believe you." When the security supervisor came back into the room, he told her that I hadn't taken the money, but the supervisor didn't believe him. She told me to leave the store immediately and never tell anybody what had happened.

I grabbed my purse and ran out of the building without looking back. I was so ashamed and filled with anger. I found out later from my friend's father that what they did to me was illegal and that I could sue them for big money. But no amount of money in the world could ever make me feel better. As I stood outside the store, I realized that the one person I wanted more than anyone at that moment was my mother. I would have given anything to feel her hug again.

I knew what I had to do. I couldn't live with my father's threat anymore. I walked over to the government building, which was down the street, and asked to see someone in the immigration department immediately. A kind gentleman escorted me into a private office, where I confessed everything to him—that I was working illegally in the United States and that my own father was blackmailing me. I was lucky I wasn't thrown in jail. Instead, I was given 120 days to get my life organized and get back to Canada.

During that time, I had a sort of breakdown. I spent a lot of time thinking. The desert was my refuge and I went to Mass and prayed a lot, just like Mother Bertillo taught us in school: I could hear her now, "Pray for your enemies— to err is human; to forgive is divine."

My friends took care of me until it was time to go. When I had everything in place, I called my Mom and told her I was coming home.

CHAPTER TWO

Off to the Races

When I got off the plane at Toronto's international airport, I couldn't wait to run out of the Arrival section and into my mother's arms, but she wasn't there to greet me. Who could blame her after what I'd done?

There I was, standing in the middle of the terminal holding my suitcase, and hoping that at the very least, Robert would come running toward me at any moment. When I realized no one was coming to greet me, my eyes welled up with tears and I called Mom collect from a telephone booth. When she answered, she was coughing with bronchitis. I soon learned that a lot had happened while I was away.

Mom had sold Fashion Court and bought a small house where she continued her dressmaking work for some of her key customers. She gave me the directions to my new home, 44 Queen Street North, and hung up. Robert was now a teenager and into his own thing and was still upset with me for leaving him and Mom.

As I boarded the bus home, I thought to myself, *I have to make it up to her.* There it was, the purple house she had described. I had to smile—Mom hadn't lost her artistic flare. She knew how to take an old shanty house like this one and turn it into something really beautiful—even on the outside.

I was nervous as I rang the doorbell. Mom answered the door and stood there, wearing her pink housecoat. I couldn't tell if she was shorter or I was taller. With a hacking cough, she insisted on showing me around the house. It was smaller than our old place, but Mom had made it warm and inviting—especially with the purple wall-to-wall carpeting. She led me up to my bedroom, a wonderful little retreat all decorated in bright colours.

"Here's your dresser," she said. "You can put your things in these drawers and hang your clothes over here." You could barely hear her words over the draining cough.

I was happy to be home in a comfortable bed after sleeping on all those couches. As I lay in bed that night, praying to St. Theresa, my patron saint, I felt lonely and empty inside. I felt like the spirit inside me was gone. I was 20 years old, a high-school dropout, with no job, no boyfriend and no father.

I spent weeks feeling sorry for myself. I never told my mother about Dad and the blackmail. I never even told her about that terrible ordeal at the department store—but somehow, I knew that she knew I'd been through a difficult time. Just the same, she never brought up what I did, or how I must have hurt her. She always looked toward the future. *If a plan doesn't work, you reinvent the plan. You turn lemons into lemonade.* That has always been my mother's philosophy.

One afternoon, as I was looking for a pair of shoes in the storage room, I noticed my old puppet theatre tucked away in a corner. I pulled it out, dusted the box and opened the lid to find my old friends, Punch and Judy, smiling up at me. I was surprised that my mother had kept my hand puppets after all these years. And I'd never realized how much I missed them until I slipped them on my hands. It felt so good to rub them against my face. The puppet theatre, however, was too small for me now and I could never fit into its small space.

I had a spontaneous idea. I remember thinking that maybe, just maybe, I could go into business for myself, performing puppet shows at birthday parties. By the time mother had come home from her opera rehearsals with the Hamilton Opera Company, I was already rehearsing and planning my future. She was so thrilled to finally see me interested in something with purpose that she suddenly transformed herself into a New York impresario, brainstorming with me about my new business.

She designed a new puppet theatre for me—one that would easily come apart to fit inside her Volkswagen Beetle—and she found a carpenter to build it. When the theatre was ready, she painted it black with big bright flowers on it and painted a sign at the top that spelled L-O-V-E in huge letters.

Soon, my small little puppet family expanded to include a dog, a crow, a witch doctor, a mouse and a swan. Mom could take simple puppets like Punch and Judy and dress them up with accessories to make them look like stars. The furry moustache on Mr. Evil made him convincingly sinister and the Canadian Mountie we added later to the entourage of characters looked stunning in his bright red uniform. Then came a uniformed police officer to arrest Punch after he'd beaten up Judy. But I couldn't continue with Punch and Judy. Mother Bertillo's words haunted me: "He is troubled. Pray for him." Poor Punch, he was troubled just like Dad. So I changed the characters of Punch and Judy to George Burns and Gracie Allen, hosting their own variety show.

Mom had so much faith in my new business that she encouraged me to find an agent who could book shows for birthday parties and shopping centres. With her help, I found a photographer who could take publicity shots of me in action. My mother even changed my hairstyle to make me look more glamorous.

The agent I found teamed me up with an aspiring talented magician. He kept us busy—we performed every Saturday at birthday parties and company parties. We were paid $50 a show, which we split, minus a 10 percent commission for our agent.

Doug, the magician, and I became good friends, frequently chatting about our hopes and dreams as we went from one job to another over the year. He was a lot like me too, with many ideas always flowing from his mind. We encouraged and applauded each other after each show. I was very proud of Doug and his accomplishments. A few years later, he became the famous magician that he had aspired to be—the late Great Doug Henning.

When I was performing at the Ancaster Theatre on Saturdays during the summer, I decided to incorporate a sad dog in my show, singing Bobby Vinton's "Mr. Lonely." I sped up the music so it would have a chipmunk sound to it, and the kids loved it. Many of them often asked to hug the dog because he looked so sad. I had another idea during these performances, a sort of magical trick of my own. I could see everyone in the audience, but they couldn't see me because my peephole was disguised as a flower. I had the puppets speak directly to the children.

"Hey you, with the red hair," Punch would yell.

"Me?" one of the kids would say.

"Yeah, you. Step on up—I want to meet you." The kids would scream with laughter.

In the meantime, Mom would stand at the back of the theatre, cheering and applauding. After the show, she was always quick to make repairs on the puppets. She became my biggest supporter. But when I tried to thank her for being by my side, she would start to criticize me. She'd nag me about what hadn't worked in the show and that would bring me down—so I never thanked her. That was my mother's way of trying to get me to settle down and focus on my career.

The crowds started to get bigger—and so did the pay. I was up to $75 a show. That seemed like a fortune to me, especially because I was getting paid for doing something I loved to do!

But after a busy holiday season, the party circuit would stop and there wouldn't be any work until around Easter. I decided to take a job at a department store to fill in the gaps.

One day, just before lunch, a petite, friendly looking, dark-haired girl about my age came into the store with a girlfriend of mine named Helen, who worked in the next department.

"Diane, she needs a bra. Got any cheap deals?" (Yes, I was working once again in the lingerie department!)

The conversation led to lunch, where we chatted like old girlfriends who had known each other all their lives. Helen's friend, Judi Schwartz, and I became instant best friends and it was the start of a lifelong relationship.

The job, however, was far from becoming a lifetime career. A month later, I was fired from my job at the department store because the manager found out that I had lied on my application when they later checked my references —I wrote down that I had a Grade 12 education when I hadn't even made it to Grade 10. I was depressed and my self-esteem was lower than a snake's wiggle. Judi knew I was hitting bottom and she suggested we take off for a week and fly to Arizona.

I was curious about my old friends and what they were doing, so I agreed to go. I wanted to show Judi the beautiful desert, Red Rock Country, and the Camelback Mountain I had once climbed. But on this trip, I would not be seeing my father. I had made up my mind when I'd left Arizona that I would never speak to him again. (This was a decision that has come to haunt me over the years and one that I deeply regret.)

We had a wild trip through Arizona. We saw most of the beautiful state on motorcycles with two guys that we just met at an apartment complex where we stayed, riding from one magical scene to another over the 10 days we were there. I don't think we had a good night's sleep during our trip.

"Maybe we'll get real rich one day, Judi, and we'll live in one of these houses on Camelback Mountain!" I recall saying as we drove through the desert.

When we came home from Phoenix, exhausted and sunburned, we slept for a week. It was a welcome break from life in Hamilton. Just the same, I was anxious to get back to a normal routine.

I got a job at Holt Renfrew in Toronto, hoping that the store would not check my references. I knew one thing for sure—I certainly wasn't going to find my life's aspirations in the lingerie department, but I needed the job to make money. I would stay at Judi's house during the week and make the 45-minute bus ride home to Hamilton on weekends.

While at Holt Renfrew, I took the opportunity to further my burgeoning career in theatre, so when Easter approached, I went to the promotions manager at Simpson's about hiring me to perform with my puppets in the toy department. Judi waited outside to hear about his decision. I went into his office at noon and by 12:30 I had the job! The schedule was tight—I would be working at Holt's during the week and weekends at Simpson's—but I was committed to making it work.

"I love doing this," I remember telling Judi. "It certainly beats selling bras." We laughed all the way back to Hamilton to tell Mom.

But my job at Holt Renfrew did not last, especially after an incident when a customer asked me for the price of an alligator handbag on the shelf. It was a tiny little chic bag and the price tag on it read $800. Surely, there was a mistake, I thought, and sold it to her for $80. The store manager had a fit and I was fired. I wasn't there long enough for them to check my references.

Judi was in stitches about the ordeal and told everybody about it. One by one, all her hippie friends who were selling flowers on Bloor Street had to go into the handbag department at Holt Renfrew to see the purses that cost so much money.

My mother, who couldn't believe I had made such a mistake, was determined to get me back on track—that is, to turn lemons into lemonade. "They're looking for talent for the Canadian National Exhibition. If you get the job, it will be for three weeks. It opens in August and closes Labour Day weekend," she said firmly.

I was definitely interested in the opportunity, but I needed a new act—something really different that would catch the attention of the crowds at the Exhibition. At that time, the press was filled with stories about Prime Minister Trudeau's affair with Barbra Streisand, and I came up with an idea to use them in my puppet show. Streisand would sing "Lover, Come Back to Me" to Trudeau.

Mom made a beautiful burgundy smoking jacket for the Trudeau puppet and Streisand was dressed in a sailor suit like the one she wore in *Funny Girl*. I rehearsed the skit until I started to dream about it. When everything was in place, I arranged an audition with David Garrick, the general manager of the Canadian National Exhibition. When he saw the puppets and my performances, he laughed so hard he almost fell out of his chair.

"Trudeau and Streisand need no introduction—the puppets look just like them," he said.

I was hired—and I almost fell out of my chair when he told me he was paying me $500 over the three weeks, plus all the food I could eat from the Food Building! (In those days, the Food Building had a large assortment of food booths by some big companies.)

Judi was really excited I got the job. She kept telling everybody, "Diane could go to Holt's and buy six more bags. One for each of us."

The Punch and Judy routine, which I brought back, still got big applause, but it was the Trudeau and Streisand duet that got all the attention. We even made front-page news in the *Toronto Star* about their performance. And the crowds kept getting bigger.

I'm on to something, I kept telling myself. I expanded my repertoire to include puppets of local media celebrities, such as CBC-TV weatherman Percy Saltzman, and TV talk show host Elwood Glover. People came from all over to see me perform at the EX. I was so busy I didn't have time to run to the Food Building. Instead, Judi ran back and forth between shows and we crammed in as much food as we could.

During one of my shows, when Punch was making fun of the parents in the audience, my eyes scanned the crowd and stopped when I noticed a familiar face. *Now where have I seen that face before?* I wondered. But before I figure it out, a little girl tugged at Punch's clothing, "Hey Punch, you're a bad boy—I'm going to come back to get you."

"Okay, okay, I'm leaving," Punch said. "But before I go, I'm going to introduce to you the greatest singing dog in the world." Then I brought out my sad puppy to sing "Mr. Lonely." It was a great feeling to hear all the cheers and applause from the hundreds of people who sat on the grass watching my show.

After the show, there was a knock on the door of my puppet booth. When I opened it, I couldn't believe my eyes. That familiar face in the crowd I saw had been none other than Bill Cosby!

He started to talk about how much he liked the Trudeau and Streisand routine and about his love of puppetry. I was listening, but distracted by his face. My mind kept saying, *It's Bill Cosby, from the* I Spy *TV show that I watched faithfully with my brother, and here he is talking to me.*

"Have you ever heard about black light?" he asked.

"No," I said, shaking my head.

"You must try it—it would be great with puppets."

A minute later, the crowd was swarming him for autographs and he disappeared.

I met Bill Cosby, I kept thinking. *Bill Cosby came to my show!* I was so happy I felt like I was floating high above the Exhibition grounds.

Black light? I was curious about it, so I went to the library to find out more about this technique Bill Cosby mentioned. I learned that black-light theatre originated in Japan and became popular in Europe, mainly Czechoslovakia, where puppetry is a cultivated art form. The technique uses ultraviolet lights to illuminate puppets, which are painted in fluorescent paint colours and glow in the dark. The performers can't be seen from the audience because they're dressed in black velvet jumpsuits with hoods that fit snugly over their faces. Even their hands and feet are covered in black, and a tiny black screen is fitted across their eyes to allow them to see. The stage itself is covered in black velvet—the side curtains, the floor and the backdrop. When the performers pick up a puppet or a prop in fluorescent colours and move it across the stage it looks like a cartoon. It seems to defy gravity as it floats and soars through the air.

It sounded magical. I, however, was so absorbed with my shows at the EX that I put my research on the back-burner. Eventually, the CNE came to an end, yet the work continued. The publicity I had received for the Trudeau and Streisand puppets brought more business—this time, I was hired to perform at shopping malls in Calgary, Edmonton and Winnipeg for a performance fee of $1,500 for a series of shows over two weeks. It was my first tour—and I was making a fortune. I figured that if I budgeted my money carefully, I could stretch it into the following year, when I hoped to be rehired at the CNE during the summer of 1972.

Christmas, my busiest season, was coming up, when I got a phone call from a woman asking me to come to Surrey Place Centre, a community-based organization in Toronto that provides programs to people living with a developmental disability. She wanted me to perform my show for people who were "mentally retarded."

Are you crazy? I thought. *Not in a million years.* I turned her down.

The lady, Mrs. Watson, was persistent. She wouldn't take no for an answer. "After all," she said, "many celebrities have given a lot of their time. Why can't you give some of yours?"

She put me to shame. Reluctantly, I said yes, even though I didn't want to go. I remember the kids in school calling me a "retard." It brought back horrible memories, but before I knew it, I was on my way to Surrey Place.

The snow was falling heavily that morning. When I arrived, Mrs. Watson met me at the main door. She was an enthusiastic person who headed up the volunteer program for Surrey Place Centre. She led me to a small room where all the chairs were lined up neatly in a row.

"You can set up your puppet theatre on that small riser that I have arranged for you. Here is your microphone. I hope you will find it satisfactory."

I was nervous—petrified was more like it. I kept thinking, *They're going to walk in here and make a mess of those chairs. I can hear them now, fighting, throwing themselves against the walls. The minute Punch appears I bet they're going to rip his head right off.*

I was so nervous that I almost started to cry. I heard Mrs. Watson say, "Diane, please take your place. They're on their way in and they're so excited that you're here." I could hear them coming down the hallway. I sat behind the theatre and watched the door open. In they walked. *Walked?* I thought. *They should be running.* They took their seats so-o-o normally. Mrs. Watson dimmed the lights at the back of the room and my show began.

"Good morning, boys and girls," Punch said as he popped up.

"Good morning," they all answered.

I watched the children through my peephole. They were really enjoying themselves. Nobody tried to rip Punch's head off. During the "Mr. Lonely" section of the show, a young girl in the audience had a seizure and everybody got up to help. Nobody laughed. It brought back terrible memories of the time in school when the new girl had an epileptic seizure and all the kids in class laughed. I began to think more deeply about who, in these experiences, was really 'retarded.' *It's the so-called 'normal' people,* I thought.

As I was leaving Surrey Place, Mrs. Watson came running after me. "Diane, wait. Don't go—we need you."

"You need me?"

"Yes, we do. You're young and energetic and I desperately need volunteers to help with the children. I hope you will say yes." Before she could finish, I was signing up, thrilled to have been asked.

"The bus leaves next Saturday for Orillia."

"Orillia?"

"It's an institution for the mentally retarded. I believe it'll be an eye-opener for you," Mrs. Watson told me.

Orillia was a real eye-opener. The facility was 'decorated' in drab colours, pipes were hanging from the ceiling and the washrooms had no doors or toilet paper. It looked like a huge basement that went on for miles. It needed my mother's touch to give the walls a much-needed lift with paint in beautiful rainbow colours. It was a cold place. Even the staff seemed cold and grim. It was the most inhumane place I had ever been to in my life. People were herded from room to room; when dinner was ready, they'd be herded from their bedrooms to the dining area. I never knew people lived like this and it broke my heart. After all, I always believed that in God's eyes, we are all sacred.

On my first day there, I took the young people for walks around the huge gymnasium that reminded me of a dungeon. There were no planned activities for the residents. In fact, we were brought in to provide the activities. All I kept thinking was: *They have to call this horrible place home.* These young people seemed to be dying inside. It made me angry—I wanted to save them, like the Lone Ranger riding furiously on Silver to save a whole town. All I knew was that the people who lived here needed lots of unconditional love and once they had that, their lives could be better.

That night, as the bus inched its way home through a snowstorm, I kept thinking of the kids I had left behind. I felt so helpless. I realized that I was one of the lucky ones, to have been born the way I was and was suddenly grateful for what I had in my life.

When I got home, I tried to describe what I had seen to my mother and Judi. They assured me they understood as they nodded their heads, but I knew they couldn't fully grasp it because they hadn't seen what I'd seen. I was determined to find a way to reach out to those people, but I wasn't sure how just yet.

A few weeks later, I got a phone call from Judi, who sounded nervous. She was telling me about a receptionist job at the Artists' Workshop, an art school with courses on art, pottery, painting and more. She wanted the job, but wasn't sure how to go about getting it. Before she could finish, I said, "Judi, you just go right in there and say, 'Where do I hang my coat?'" She got the job and soon worked her way up to manager.

Running my own puppet show business was having its share of ups and downs. Sometimes I earned good money, but then I'd be out of a job for months. I needed something steadier, so I went to Judi's office and asked her, "Where do I hang my coat?"

She offered me a job, although it certainly wasn't glamorous—running errands and cleaning the ceramic room. But, as a bonus, I got free classes in painting and pottery and met some of Canada's future artists.

During my stint there, a company called Black Box came to perform at the Poor Alex Theatre. The theatre was attached to the workshop and every week people came there to perform. I caught a show during rehearsal and I got really excited about what I saw. Black Box was performing black-light theatre, the same concept Bill Cosby had told me about after my show at the EX. I sat entranced by the magic. It was an explosion of colour, dripping all over the stage. There was even a scene where a clown named Joey went from big to little right before the audience's eyes. The colours appearing and disappearing in the dark reminded me of the hours I'd spent as a child in the basement, pretending to talk to characters and letting my imagination run wild.

Other shows by talented groups followed after Black Box's run at the Poor Alex. Some of them had a big influence on my future. There was The Jest Society, a group of young kids who wrote and acted out satires about well-known politicians—just like my skit about Trudeau and Streisand. They went on to become the Royal Canadian Air Farce and landed their own show on CBC-TV.

I loved watching talented people and saw it as an opportunity to learn a new craft. Whether it was getting the crews coffee or cleaning the toilets in their dressing room, I soaked up all the knowledge I could about the stage. Without even realizing it, a new dream was forming inside of me.

I was working so hard at the Artists' Workshop, performing my puppet shows and taking art classes, that there was no time for socializing. That is, until a friend of mine, Joseph Fodor, called me and asked if I would go out with a friend of his.

"Who?" I asked.

"The French man who played the guitar the other night at my house."

"Him! He doesn't speak English. What would we say to each other?"

"Please, for me, go out with him," said Joseph. "He's from Bordeaux. He's a nice guy and he's learning English. Besides, once you get to the movie theatre, you'll be watching a movie instead of talking."

I was skeptical, but I remembered the times in Arizona when complete strangers had made me feel welcome in their country. So, reluctantly, I agreed.

When I opened the door that evening, I almost fainted. There stood a drop-dead gorgeous man.

"My name is Bernard, mademoiselle. I have my car out front, if you're ready to go to dinner. I found a nice French restaurant called the Surf and Turf that I think you will like."

He walked me to his fancy Citroën Maserati and opened the car door for me as I got into the car. We were both silent as he drove to the theatre, but as I looked at him out of the corner of my eye I was thinking, *I don't remember him being so good-looking.* He was beautifully dressed, and, oh, those sideburns!

My life began to take a turn—a wonderful turn. I was falling in love. Bernard was interested in me and he showed it. He treated me with respect, dignity and supported my creativity. Unlike others who had shunned my creativity, Bernard loved it when I exploded with ideas for my puppet show. He would laugh at my silly jokes and looked forward to seeing my show. Following that one wonderful blind date, I began to see Bernard every night.

Then one morning, still tired from my date with Bernard the night before, Judi came up behind me and gave me a big kick in the butt. "You're fired!" she told me briskly. "Look Diane, you're too talented—you've got too much going for you to be here cleaning the ceramic room and being someone else's gopher."

In an amazing coincidence, that same morning I was offered a job at the National Program for the Mentally Retarded as a receptionist. I went to the unemployment office and the lady pulled from her files a job for receptionist.

I enjoyed my new job—answering the phone, doing research for fundraising. This was a campaign office and I was involved in all kinds of activity, but I hardly ever saw any mentally retarded people. Sometimes I saw them featured on a poster working in a sheltered workshop, but that was all. *Why is it that they think that's all they can do?* I remember telling myself. *They can make beautiful Christmas cards and wonderful pottery, but they could do so much more.* At fundraising dinners, there was usually a table full of beautiful items for sale, such as teapots, candles and paintings, made by mentally retarded people, yet the people who made these gifts weren't selling them. They were never able to witness the joy their creations brought to the people who purchased them.

When I mentioned this to my boss one morning, he laughed, and said, "They can't come out and sell. It requires supervision, transportation. It's unnecessary. Besides, we're the campaign office, we don't get involved in those politics."

Well you should get involved with those politics if you're out raising the money, I thought to myself as I went back to answering the phone. I nearly said, Hello, The National Program for the Dull and Unimaginative, the next time the phone rang.

I could hear my heart beating to the beat of Silver's gallop. Then my boss came over and put a grant application on my desk: "Opportunities for Youth, Federal Government."

"File this away," he said. "We don't need it." I picked it up and was intrigued by what it said. "Job creation. 18–23 years of age." At 23, I just made the requirement.

That's Trudeau for you, a visionary, a dreamer, I thought about the program his government created. I snuck the application in my bag and took it home.

My mind was churning furiously that night. "Why can't the retarded do something other than janitorial work? Who made the law?" I said, pacing back and forth in front of Bernard. "If something isn't done about it they will remain that way for the rest of their lives."

There was no planning, no careful strategizing when it came to creating programs for the mentally retarded. If it didn't exist, then I just knew I had to do it. I was going to set up a theatre company with puppets, of course. After all, that's what I knew how to do. I was sure there was a reason I'd been fired by Judi and hired by the National Program, and I wasn't going to waste the opportunity. I sat up all night to fill out the application, knowing in my heart that this had the potential to make a huge difference. As I completed the application, I thought of those children at Surrey Place and those young people in the horrible institution in Orillia.

I suddenly realized, my life had a purpose—it had meaning. I was excited and relieved at the same time. *I have a calling. I'm going to change the lives of people who are mentally retarded. Take away the hurt, surround them in bright colours like the sun. It will be my puppets, my imagination and my pretending that will make the world a better place for others!*

A week later, I noticed a newspaper ad for Liberace's show at Toronto's O'Keefe Centre on November 12. Liberace was my mother's favourite entertainer, and he was coming direct from Las Vegas.

When I was growing up my parents had always remarked, "If you ever have the opportunity to see Liberace in concert, you will love it." I don't think there was a kid on Kingsway Drive who was learning to play the piano that didn't have Liberace's sheet music with his picture on it. It was that same picture that shone from the newspaper ad. I remember thinking what a great puppet he'd make.

I managed to get four tickets to the evening performance. Mom and Judi couldn't come, so I took Bernard, a girlfriend from the Artists' Workshop—Ann Laitin—and Robert, who had grown into a rebellious teenager who was fun to be with. We dressed to the nines. I wore a long red gown, Ann was in purple, and our dates wore tuxedos—we were going to have a blast. We sang in the car as we headed for the O'Keefe Centre.

When we got there, the lobby was buzzing with anticipation before the show even started. "Two minutes to curtain. Please take your seats, the show is starting." I was so excited.

But as we walked into the O'Keefe Centre, the usher looked at our tickets and told us that the four of us weren't sitting together. Robert was in the balcony, Ann was in the second balcony, Bernard was in the mezzanine at the back and I was in the mezzanine in the middle. Robert was a little annoyed that I didn't get four tickets seated together. "That's all they had left," I said, and went to my seat.

The overture began and the curtain rose. Liberace entered wearing a long, white fur coat. "It's made from white virgin mink, and you know how hard that is to find!" he drawled.

He was hilarious, walking into the audience to show off his rings. "Oh darling, I see you have a beautiful diamond," he said to one woman, "but I didn't have to do anything to get mine." The audience roared.

"Do you like my outfit?" Everyone applauded. "I had it made for my royal command performance for the Queen... I was the only one there with one like it."

At intermission, the four of us met in the main lobby. I saw Ann first and ran up to her to tell her how I thought Liberace would make a great puppet. "The smile, the hair, the hand gestures, the piano, the candelabra. Can't you just imagine this all in black light?" Ann loved my ideas and was excited to see them come to life.

The rest of the Liberace show was an incredible spectacle featuring many of his lavish costumes that were paraded one after the other. In his last set, he came out wearing hot pants in the colours of the American flag. He danced to the Stars and Stripes and then the lights went off. In complete darkness, he lit up like a Christmas tree.

The money I had spent on those four tickets was worth every penny. After the show, I met my friends. "We have to go backstage to meet him," I insisted. Pushing my way through the crowd, with Bernard, Robert and Ann following me, I reached the stage door. A young usher was standing against the wall. "Look at him," I said to Robert. "This is going to be a snap."

"Yeah, just like Christmas caroling was."

"Give me $10," I demanded.

"Ten dollars?" Robert asked. "What are you going to do with $10?"

"You'll see, Tonto."

He handed it to me saying, "Why do I feel that this is Christmas caroling all over again and I'm the one who gets left holding the mug?"

"Hi." I smiled at the cute usher, in his conservative uniform. Then I gave him the $10.

"What's this for?" he questioned.

"I want to get backstage and see Liberace."

"Backstage? You'll never get backstage." He looked at the $10 and handed it back to me. "Not on your life! No visitors are allowed backstage."

"Wait a minute—this always works in the movies."

"Well, this isn't the movies. Your $10 is not going to cost me my job."

I went back to Robert, deflated.

"Give me back my $10," he said and grabbed the bill from me. Bernard put his arm around me, knowing I was close to tears.

"But it always works in the movies," I kept telling him.

We went to the lounge to have a drink. The audience was still buzzing as it left the theatre with souvenir programs in hand.

"Here," Bernard offered. "I bought you a program. Feel better?"

My eyes started to well with tears. Why hadn't it worked out as it always does in the movies?

Then Ann nudged me in the shoulder, "Look, there's Liberace."

"Where?"

"Over there." She pointed to a roped-off area that was specially arranged for Mr. Showmanship and his guests.

"How do I get in there? There are too many security guards. Oh look, he's dancing with that lady."

"Wait! What are you doing?" Ann yelled.

I still don't know what possessed me, but I had absolutely no control over my actions. It was as if my guardian angel picked me up and dropped me over the rope. I tapped the lady on the shoulder who was dancing with Liberace and said, "May I cut in?" I couldn't believe it. *I'm dreaming*, I thought. *I can't believe I'm dancing with Liberace!*

Liberace swirled me around the room like he was performing on stage.

"I'm Diane, and I performed at the London Palladium." *Now why am I saying that?* My mouth was moving faster than my feet.

"I love the London Palladium," Liberace said, smiling.

"Then you must know Des O'Connor," I said, hoping he wouldn't catch me in this lie I was creating.

"Oh yes, I love his act. He's a great British entertainer. Have you worked with him?" Liberace asked me.

"Oh yes—that's why I had to cut in—to tell you that we made a life-size puppet of you. Your piano flies in the air, chasing after the candelabra. Musical notes appear every time you pound the keys. And *our* Liberace, well, he plays the piano with his feet!"

Liberace stopped dancing. His eyes opened wide.

"Seymour!" he shouted across the dance floor to his manager. "Look, come with me," he said, taking me by the hand. "Seymour, you must meet this delightful young woman. Diane, is it?"

"Yes. Diane," I nodded.

"She has a puppet of me. Wait till you hear what I can do. Tell my manager." Liberace was like a little kid who had just discovered a new toy—a puppet of him.

"Well, I performed with the London Palladium—and we made a puppet of Mr. Showmanship himself," I knew he'd like that "and it's all painted in fluorescent colours—it's black light and everything—and Liberace's piano bench and candelabra fly across the stage. Instead of the cow jumping over the moon, it's Liberace who does the jumping!"

"Isn't it wonderful?" Liberace laughed.

Then all of a sudden the general manager of the O'Keefe Centre, Hugh Walker, came over to join us. *Uh-oh,* I thought, *he'll know I'm a fake. What a stupid thing to make up such a story.* I had forgotten that the London Palladium had been here just the week before performing in this very theatre. *He'll know my story is as phony as a three-dollar bill. Maybe if I keep talking, nobody will get a word in edgewise.* So I kept chattering away.

"Seymour," Liberace eventually cut in, "give Diane your card." Seymour opened his alligator wallet *(hmm... I wonder how much that cost?)* and handed me his business card with Liberace's trademark piano keys.

"Now, you hang on to this card," Liberace told me. "And keep in touch with Seymour. I want to see your act."

With that precious gift in my hand and a big hug from Liberace to make the evening perfect, I bolted from the reception area and hopped over the rope before I could be found out.

Bernard, Robert, Ann *and* I were in shock, but I enjoyed every minute of it. "I got his card—I got his card!" I looked up at the stars and made a wish to my guardian angel. *Help me achieve my dream. Guide me to find my players. Dear God, thank you for tonight.*

Liberace was my inspiration. Suddenly, the idea popped into my head: *Famous PEOPLE Players—that's what I will call my theatre company—it's perfect! We'll use life-size puppets of famous people, and Liberace will be the first.*

The next morning, I woke up and thought it had all been a dream. It had never happened. I fell back onto the pillow, looking up at the cracks in the ceiling of my room. I almost started to cry. Then I got up and ran to my closet. I opened the door and reached inside my coat pocket, and there it was—Seymour Heller's business card! It wasn't a dream; it was for real. I read that card over and over again until I had it memorized. Then it hit me. *Oh my God! I told him I was with the London Palladium—that I already had a puppet of him. I have to make the story true,* I thought. *Why did I make up the story?* As I looked at my face in the bathroom mirror, I knew why I'd done it. If Liberace had any idea that I was planning to start a theatre company with people who were retarded, he wouldn't be interested. He'd think that we wouldn't be any good. Besides, I could just imagine him saying, "What do they know about showbiz?"

No. We're going to be professionals—as good as anyone at the London Palladium, or Broadway, or anywhere else in the world. I was going to pull this off; I wasn't going to fail this time. I have my imagination, I have a dream and I will make my dream come true.

I went to the dresser drawer and pulled out my application for Opportunities For Youth. I picked up the phone and called the federal government representative, Sybil Powell.

"Opportunities For Youth," said a voice at the other end of the line.

"Is Sybil Powell there?"

"One moment, please."

"Sybil Powell speaking."

"Miss Powell, I'm Diane Thornton. I'm hoping I will have the opportunity to meet with you personally. I'm applying for an Opportunities For Youth grant."

"You know this is a three-month program," she said.

"Yes I do, and well, I've got some great ideas I'd like to share with you."

"When can you come in?" she asked.

"Right now. I mean today, if possible."

"You're certainly ambitious," she laughed.

"Oh yes—but I'm excited."

"And you want to share your excitement with me?"

"Yes!" I replied.

"Then I expect to see you here today at 2 p.m."

I tore open my closet, throwing one outfit after another on the floor until I found exactly what I was going to wear. *I have to make a good impression.* I hopped into the shower and sang the lyrics, "Aruba Liberace, then mambo for me" reliving his performance from the night before.

When I got to Sybil Powell's office, I sat straight with my legs crossed, a briefcase by my side, and tried to look smart. ("Don't touch your hair," I could hear my mother saying.)

"I don't like the way we treat the retarded and I feel my project will change that," I began.

"I'm listening." Sybil Powell leaned forward.

"We hide them away. The charitable associations contradict themselves by saying that these people are capable of working, but they just give them janitorial work. I feel that they are creative people wanting to burst out of themselves."

"What makes you think that?" She stared at me.

"Because they make beautiful Christmas cards and pottery," I said firmly. "I don't know if you remember the puppets of Trudeau and Streisand that made front-page news?"

"Oh, I remember. I thought you looked familiar— you're the puppet lady."

I smiled and felt proud. I had a reputation. "I want to do that with them—start a theatre company called Famous PEOPLE Players, and do life-sized puppets of famous people." I described to her in detail how it would all unfold. I had always seen everything larger than life. It was magic and I wanted to share it. The words kept flying out of my mouth, "The puppets are painted in fluorescent colours, you turn on the ultraviolet lights and you can't see the puppeteers...they disappear. It's magic."

"That sounds wonderful," she smiled.

I added that the performers would learn to become self-reliant.

"That's a very interesting idea," she said, turning the pages of my application.

As she was reading it, I said, "You know what?"

"What?" She looked up.

"You would get the credit—because you saw an opportunity to change the world's attitude about the mentally retarded. You would be giving an opportunity to young people who would never have a chance like this come their way."

Shut up, Diane! I screamed in my head. *Don't push too hard.* I leaned forward to soften my approach when Sybil closed my application.

"I think your idea, or should I say dream, is wonderful, Diane. I'm going to try and help you in any way I can," she said.

We spent the next hour fine-tuning the application—specifying how many people would participate, how many people would be needed to help train the players, where we would rehearse, and most importantly, "You need to get three support letters from the community or it is a no-go," she said firmly. "You can call me anytime you want and when you have everything in place, the application will be forwarded to Ottawa. I can't promise you'll get the money, but I think you have a very good chance."

A very good chance? To some people that wouldn't be much to bank on, but Sybil's encouragement was money in the bank to me. I left her office, not realizing the mountain ahead of me I still had to climb.

I started with Audrey Watson at Surrey Place.

"You'll have to go to the Toronto Association for the Mentally Retarded and see the president or the executive director. They are the ones to give you a support letter for your application."

"What do you think my chances are?"

"Well, I don't know. This has never been done before."

"You like it, don't you?" I needed some kind of encouragement.

"I do, Diane, but I'm just a small fish in a large pond, and besides, I don't have your imagination to picture it."

Surely, if they were really committed to the mentally retarded, as they say they are, they would leap at the opportunity, I kept saying to myself.

I phoned the schools for the retarded, the sheltered workshops in the Toronto area, and all I got was: "What experience do you have?"

"I have lots of experience with puppets. I was on the front page of the *Toronto Star.*"

"I don't mean that," one principal I visited said. "I mean with the mentally retarded."

"Well, I volunteered up in Orillia, and performed at Surrey Place Centre."

"Do you have a degree in psychology?"

"No."

"Do you have a diploma in early childhood education?"

"No."

"What education do you have?"

He brought me up short. I had no education. Dejected, I left.

The dream can't possibly stop here, I cried to myself. *I have a heart, I care, I know I can do this.* But I didn't have the courage to stand up for myself.

"It's a nice idea," said one teacher of a special needs school. "But it's just not practical."

The more I tried to convince them, the less they wanted to hear about the project. One of the most painful encounters was with a staff member at yet another training centre.

"These mentally retarded people have to be prepared for the future and just what kind of a future would you be offering them, sticking them up on stage? It sounds like a freak show to me."

"Freak show!" I gasped. "How dare you accuse me of making freaks out of them. They're people, not your so-called 'mentally retarded,' which you, with all your education, label them. It's you who are making them into freaks just by thinking such an awful thought. When you address them, you should always address them as people first, handi-capped second. And you call yourself dedicated!"

"Look, I'm sorry…I didn't mean to…I was just trying to put this into perspective, as to how the public would react."

"React! There is nothing to react to because the public isn't going to know. It's black light; nobody will see them. The public will just see and hear the puppet of Liberace—not the players."

"But their future?"

"Their future would be a lot brighter if they were doing more than putting pencils into boxes," I retorted.

"I'm sorry, but there are certain realities involved when working with these people that you certainly don't understand." She turned her back and said, "I'm late for a meeting. I have to go." She left me standing there in her attractively decorated office, while just outside her door and down the corridor, there was a grey room where people sat in an assembly line, stuffing pencils in boxes.

School after school, expert after expert, I was still on the ground looking up. I tried everything, and I even began banging on the doors of all the training centres again. I tried getting appointments with officials in municipal and provincial governments, as well those in social services. Nothing was working and I turned to Judi for support. "I don't have a chance at the Opportunities For Youth grant unless I have three solid support letters, and I can't get anyone to believe in my project!"

"Give up. It's not going to work," she said.

"But it is—and I'm going to make it work."

"How, Diane?"

"How? You need a letter from someone important, someone who would have credibility. Anne Murray. I'll get one from Anne Murray!" Judi almost choked on the apple she was munching.

"Yeah. She is the honorary president of the Canadian Association for the Mentally Retarded—I'll write to her, then I'll go to the mayor of Toronto." I kept babbling about all my ideas out when Judi said, "Good luck. They say if you can't get a response, go to the top. Besides, you have a lot of chutzpah."

"What's that mean?" I looked up at her.

"It's Yiddish—and it means something in between confidence and arrogance, with a huge scoop of nerve thrown in."

"That sounds like me," I laughed. "Talk about chutzpah —you certainly let them know where you were hanging your coat when you took that job as curator of the Hart House Gallery at the University of Toronto."

"I love that job," she said.

"Would you ever consider giving it up and joining my company?"

"Now that's a perfect example of chutzpah! You've got to be kidding, not a chance," Judi said. "Try someone like Ann Laitin. She has spunk, she dances, she's creative— and she's 18, the right age for the project qualifications. She'll have the enthusiasm to go along for the ride. Oh yeah, she can type too. Get her to type up your letter to Anne Murray!"

We were a great team. Ann typed my letters and I banged on doors.

When I went into work one day, I convinced my boss, Dave, to help me. "I need you to write a letter—a really good support letter to help me get this grant. Please!" I begged.

"We're a campaign office, hired to raise money for the Canadian Association for the Mentally Retarded. Once the campaign is finished, I go to work on another project for another charity," he explained. "My letter, Diane, is not going to help you."

"They won't know the difference. The letterhead is perfect—the National Program for the Mentally Retarded, and you're the president. Please!"

"*If* I write you a letter, I will write about how great you are to work with, the kind of person you are—determined and full of spunk," he said, winking at me.

"A job reference letter, I'll take it! And could you add one little tiny line that says that if anybody can make this project work, it would be Diane. She can make a big difference?" I winked back at him.

"I suppose you would like to type up this letter yourself and let me sign it?"

I made a beeline for the typewriter, and tried to type, even though I was (and still am) the world's worst typist. In the meantime, Ann typed up the letter to Anne Murray. I continued answering phones, running errands for my boss and turning my little reception desk into my own little business on the side. When Dave read my draft letter, he said, "You know those awful posters you don't like that we used in the campaign, with that word 'Normalization'?"

"Yeah?"

"Focus on that slogan," he suggested. "Get them to put their money where your mouth is, with their own philosophy."

Why didn't I think of that? I hit myself on the head.

Dave was now getting into the spirit. "Call Dr. Allan Roeher. He's a strong advocate for normalization. Here's his number. A letter from him would go a long way."

"Dave, I can't thank you enough."

"If it doesn't work out, you always have a job as receptionist on my next project."

I started to get tears in my eyes. This was the first boss I ever had who didn't want to fire me.

I got an appointment with Dr. Roeher, a distinguished man who was also the executive vice-president of the Canadian Association for the Mentally Retarded. I enthusiastically described my project to him. He got up from his chair, walked around his desk, and leaned against it. He was skeptical, but in a kind way. "It sounds like a wonderful idea, but the grant is for three months. Then the performers have to return to their sheltered workshop. This is not a long-term solution."

"Oh, yes, it is." I jumped up from my chair. "These people will have careers. They will be professional performers."

"Diane, everyone knows the entertainment world is full of disappointments—up one day, down the next. It's not stable." He expressed sincere concern. "How can you speak in terms of a career when 'normal' people, with all their training in theatre, have great difficulty?"

"Well, I got an audition with you."

He laughed, which broke the ice, and our conversation became more relaxed. "See me next week for a callback," he said. "And I'll think about it."

The next week, I was waiting for him outside his office at 8:45 a.m., even before his secretary arrived. I brought him a coffee.

"I have a feeling I'm not getting rid of you," he said as I entered the room.

"No. I want you to hear all about the show that we're going to perform."

He leaned back in his leather swivel chair, took the lid off his Styrofoam coffee cup, and started to sip it. Again, for what seemed like the hundredth time, I explained my idea of black light, flying musical notes and Liberace. "I even found a great design student who will build the puppet, and my friend, Ann, who can perform." Ann would lead the performers on stage to help them find their way until they could do it on their own.

"We are committed to finding the right support. You're the right support!" I watched him take another sip of coffee. He was silent, but I knew I was getting to him. Then I went in for the kill. "We need you, Dr. Roeher." I pleaded. "The people called 'mentally retarded' and the whole world need you. You have dedicated your life to normalization and now this is the opportunity of a lifetime to put it into action and see it bloom."

"You're good Diane, real good," he laughed. "I do believe you're sincere, and that's all I'm going to tell you right now. You're going to have to be patient and give me a few days to think over these ideas of yours."

"A few days! Why a few days?"

"Because I say so. And because you must learn to be patient." He escorted me out of his office and thanked me for the coffee. "Next time, don't forget the cream."

He liked me. I knew it. *Dear God, bless him, and whisper in his ear to say 'yes.'*

The next hurdle was trying to recruit performers, which no teacher would give me. I knew I was getting ahead of myself but I started to worry more and more about whether I was ever going to make this dream happen.

On Valentine's Day, Dr. Roeher phoned me. "Well, I gave it a lot of thought," he said.

I held my breath. "You did? And…what did you decide?"

"To support you and your dream," he replied. "You can pick up your support letter, and bring donuts."

I screamed for joy. "I can't thank you enough, Dr. Roeher. You'll never regret this decision." I hung up. Then the doorbell rang. I was now living in a rooming house with other women. I ran down the stairs to open the door before my landlady got there because we weren't allowed male visitors.

There stood Bernard with roses in his hand.

"Bernard!" I shouted, "I just got a call from Dr. Roeher. He's supporting the project. The executive vice-president of the Canadian Association for the Mentally Retarded is supporting the project!"

"Okay," he said, waving a velvet jewellery box under my eyes.

I soon forgot about Dr. Roeher. The box sent shivers down my spine. I opened the box while I stood in the doorway and in it was a diamond ring. Bernard had asked me to marry him. His eyes were sparkling even brighter than the ring he slipped on my finger. Over the previous several months, our love had grown to be the most natural thing I had ever experienced. We were a great team—his quiet humour and strength balanced my outgoing and energetic persona. I knew he was the man I wanted to share my life with. And he became my biggest ally.

We had lots to celebrate that evening: our engagement and my coup with Dr. Roeher. We broke open a bottle of champagne with my mother, who still lived in Hamilton. She was thrilled with both events, but she still remained my biggest critic. She didn't believe Famous PEOPLE Players would work.

"To prove it, I will help you," she offered.

"Now that doesn't make sense," I said. "Are you going to help me not make it work?" I said angrily.

"I am going to help you make it professional. I'll show you how to make the costumes and paint. Diane, need I remind you that you failed home economics? How are you going to build props and make clothes for your costumes when you can't even thread a needle? I don't want you to fall flat on your face."

She thinks I'm a failure. I sank into my chair and said nothing. As we left Mom's place that night, Bernard held my hand and said, "I know you're going to make this work." That was all I needed to hear.

Once Dr. Roeher's letter came, the others followed: my member of parliament supported me and so did the wonderful Anne Murray. "The benefits of such a project can be rewarding for all of us," she said in her letter. Our Canadian snowbird did not let us down.

Next came the search for qualified professionals with dance training. Finally, after months of searching, we found Lisa and Cynthia.

Then came a location. Dr. Roeher, who proved to be a great advocate for the project, even arranged a place where we could rehearse—the office down the hall from him. I think he wanted to keep an eye on me to make sure I didn't get out of hand. Everything seemed to be falling into place nicely, except the most important thing—the performers themselves.

I was facing resistance. One woman waved her finger in my face. "The parents are questioning their kids' futures. What happens when your three-month grant is up? What about their pensions? If you take them off their pensions and give them a paycheque, they'll never get back on."

I needed the parents' support or there would be no project. The minimum age for Opportunities For Youth was 18, and even though this was the legal age to consent to participate, I still needed the parents' consent. "Let's say if something happened to the parent," the counsellors started to educate me, "how would they know for certain that their son or daughter would be provided with an income?"

Sybil Powell, who was starting to become a friend, knew how to get around this. "To avoid losing their pensions, we'll pay them for two months instead of three. They are allowed to earn additional money up to a certain maximum," she said with authority. I was disappointed, but Sybil had the answer. "You won't find anyone to join the project without parental consent if you don't do this."

Parents weren't the only problem. One teacher at a training centre thought she was being helpful when she suggested that I recruit eight-year-olds to be the performers. "You don't understand. This is going to be a professional black-light theatre company," I explained—again.

I'm not going to give up, I told myself. *I'm going to find the Famous PEOPLE Players if I have to go to every school and training centre in Canada! I know they're out there somewhere.*

My former boss, Dave, told me about a place called the Haney Centre, headed by a woman called Doreen Crystal. It was experimenting with a relatively new concept in training and he thought I should look into it. When I called Doreen, I didn't even have to finish my spiel before she responded. "I might have several kids who would be interested. Let me arrange for you to meet them in a couple of weeks' time."

Meanwhile, the grant application needed the names of each candidate. "Here's what we're gonna do," I told Ann, who was on board with me.

"Uh-oh," she said.

"We're going to fill out the application and we're going to say that we have the nine participants. We'll give the names later, along with their social insurance numbers."

"There's one problem," she said.

"What's that?"

"We don't have nine participants."

"Yes we do, from the Haney Centre."

"But that's not confirmed. Besides, what about their parents? You still have to get approval."

"Look, we'll take care of the parents later—just fill out the final page of the grant."

The next morning, I delivered the application to Sybil. Within two weeks, it was finally accepted—thanks to Sybil, who pushed it through as if it was a bill being passed by Parliament.

Our grant was for $18,000, including salaries of $70 per week for the performers and staff, and $86 a week for me as the project leader. I decided not to take my salary, so I could use it to buy materials to build the puppets.

That week, the Haney Centre called to say I could meet everyone the first week in May. It was a day that I will never forget as long as I live. It was the first time that I had ever spoken to a group of people who were mentally retarded, and talked to them about my dream.

I was surprised to find that the Haney Centre was a house, with a living room, kitchen and bedroom on a nice, quiet street. Most of time, I'd meet mentally retarded people in workshops or classrooms, but never a house. I was nervous walking into the unexpected. They all sat around, some on couches, others on living room chairs, another leaned back on a La-Z-Boy chair.

When I was introduced, many of them laughed. I sat down on a piano bench and looked at their faces. One tall, lanky guy with bent shoulders was shouting at a small, elfin young man who wore a black leather jacket with lots of silver rings on his fingers. He looked tough. Others sat up nice and straight. They seemed polite, and they weren't laughing at me. One girl sat on another guy's lap playing with his hair. The teacher pulled them apart.

It's the nice ones on this side of the room that I want to join the project, I thought.

I started to talk about Famous PEOPLE Players, but the shouting was deafening. "Shut up," yelled one kid. "I can't hear her."

"It's going to be a puppet theatre, and you're going to learn to perform on stage."

"Do we swim?"

"No."

"What about canoeing?"

"No, it's puppets."

"Do we play baseball?" asked the tough little kid with the leather jacket.

"What about the potato sack race? I can beat Brian," the tough girl in men's clothes said.

"I'll get you," he replied.

What on earth are they thinking about? I was puzzled by their reaction.

Then one of them said, "We go to camp every summer, and it's lots of fun and we get to play all the time."

"Don't you want to earn a paycheque?" I asked.

"Nah, I'd rather go to camp."

Suddenly, the sloppy guy with the bent shoulders said, "This sounds great!"

"Yeah," piped up the kid with the leather jacket.

The girl who had been sitting on the guy's lap was inching toward another guy on the couch. Playing with her hair, she looked at me with her baby blue eyes, and said, "I'd like it."

I felt confused. I don't want those people. I want the other ones, the well-behaved teenagers. At the end of our meeting, the loud and abusive ones were all putting their hands up to join Famous PEOPLE Players. The quiet ones got up to leave.

I was left sitting in a room with the rejects. They couldn't sit still for one second, and appeared to have terrible coordination. One had a speech impediment that made it impossible for me to understand what he was saying. Eleven—there were 11 of them, and I felt like Lee Marvin in the movie *The Dirty Dozen*. How was I supposed to make professionals out of this group?

A funny-sounding voice interrupted my hysterical thoughts.

"Hey, dearie, how ya doin'?" A young man with puppy-dog eyes smiled at me, but a small, dishevelled teenager in a black leather jacket interrupted him. He looked at me and said, "Grizzk."

"Pardon me?"

"Grigozik"

"Slow down," I said, "I'm having trouble following what you're saying."

"His name is Greg," yelled the tall guy with the bent shoulders.

"Say your name for me, Greg, only slower."

"Greg Kozak."

One by one, I sat with them, writing down their names and addresses. It took more than an hour. I spent another hour explaining to all of them that they would have to apply for a social insurance number to get a paycheque. They also had trouble understanding that they were to report at the association office of the National Program for the Mentally Retarded at York University, not the Haney Centre.

Finally, on 11 pieces of paper, I wrote down the address, date and time they needed to meet me. I told them to give this information to their parents since they were now a part of the Famous PEOPLE Players.

As I left the Haney Centre, I looked back and saw the kid with the bent shoulders trying to crawl through the front window.

CHAPTER THREE

X Marks the Spot

June 1, 1974. I'll never forget that day as long as I live. It was the most important and memorable day of my life: the official founding of the Famous PEOPLE Players. In fact, it was more than that. The first day of starting a professional theatre company actually turned out to be the first day of learning how to find the strength and determination within myself to never give up.

Ann and I, along with the newest member of the team, Ron Dick our prop man, got to our designated office really early that morning. We made our way through the offices on the second floor, avoiding the dark, empty desks and the line of filing cabinets that led into our tiny corner space.

"Can you find the light switch?" I asked Ann, who was carrying a box that contained a record player and Liberace records. She put it down on the desk, which sat in the front entrance to the room.

"It's here, I think," she said as she pressed the switch and a row of lights popped on one by one. "So this is it," she said as she looked around. "It's small. How are we all going to fit in here?"

Just past our tiny front office was our designated rehearsal space, an adjoining room about 12 by 10 feet. The desk in the front office had one chair for a visitor and one for the person behind the desk. "We'll need a typewriter."

I was looking at the typewriters in the main office. From our little corner we could see out to the main administration offices from a small window.

"Let's put the record player in this corner." I bent down to find an outlet for the cheap portable record player I had owned for years. "We need a table to prop it up on, Ann." I looked out to the main office and there was a tiny one over by the third desk.

"It's not ours," Ann stared out the window.

"Oh, I'm sure they won't mind." I walked out of my office and headed to the small table, removed the books on top of it and wrote a little note to the secretary. "Dr. Roeher needed the table for a special project on the breakthrough of the mentally retarded. Thank you."

"That's nerve," Ann said, following me.

"Never mind—we've got only three months to pull this off."

The record player fit nicely on the table. "Now, the first thing we're gonna do when they all arrive here is stretch exercises, then assign parts and rehearse with music."

Before I could go any further, Ron walked in. "This place is far. Couldn't you pick a place closer to Toronto? It took me an hour and a half by bus and subway to get all the way up here. We're in the boonies."

"This is the York University campus and I'm going to go to school to take psychology here," Ann said.

"Well I'm going to need a dorm—the commute is going to kill me." He had a sketchbook and a small box of paint. "I didn't know what else to bring because I'm not sure what we need to start building."

"When everyone gets here, we'll sit down and talk about how the shows are going to look," I replied.

By now, many of the secretaries, who worked for various departments of the National Program for the Mentally Retarded, were coming up the main stairway to take their positions at their desks. There were 14 desks in the main room, which was in the centre of the second floor. Surrounding the main central offices were private offices, each with a window looking into the main administration area where the secretaries sat. Dr. Roeher's office was at the opposite end of the second floor, tucked away in a corner. The place was starting to get busy and the phones were starting to ring.

"I think it's time to get ready to meet the future Famous PEOPLE Players," I said proudly. As we walked past the desks, each secretary looked up at us with curiosity—we were the new tenants who had invaded the corner office.

"Uh-oh," Ann said, "that secretary is reading the note you left."

We kept walking—and I glanced out of the corner of my eye. "Just smile," I said.

"Good morning," we said as we went by.

We went and stood at the top of the winding staircase to greet our future performers. Over the next couple of months, we would be getting plenty of exercise going up and down these stairs.

The wall was covered in beautiful artwork, from the bottom to the top of the stairway. We stood there admiring the beautiful building, which was the headquarters for the National Program for the Mentally Retarded.

"It hasn't been open for long, according to the plaque at the foot of the steps," I said. "I feel like Scarlett O'Hara running up and down this staircase. It's nice and wide."

At the foot of the stairway was the main lobby, lined with glass cabinets that displayed artwork by the mentally retarded. We stood at the top of the staircase, about to go down the steps when, without any warning, the main glass doorway burst open and the screaming began. It sounded like a stampede of elephants going up the stairs.

"Oh my God! I'm not going to make it. My appendix!" yelled one of the boys, huffing and puffing. He collapsed at the top of the stairway and rolled down a few steps.

"Quick! Call an ambulance!" I shrieked to Ann.

As she raced to the office to call an ambulance, he picked himself up and leaned against the wall behind him, almost knocking down the paintings. He started to laugh hysterically. "I'm only kidding," he said.

Ron ran to tell Ann to stop calling the ambulance. The others were all applauding the boy and laughing. They thought it was funny. I grabbed the class clown by the shoulder.

"You scared the hell out of me." He didn't answer. "I said you scared me. Why did you do that?"

He started to squirm with embarrassment. "I don't know," he said with his tongue hanging out of his mouth.

His eyes looked up to his brain as if he could find an answer there.

"You played a mean trick on me and now we've got to call the ambulance back and tell them not to come. I want to know why you think it's so funny."

"I don't know, Miss," he looked like he was about to cry. "I'm scared. I won't do it again."

"What's your name?" I put my arm around him to take him up the stairs toward the office.

"Fred."

"Fred what?"

"I don't want to go with you!"

"Yes you do, Fred. And everything's going to be all right, providing you don't play any more tricks."

I was so busy walking Fred to our little office, I didn't notice all the secretaries standing up, staring at us in shock. When we reached our room, there was a scene of complete confusion. One of the girls, Alice, was locked in a passionate embrace with one of the boys. Two others were rolling around on the floor punching each other. Another girl, Daphne, who was wearing a flowered, cotton housedress that looked like it belonged to her mother, was sobbing and clutching her plastic purse in fear. One boy was spinning around in circles, and the others were leaping around the room like kangaroos. In the middle of our circus stood Ann, Ron and I, staring at what looked like a scene from *One Flew Over The Cuckoo's Nest*.

Then Fred went over the top as he yelled "Retard!" to a girl who wore men's overalls, work boots and a plaid shirt. The room went silent. He pointed to her and yelled again, "RETARD!" Everyone froze. The girl burst into hysterical tears and ran out of the room, past the secretaries, down the winding staircase, and out of the building. I followed her, only to watch her throw herself on the sidewalk, crying. Behind me, the secretaries jumped to their feet and watched the excitement.

She was crying hysterically as people walked by, staring at her. As I got closer to help her up, I could hear her crying, "LABEL, LABEL, LABEL..."

"What label?" I asked. She sat up, cross-legged, and looked at me with such great hurt in her eyes that I wanted to cry with her.

"What Fred called me."

I helped her up, took her to the bench on the front lawn, and sat down with her.

"What's your name?"

"Eleanor."

"Eleanor what?"

"Eleanor Lawrence."

"Okay Eleanor, I'm Diane; Diane Thornton. Now what's the label that Fred called you?"

"You know what I mean—it's because I wear my dad's clothes that he calls me that mean word: retard."

"Why do you wear your dad's clothes?"

"Because I like to, that's why, and besides I don't have any dresses. I don't like to be labeled—labels go on jars in the supermarket." Her tongue was beginning to poke out the side of her mouth.

"We should never use the word retarded?" I asked.

"Don't say that," she cried.

"Eleanor, we have to get rid of that label and give you a new one."

"A new one?"

"Yes, it's called professional. You and I, and even Fred, are going to work hard to change the label."

"How?"

"We're going to put together the Famous PEOPLE Players and we're going to be so good that no one will ever call you mentally retarded again. They are going to say you are a professional."

She wiped her eyes and we started to walk back into the building and up the winding staircase. "Eleanor, when people see you lying on the sidewalk crying—a grown woman—then you are acting like a retard. You have to start changing your behaviour so that no one will think or call you that. Do you understand?"

We stopped walking for a moment and I hugged her.

"Yes," she nodded.

We got to the second floor and walked past the secretaries, who stopped typing to look at us. This was my first lesson: You don't know anyone until you've walked a mile in their moccasins.

We rallied the 'troops' again and handed them over to Ron. Ann and I stood in our little reception office, staring at the kids through the clear plastic window. We felt like detectives who watched the suspects through a one-way mirror to see how they behaved while being interviewed. Ron was trying to show the group his sketchbook with beautiful drawings of animals. But they were still uncontrollable.

"You want to start a professional theatre company with these people?" Ann shook her head. "It will never happen; not with all these problems."

I marched back into the room, and what I did next surprised even me. "STOP IT! STOP IT! STOP IT! JUST STOP IT!" I screamed over their loud yelling. "SILENCE! SIT DOWN! SIT DOWN NOW! YOU'RE ACTING LIKE A BUNCH OF RETARDS!"

There was dead silence. Everyone sat down and lowered their heads. You could see the anger on my face. "Don't MOVE. And SHUT UP, you're behaving badly." I pointed at each of them, "You hurt people's feelings. You're mean." I paced the room like an army general. "How *dare* you come here today and treat us this way."

"Sorry," said a faint voice from the corner.

"Sorry, my ass. You'd better be better than this—because it's not happening again."

They looked scared and shocked. I bet no one had ever spoken to them like that in their whole lives.

"You smell, you're dirty, and you need to take a shower."

A hand went up slowly.

"YES!"

"I took a bath last night," said one boy.

"Well, I bet you're wearing the same clothes you've worn all week."

"I don't have any other clothes." He wanted me to feel sorry for him.

"Then you need to learn to wash the ones you have," I said severely.

I pulled up a chair in front of him, sat on it and said, "Let's be straight with each other. Eleanor's hurt because you," I pointed to Fred, "called her a retard."

Everyone started to perk up.

"Don't use that word," said Greg, the kid in the black jacket.

"Yeah, don't use it," added the kid with the bent shoulders, who started to straighten up. His name was Brian.

"Let me tell you something. When you behave the way you do, rolling on the floor, punching each other, screaming and hollering at the top of your lungs, and you—" I pointed to Alice, "throwing your body all over Mike in public, then you are acting like a retard."

They stiffened in horror.

"You came into this office this morning—into this beautiful building—screaming like bats out of hell." They started to laugh. "It's not funny," I said. "You're acting retarded. Your behaviour is terrible."

"I want to be normal," said Fred, perking up. "Don't you think I look normal?" he asked.

"No, you're too busy throwing yourself down the staircase screaming that you're having an appendicitis attack and calling people retards."

He was silent.

"Do you want to be normal?"

"YES!" Their hands went up.

"Then I'll help you to be normal. We're going to change together, you and me, Ann and Ron. We're all going to change because we're going to be in the Famous PEOPLE Players. We're going to act and behave professionally, normally, and when you do that, *nobody*—not even me—will ever call you retards again."

I went on to tell them that I knew how it felt to be different. How kids at school had made fun of me. How I couldn't hold down a job because I was fired from every place I worked. How I felt like a failure and, because of that, I couldn't amount to anything.

"At Famous PEOPLE Players, things will be different because we're going to succeed together. We're going to help each other, support each other, and not call our friends that we go to school with retards—like you did to Eleanor this morning. Instead, with the wonderful show we are going to create, we are going to make all of that disappear because *you* are going to disappear."

"Disappear!" they all said. That made them laugh.

"It's like the movie *The Invisible Man*. Ron will build a piano and piano bench and you'll lift up puppets and make them float in the air. But first we have to act like…"

"—like norms?" said Fred.

"We're going to be like the pioneers who built the railroad and the first highways. We're going to build a path for others to follow. It'll be lots of hard work, but we are going to do it for the people who come after us. We will change the attitude of people who don't understand people like us."

"We're going to be GREAT!" shouted Kevin. His big, puppy-dog eyes reminded me of Paul McCartney.

"Yes we are!" said Ann, supportively.

"Hey, Ann," Kevin said, "You and I make one good couple. Someday we got to go out on a date."

Everyone laughed.

"I want to show you something," I said, waving the business card of Liberace's manager, Seymour Heller. "We're going to make a puppet of Liberace and he will come to see our show. The curtain will go up and reveal the piano, the bench and the candelabra—all painted in bright colours. Then, at the very end of the show, we'll come out to take our bows, and, boy, will people applaud."

Everyone got excited and the screaming and yelling started up again.

"STOP IT!" I yelled over the noise. "We have to behave like professionals—like norms, as Fred said—if we are going to fool everyone."

I noticed one girl who was very quiet, sitting in a corner away from everybody.

"What's your name?" I asked. She wouldn't look at me.

"S-A-N-D-R-A."

"Sandra, come with me," I said quietly. When we got out of the room, I said, "You're bleeding—I believe you're having your period." We went to the bathroom and I bought her a pad from the dispenser.

"I don't know what to do," she spoke slowly. Apparently no one had ever told her what to do when she had her period, or maybe she forgot. I bought her three more pads and told her to keep them in her purse.

Before I knew it, it was lunchtime and we hadn't accomplished anything, except yelling and screaming. All I kept thinking was that we had three months to turn this group into professionals and create a show.

But there were some basics I had to teach the group first. "Today, we're going to learn how to behave like professionals. We wash, shave and take care of ourselves. When you go home tonight, remember that washing is like having a part in the show—only it's a part that will start getting rid of that label. Wash it away. We're going to work hard, learning our stage parts, and I'm going to call the CNE to have you perform there."

They started cheering and yelling again, but my voice was louder. It had to be to get their attention. "STOP IT! Remember—act professionally. You can clap and cheer, but screaming all the time has to stop, especially in this office. It's okay at a hockey game, but when we are in this office we have to behave like professional workers."

My challenge seemed to appeal to them. Alice stopped flirting for an hour, John stopped punching Keith and even Sandra smiled a little. I put on the record player and started to play "Aruba Liberace." Everyone got up to dance around the room. Every time the Liberace song said "Oomph," we all started to move our bodies and say, "Oomph." Sandra couldn't dance. Instead, she moved slowly—like a monkey with her arms and shoulders bent and sweeping across the floor. Brian refused to dance. Instead, he watched from the corner of his eye, arms folded.

"Come on, Brian, it goes like this," I said.

He giggled, "I know, I know."

The group was now lined up like a chorus line and Alice was chasing after Mike to get closer to him, and I was chasing after Alice to get between her and Mike. I looked up at one point and noticed all the secretaries outside our office watching us in disbelief. We turned to them and bowed. They hesitated, looked at each other, and then started to clap.

It was almost the end of the day, but we kept going. We decided to assign everyone a part, even though we didn't have any props yet. I could tell that Mike had great rhythm, so I put him on the maracas. Kevin was the piano. The small elfish boy, Greg, would carry the bench. Alice was the tambourine and Brian, who had difficulty moving, would be in charge of hiding the musical notes with a black cover before they floated from Liberace's piano.

"What do I do?" Fred started jumping.

"No jumping—you're the candelabra."

"Oh boy, I'm the candelabra, I'm the candelabra," he kept repeating. "Diane, what's a candelabra?" I showed him the picture of Liberace on the front cover of his album sitting beside the candelabra.

"That's me—wow! I got the best, I got the best."

"Shut up, Fred!" Ron cut in, "It's 6 p.m. and we've been here all day. It's going to take me an hour and a half to get home, just to wake up and come back to this zoo."

I didn't realize how fast the first day had gone by.

"Now, promise me, when you leave this office that you'll walk down the stairs *quietly*," I pleaded.

"Yeah, dearie, I promise," Kevin laughed.

"See you first thing in the morning."

"Promise me you'll take a shower—and sing "Aruba Liberace" while you're washing." Philip, a young man, whose head moved around as he talked, said with a stutter, "Ah, ah, I'll be here first," and he pointed his finger up.

"Okay, now line up single file."

I put Mike in the front of the line and Alice at the back, so he could get a head start home, away from her aggressive pursuit.

"Remember, quiet—and you, Fred, "Aruba Liberace" 10 times in the shower."

"Yeah, yeah, I promise."

I opened the door and watched them leave, tiptoeing across the office in a single file. I had just closed my door when I heard them screaming and jumping all the way down the winding staircase. The secretaries leaped up from their chairs.

The next day was a repeat performance—they came into work screaming and hollering up the winding staircase and they smelled appalling. Some were a couple of hours late because they got lost on campus. They wore clothes that made them look like nerds—especially Philip, who buttoned his shirt right up to the top button.

Even so, Ann, Ron and I were starting to enjoy our relationship with the kids. Even when they were spinning out of control, we were getting to know them as individuals. Eleanor continued to dress in her dad's clothes, yet she was a very sensitive girl. Mike seemed to be the most together of the group. He told me he was in public school, but because he couldn't read or write, his teachers suggested he go to the Association for the Mentally Retarded to be placed in a school for the retarded. Greg still looked tough, with his black leather jacket and steel rings on every finger. He had a great sense of humour and he loved sports. He knew every player, every score, every game ever played in the history of sport. For someone who couldn't read, he could tell you more information than what you'd read in the sports pages of the newspaper and could read scores and standings of any game. Fred, the show-off, was an overweight teenager with an excess of energy and a knack for constantly getting into trouble.

The biggest challenges were Alice and Daphne. Daphne behaved like a two-year-old and threw one temper tantrum after another. "Go suck your thumb," Kevin would often say to her. She was short and round and dressed like an old lady from a nursing home. When Ann tried to take her purse away from her while she was learning to perform, she bawled her eyes out. She worked herself into a frenzy; rolling on the floor, kicking her feet, holding her plastic purse close to her chest. We had to call her parents to come and take her home for the rest of the day.

The sex-mad Alice was particularly hard to take. Several times I caught her necking with Mike or Fred in the office.

"Look, I've told you before, no sex on the job. It's something you do at home and you keep it private. Do you understand?"

"Yes," she'd reply.

But by the next day… she was back at it again.

It was no wonder we were always starting rehearsals late. Some of the kids would arrive early, but others would get there hours late, like the time one of them forgot the route and ended up riding the subway for hours until a TTC supervisor came to the rescue. Even when rehearsals got underway, they were slow and painful and marked with constant interruptions.

The hygiene issue wasn't improving either. "I just don't get it," I'd say to Ann. "What are their parents teaching them? I feel like hopping into the bathtub with them and scrubbing them silly."

Ron usually worked quietly putting together a piano, candelabra and Liberace puppet. When the bench was finished, I played the voice of the announcer, from Liberace's record, introducing Liberace at a live concert. Sandra was supposed to hold the white hand that would point to Liberace when the announcer said the name. Over and over and over again we tried to help her memorize this movement.

"When I say 'Liberace!'—lift the hand and point to him." She never lifted the hand; she just stood there, staring.

Greg's piano bench always came out upside down and Kevin's piano was never in the same place twice. Greg and Kevin constantly mimicked each other, then would give me a thumbs up and reassure me they would get it right. But no matter how much Greg tried, the bench came out upside down.

Fred shook the candelabra so violently that the foam candles flapped back and forth until they broke off. Kevin usually pushed the piano past centre stage and right through the door of the office—into a secretary's desk. The secretary got used to pushing the piano back with her foot while she typed.

"CENTRE STAGE! Pretend there is an X on the floor—don't go past the X," everyone would often hear me yelling.

To make it easy, we actually drew an X on the floor. But Kevin had a way of zooming right by. After he'd miss his mark, Kevin would walk to centre stage, look at the X, shake his head, shrug his shoulders, scratch his head, and then walk back to get his piano and start all over again.

The office was just too cramped and we needed more space. I finally went to Dr. Roeher's office to ask permission to use the lecture hall downstairs. It had a tiny stage and more room for everyone. Ron would set up his cardboard piano on stage and we would sit out in the audience to give Kevin his cue. He pushed it right across the stage and smacked into the concrete wall.

"The X—don't you see the X?" Ron would yell.

He'd stop, look at it, walk around it, brush his foot over it, even thump on it, then he'd look up at me and say, "Okay, dearie, I'm on a roll, and I'm gonna give you the piano right there," he'd say, pointing to the X. Then he'd push the piano out slightly, nowhere near the X.

"Come on, Kevin—further." The piano moved a little bit, but never made it to the X. Ann tried guiding him to centre stage. After a few days of this, the piano legs came off and Ron had to rebuild them.

Introducing black light created a new problem. The performers couldn't understand the effect of being invisible. So I brought an old pair of shoes into work, a hat and a cane. Ann put on the hat, a pair of gloves and shoes, which were covered in fluorescent paint to glow. With the cane in hand, she started to dance around in the dark.

Without realizing it, we had created a number in the show that would become our company trademark—the invisible man. I chose the song "Me and My Shadow" from Liberace, which worked perfectly with our new logo. The performers all laughed and cheered as our logo danced around the stage. Then they ran up on stage and stood in *front* of the piano—showing their black bodies in front of the florescent image. They still couldn't understand that they could see themselves, but no one watching would be able to see them. So, Ron, Ann and I took turns positioning them *behind* the piano.

When Liberace's body was finally built, we knew it was going to be too difficult for anyone to handle. I became the head and body, Ann did the hands, and Ron handled the feet. You should have seen us learning to coordinate our movements!

Ron pulled down on the legs and I pulled up. Ann would try a balancing act between us. I was performing Liberace with one hand, and directing everyone's cues at the same time. When I was tired of lifting Liberace, Ann would lead rehearsal, and Ron and I would collapse from exhaustion. She was always trying to teach everyone to move in time with the music, with no success, except for Mike on the maracas, who was the only one who had rhythm.

Learning to move the musical notes came next. "Tiny, little notes—that should be real easy," I said to Ann. I was wrong. The notes kept bumping into each other and fighting for position. The fighting was even more intense behind the cover that Fred was holding to hide the notes at times. "Lift it higher!" yelled Alice.

"I'm doing it, I'm doing it," he yelled back.

In the middle of all this, I was trying to do and be everything to everyone. I was performing Liberace, directing the show, organizing the performers, and pleading with Dave Garrick, the general manager, to book Famous PEOPLE Players at the Canadian National Exhibition in August. After a week of frantic phone calls, he agreed—but there was a huge catch.

"Famous PEOPLE Players can do it, providing you perform *your* show, Diane, as always, in the park." He was referring to my puppet show. "Remember—it's 16 shows a day."

I tried to get Liberace himself to come see our show at the EX, which we endearingly called *Aruba Liberace*, after his hit song. I was careful never to tell him who we really were, but I could never get through. Whenever I called Seymour Heller in Hollywood, I got some snotty secretary on the other end of the line who would put me on hold for five minutes. Then she had the nerve to say, "Mr. Heller is in conference." And there was no response to my many letters.

Everyone at Famous PEOPLE Players was thrilled to be performing at the EX, but weren't making progress with our rehearsals. The ensemble was becoming more and more disorganized and it was a constant battle to achieve the simplest results. We had to constantly remind the players how to hold their props, stop the fighting and learn their cues. They'd hear my endless rant over and over: "we're here to change the label; you've got to be professional."

Then there were the parents. As rehearsals grew longer, my phone started to ring off the hook.

"Why is my kid at work till 7 p.m.?"; "Why are you yelling at them and calling them retards?"; "What's this crazy story about Liberace?" And, the worst one of all—"Are you exploiting them?"

I bullied them right back. "Look, Mrs. So-and-So, I don't have your social insurance number on file; I have your son's. If he has a problem, he should be man enough to speak to me directly."

Or, "If anyone should bitch here, it's me. Why should I have to put up with your daughter's behaviour?"

I don't know what possessed me to stand up to the parents when I couldn't even stand up for myself for years, but somehow I now had the strength. Perhaps it came from the fear of failing again. Or that we were running out of time. Or maybe it was because I had come to love each one of the players. My passion was their passion and we were all becoming a very special family. We believed in each other.

Still, I was being challenged. It wasn't long before I was hauled into Dr. Roeher's office to explain my methods. "Why is it all right for them to scream and yell because they're retarded, but it's exploitation when I do it, because I'm 'normal'? Let me tell you, Famous PEOPLE Players is going to be a major breakthrough for this disability. You'll see—and every one of those parents will eat crow. We're going to get rid of those labels, 'retard,' 'normal,' and we're going to do it together because it's what we all want."

Dr. Roeher smiled and said, "I can't keep up with you. Please, do me one favour? Lower the sound on the record player. I'm hearing "Aruba Liberace" in my sleep."

Among all this chaos, I was planning my wedding. There were days when my mother came to the office to fit me into my dress—taking it in, lifting up the hem—while I was trying to direct the show. She was growing frustrated because I'd usually have to run down the winding staircase to the lecture hall in the middle of a fitting. It wasn't unusual for me to be running around while I wore my veil and pins were stuck everywhere. I had always had a problem sitting still.

June 22, 1974—my wedding day. It felt odd not to be wearing blue jeans under my dress. My brother gave me away because Dad did not attend the ceremony. I hadn't invited him, which wasn't a nice move on my part, although I'm sure my mother invited him secretly. As we were walking down the aisle, I was as nervous as a cat. My brother, the comedian, whispered in my ear, "You should see the hat Auntie Ray is wearing." When he gave my hand to Bernard he said, "Whatever you do—don't fart."

When Bernard slipped the ring on my finger, I noticed spots of fluorescent pink paint all over my hand. "Please don't get paint all over my beautiful ring," he smiled.

The reception was wonderful. As usual, my mother outdid herself, cooking the entire meal—16 courses for 150 people. But this time I didn't have to carry the spaghetti strands to the broomsticks!

We couldn't afford a honeymoon, so we both went back to work at our jobs the next day. Bernard went back to the car company as general manager and I went back to directing at Famous PEOPLE Players. Everything was the same, except now I was living happily in a two-bedroom apartment in downtown Toronto with Bernard.

Just weeks to go until show time and we still had a lot of work ahead of us. I was getting more and more exhausted trying to whip everyone into shape. The three of us who were holding the Liberace puppet weren't getting any better—the head would usually go one way, the feet another, and Ann would scream for mercy in the middle. Fred was still shaking the candelabra violently. Greg was consistently inconsistent, bringing in the piano bench upside down. Meanwhile, his sidekick, Kevin, would invariably miss his mark—taking the piano right into the next wing, so we nicknamed his move 'the flying piano.'

Sometimes I felt like I was back in school and my teacher would make me repeat things over and over until I understood them. I remember how agonizing it was and I didn't want them to experience the same frustration, so I tried to make it fun for them.

One day Daphne threw a fit, screaming at the top of her lungs because I had corrected her for holding her musical note upside down. She rolled around on the stage, pulling her hair and kicking the piano until it broke. We tried to calm her down, although it didn't help. I had no choice but to call her mother and fire her. This was the first person to leave Famous PEOPLE Players.

July came quickly and it was the first time we'd be seeing a paycheque for our work. Everyone was so excited, especially me. I thought I was going to burst. In my joyous state, I wanted to do something special for overcoming our first hurdles.

"Ann, let's have a party—turn the whole affair into the Academy Awards."

We sent out invitations to all the performers for our make-believe award ceremony and everyone was all gung-ho. This party, we thought, would be a way for all of us to bond as a family. Ann and Ron cooked chicken tetrazzini. Ron brought wine, Greg brought beer and everyone dressed up to receive their 'Oscar' awards. I took Eleanor to my closet and picked out one of my dresses for her to wear. After Ann and I got through dressing her and applying some makeup on her, she blushed with embarrassment.

"You look beautiful," said Ron.

Everyone looked great. Even Greg shed his black leather jacket for the occasion. We all sat cross-legged on the floor office with our food in our laps.

"Ladies and gentleman, this is the day we have been waiting for—your paycheques."

The kids went wild. Ann, Ron and I announced each person's name and each one came up to receive the envelope.

"Now I can marry Sandra," Philip said. Everyone laughed as Sandra collapsed on the floor.

"Oh no, no way," she howled.

Everyone was so proud that I started to cry.

"Why are you crying, woman?" Greg asked me.

"Because I'm so proud of all of you."

"And we're proud of you," Mike hollered from across the room.

Kevin kept looking at Ann, who was out in the kitchen washing the dishes. "Hey dearie, you and I have to go out on a date soon."

It was a wonderful way to spend the afternoon. We all welcomed the break from the drain of rehearsals.

By the next day it was back to the grind. We needed to get Liberace to move in one piece, among other challenges. We also needed the musical notes to float without fighting behind the black cover, the candelabra to stop moving like a house on fire, the piano bench to appear right side up and the piano to hit its mark. We still had lots of work to do.

But now we had an encouraging 'audience' to push us along. The secretaries always looked forward to seeing the gang come up the stairs for work. On their coffee breaks they watched our rehearsals, applauding and cheering us on.

"You're great," they would yell. "BRAVO!"

We were just two weeks away from meeting a real audience—our first performance would be in front of all the parents—our own parents' night. "Finally we're going to meet the parents behind some of those phone calls," Ann said.

"I can't wait," Ron added.

After two months of rehearsals, Ann finished typing the invitations for the parents' night. Even though we were nervous about our first show, it actually helped us stay on track. The performers seemed to work harder because their parents were coming, and it made for high energy and ongoing enthusiasm during rehearsals. Mike was showing remarkable progress beyond his role to control the maracas on stage. When he wasn't on stage, he helped Ron carry supplies for the props. He even stayed late many nights to help repair the damage to the candelabra and piano during rehearsals. The others were slowly showing signs of progress—their hygiene was getting better and they were even setting up their props without a word from me.

On parents' night, I was really nervous, understandably. Besides, I had something to prove to many who didn't think it was possible to train my players. I wanted their parents to be proud of them and me. Ann and I stood quietly in the wings, trying to figure out who was who. In a show of support, all the secretaries from work came to watch too. Just as the lights were starting to dim, I saw Dr. Roeher slip in and take his seat at the back of the auditorium.

Ron turned on the record player. At first the needle got stuck, but then it got over the bump and the show began.

Sandra, who was the hand of the announcer's voice, never showed her hand—until long after her cue. Kevin brought the piano out only three feet from the wings.

"There's no room for the piano bench!" I yelled.

Greg was standing in the makeshift wings, with his bench held sideways, saying, "I gotta go. My mother's out there."

"NO!" I yelled at him as I held the Liberace puppet.

He tried forcing his bench on stage. I kicked it off. He persevered and then rammed it right into Liberace—

pushing Ann, Ron and me right into the piano, which fell into the candelabra, which crashed into the musical notes. The audience was cheering and there was an instant standing ovation at the end of the show.

After our clumsy and awkward performance, we all gathered in the lunchroom to meet with the parents. The ones that had given me a hard time didn't show up and the ones who came were truly supportive of their children and the project—particularly Greg's Mom, June Kozak. She was a delightful woman with a soft complexion and blonde hair. She couldn't thank Ann and I enough for all the work we had put in with Greg.

"I've never seen him so excited."

Brian and Kevin's mothers echoed the same sentiment. "They're up at the crack of dawn and can't wait to get to work," said Brian's mother.

"And Kevin—I have to tell him to wait, as the subways aren't running that early in the morning."

"If there's anything I can do," said June Kozak, "you've got my number. If you call, I'm willing to help you in any way I can."

For Ron, Ann and I, it was a relief to know there were some thankful parents out there who supported our work and appreciated our efforts. It gave us the courage to carry on.

The next day when I came into work, the secretaries all congratulated me on a wonderful show. But I couldn't accept the praise.

"You've got to be kidding—we were awful," I said. "Stop applauding, stop telling everyone how great they are—they suck. If you really want to help us, boo. And boo hard."

"Boo?" said one secretary. She looked horrified. "You can't do that to them!"

"Why? Because they're handicapped? If they were normal, everyone would be booing."

"But that would upset them."

"Oh really. You think that's going to upset them? Not as upset as they're going to be when they find out at the CNE that the public doesn't think they're so great. Because, you see, *that* audience doesn't know who they are—there'll be no pity."

I marched into Dr. Roeher's office. The secretaries watched me talk to him, demanding that everyone come down to the auditorium and watch them perform, only this time, they had to BOO.

"Boo? Why?" he asked, looking up at me.

"Because if I'm not mistaken—and I know the EX— that is *exactly* what's going to happen to them when they get there. I'd rather find out now what they'll do when they hear the catcalls from the EX crowd."

Dr. Roeher knew I was right. With his support, the company got ready for another go of *Aruba Liberace*. "Lights out! Action!" said Ron.

This performance wasn't any better than the one that took place the night before. The reaction was immediate: in fact, if I hadn't known better, I would have thought we were at the EX. There was a riot of catcalls and boos. One secretary even pretended she was a little girl, saying,

"Mommy, I want a balloon," and got up and left during the show.

The performers reacted immediately. Alice leapt off the stage and shouted, "You're a bunch of idiots! How dare you not like our show!"

"Yeah," Brian said, throwing down his musical notes. "You're mean."

The show stopped and all the performers, one by one, started to jump down off the stage to pick a fight with the audience. Eleanor came out like a prizefighter. "I'm ready to take you all on," she announced. The phony audience was in shock.

"My God, if this had happened at the EX," said Ann, "we'd all be up to our asses in alligators."

Afterward, I lined them up and went into my Lee Marvin routine.

"You blew your cover—you lost the war. You can't do that at the CNE," I told them. "If you *ever* jump off the stage and yell at an audience, then they'll know you're retarded. You can't act like that—you have to act like professionals. A professional would continue the show with dignity and not fight with the audience."

My talk worked this time. As the CNE date was getting closer, the performers were trying harder. It was a race to see who would show up for work first and who would be the last to leave. In the middle of all this craziness, we got bad news that almost meant the end for the show. The Toronto Transit System workers were going on strike. The TTC was the main mode of transportation for my performers and most people in Toronto who wanted to get to the EX.

Parents started calling and assumed the project was over. "Well, thank you for the summer job but with the strike, Eleanor will not be coming into work."

One after another, the calls kept coming. Everyone was deserting the ship, and slowly, the entire ship was sinking. But I wasn't about to go down without a fight—I had a thought and an imaginary life preserver reached out and saved us.

"They can all move in with me."

"What!" Ann was aghast.

"Yeah, they can bring sleeping bags and live with Bernard and me."

"You live in a small apartment—you just got married," Ron yelled back.

"You'd better ask Bernard. Ten to one he'll say no," said Ann.

"No he won't. I won't tell him."

"What do you mean, you won't tell him?" said Ann.

"You have to tell him," Ron said. "What are you going to do, hide them all in your closet? Tell them not to snore, be quiet, no flushing the toilet, and tiptoe out in the morning before he wakes up?" Ron started laughing, "Can you imagine?"

"No, I'll have them come to my apartment and then when Bernard comes home and sees them, *then* I'll tell him." My eyes crossed each other.

When I went to the performers and told them about my idea, they cheered. I made my first call to Greg's mom, who laughed at the other end of the phone. "How long have you been married?" she asked. "Let me help. I can drive Greg and four others to the CNE every day. So that means you have six more to worry about." I felt a sigh of relief go through my body.

The day of the strike, we boarded the last bus leaving the York University campus at 5 p.m. We were on our way to my apartment. "The newlyweds," Ann laughed. "The poor French man from Bordeaux, France, will wish he'd stayed in France!"

When we arrived at my place, I got everything and everyone organized. "First, let's make sure the apartment is absolutely spotless before Bernard comes home. And whatever you do, when he walks in the door, *don't say one word* that you're sleeping here, not one. Do you hear me?"

"Yes, Diane," they chorused.

We scoured, washed and prepared a great dinner. *A special meal that will please Bernard*, I thought to myself. As we worked away, I kept repeating over and over, "Don't tell Bernard, not *one* word, do you hear me?"

"Yes, Diane," they all answered.

The door opened and in walked a surprised Bernard.

"Hi, Bernard," Kevin piped up. "We're all living here till the strike is over. Hee hee." Bernard stared at all of us, then turned around, slammed the door and left the apartment.

"Now look what you've done," I said to Kevin. "I told you not to say anything."

"Big mouth—you got a big mouth," yelled Sandra.

I was shocked to hear Sandra speak like that, since she was always the quiet one. I sat on the couch and started to cry. My husband, whom I loved more than anything else in the world, had just walked out the door, and my marriage was in trouble.

My mind kept wandering back and forth to Bernard and our CNE performances. *The players and I are not going to get to the CNE because of the strike and the dream is over. What to do...what to do?* I was in shock and at a loss for words.

Then the door opened and Bernard walked back in the apartment. "Okay, what's for dinner?" He looked directly at Kevin. "Don't you dare go in my fridge and eat all the food."

I jumped up and ran over to Bernard to give him a big kiss. Everyone applauded and we all squeezed into my tiny kitchen to eat dinner.

During dinner, we decided we would walk and carry our props to the CNE grounds. "It's going to take at least an hour and a half from here," said Bernard, who couldn't drive us because of an early morning meeting at the other end of town. But I was confident we could manage. Just the same, I called my mother in Hamilton to ask her if she could come to Toronto and drive some of us in her new station wagon. She sounded exasperated, but agreed.

"Just be downstairs, waiting outside when I pull up. And don't say I never do anything for you."

The next morning we were all waiting downstairs with the record player, puppets and the tall black flats, which were boards covered in black velvet to form the back drop and the wings. The flats just barely fit in the station wagon if we left the back door open, but there was only room for one person. Sandra went with my mother, while the rest of us started walking. As we were walking, Mike got the idea to hitchhike. A small truck pulled over and the five of us jumped in the back. As we were getting out, Kevin yelled, "Can you pick us up tomorrow?" and giggled.

Every day for the next three weeks, my mother would drive from Hamilton to pick us up and we'd squeeze into her station wagon, sitting one on top of the other. (Mom ended up pitching in even more—she built a box that held all the props, which made it easier for us to travel.) Greg's mother (God bless her) organized the other players from different destinations and took them back and forth from the EX.

Living and working together during those weeks was an incredible experience. Everyone in the company was learning life skills and I was learning survival skills. The performers learned to work and cooperate as a team, a family—sharing a bathroom, kitchen and bedroom, or should I say, floor space. We all chipped in for groceries, although the bill wasn't that high because we were eating Swiss Chalet every day, courtesy of Greg's dad, who we found out worked there. Eleanor was shedding her men's clothes and started wearing my dresses. The players even learned to deal with their body odour problem. I wouldn't have it any other way, so I would stand outside the small bathroom in my apartment and time the length of everyone's showers.

"Use more soap," I yelled through the door.

The shows got off to a rough start. On our first day, while we were setting up, we discovered that the flats Ron had made were two feet too tall for the small stage. I ran to the construction department and dragged a carpenter back with me to saw down the flats to fit. Once they were cut down, he had to readjust the velvet to fit the flat. By the time we set our stage there was wasn't much room for the piano, so we didn't have to worry about it flying across the stage.

But the size of the stage wasn't our only challenge. We were performing on a small stage, positioned underneath the CNE's famous Grandstand. We could hear the sound of screaming teenagers as the Osmonds performed at the Grandstand, along with other superstars who drew thousands of fans every night.

Our first performance was a disaster. The needle on the record player got stuck and Liberace sang "Aruba, Aruba, Aruba" over and over again before Ron could let go of Liberace's feet and run over to fix it. Fred talked through the whole show, even though all of us kept telling him to shut up. He danced with the candelabra even though there wasn't much room for it to dance. He yelled in my ear, "How am I doing?" I had no time to reply.

I kept coaching the performers, "Be quiet, no talking on the stage. Don't ask me how you're doing, I'll tell you after the show." They all agreed. Then it was back to another show and the talking continued. In between performances, I ran across the park to do my Punch and Judy puppet show. It took me 15 minutes to get there. So I'd do a 15-minute puppet show, then run back for 15 minutes and perform our 10-minute black-light show. I was exhausted and I had no time to go to the Food Building to eat any free food.

We were all growing tired. It seemed as though at every other show Greg brought out the piano bench upside down. It threw Ron, Ann and I off because we didn't know how to sit Liberace down on it. To make matters worse, one piano leg kept coming off. During one show, Liberace ended up playing the piano on a slant—I was holding the piano up with one knee, Ann was playing with one hand and with the other holding on to the piano leg so it wouldn't roll off into the audience. On one occasion, it rolled off the stage and I had to jump off the stage to get it. Just the same, while I was getting tough on the performers, they were getting more confident—especially Sandra, who offered to do a musical note when Eleanor didn't show up for work.

Audience reaction was mixed. At times, we received some polite applause; other times, we heard lots of talking, kids crying, bullies yelling at us, and saw audience members walking out.

"That's the secretaries," Kevin would whisper on stage.

"Yeah," Brian said, "it's the secretaries."

There were crazy moments too. During one performance, we heard a big crash. A young man was lying on the floor with pieces of the rooftop on him.

"Who the hell invited you?" I demanded.

He looked up at me and said, "Sorry Miss," as he tried getting up. "I was climbing up the roof to sneak in to see Evel Knievel at the Grandstand and I fell."

"Well, get the heck out of here before I call the police!" I yelled at him.

He ran hopping out of our dressing room, bleeding. I don't know what scared him the most—falling through the roof or landing in the dressing room of some mad-woman!

At the end of another performance, we found Alice having sex with another performer. I couldn't believe what I was seeing. "I told you a million times not to have sex on the job!"

"Well, I didn't miss my cue," she responded.

"Didn't miss your cue! Well, guess what, Alice? You're missing it from now on. You're fired!"

Firing Alice made me feel sick to my stomach. I was a mess when I went home that night. The other performer was spared because he had never done anything like that before. But Alice had been warned over and over again.

"You just don't go and fire a person who is retarded," Ron said.

"Why? Because she's handicapped? If it were anybody else having sex on the job they wouldn't have gotten a job warning—they would have been fired, too. No second chances. In fact, we spoiled her and kept giving her chances, and she still didn't change her behaviour. We did that because she was handicapped and you know what, Ron? We didn't help her one bit."

Filling Alice's spot was going to be tough. She was one of the better performers. She had the ability to pick up musical cues and had a lot of rhythm. And she did it with little difficulty in a black-light setting, with a hood over her face and her breathing cut in half. We had our answer the next morning. Mike's girlfriend, Brenda, was sitting on a park bench outside the theatre waiting for him to show up for work. She was a beautiful blonde girl, with hair down to her waist. Dressed impeccably, she jumped up when Mike and I were walking toward the theatre.

"Diane, this is my girlfriend, Brenda. Maybe she can join the company."

"I'd love to."

She was really enthusiastic. Ann and I put her into Alice's jumpsuit and helped her get used to the hood over her face. At the beginning, she gasped for breath and struggled to find her way around in the dark. Ron had to step in to fill the hole Alice left for a few performances until Brenda got it. Slowly but surely, however, she was making progress.

By the last few days of our gig, the performances were getting stronger and the audiences weren't walking out on us. Now, we were thinking about our future: "As soon as we get some money, we'll do this properly," Ron suggested. "We'll go to a recording studio and have the show put on reel-to-reel tape. Then we'll buy a tape recorder."

"They're expensive," I said.

"I know. But working with a record player that has a microphone pressed up to the speaker and the needle getting stuck is just not the way to go."

I agreed. But I had to figure out where I was going to get the money to buy the machine and speakers.

As we trooped off stage just a few days away from our final show, two police officers were waiting for us in the wings.

"Is there a Diane Dupuy here?"

"Yes, I'm Diane."

"There is a missing report on Alice Bergen."

I was stunned. "She doesn't work for us," I said with my heart in my mouth.

"She has been missing for the past 10 days. She never came home from work."

"Oh my God." I started to cry. I slumped down on the steps leading to the stage. "I fired her that day."

"You fired her?"

"I... I... didn't want to... but she kept having sex during the show... backstage... in public... and it was embarrassing... and it was wrong. I tried to help her, but she just didn't listen, so I fired her."

"She never came home." The officer's partner started writing in his black notebook.

"It's all my fault," I sobbed. Ron and Ann were at a loss for words. The other performers were quiet.

"If it makes you feel any better," the officer stopped writing, "Alice's mother didn't report her missing till this morning."

"This morning!"

"Yeah, there are problems in that family, so don't feel so bad."

"Do you mean to say for the past 10 days she has been missing and the parents never called *once*?"

"Nope. Not once." The officer took off his police hat to wipe the sweat from his forehead. They took some more details and left.

It was difficult to get through the rest of the day. In between shows, we called the police station to see if they had heard anything or found Alice. I was sick with worry, so at the end of the day, we walked over to the police station and waited. We couldn't go home until we'd heard about Alice. I pictured her lying in the gutter, strangled. I felt sick. When Alice's mother, whom I had never met, came into the police station, the officer pointed over at me. She made a beeline for me.

"How *dare* you mistreat my daughter! How dare you fire her. You'll pay for this. You will never work with people with disabilities again!"

I jumped up from the chair and started screaming at her. "How dare you mistreat your own daughter? You didn't report her missing until today." As I looked at Alice's mother, I realized that she was a prostitute. And it finally dawned on me why Alice was the way she was.

Before I could say anything more, Alice walked in with a police officer. She looked awful. She had been living with some guy over the 10 days. The officer handed her over to her mother.

"Don't blame this young lady," he said, pointing at me. "It's not her fault. As Alice was leaving the CNE grounds, she met someone and, well, the rest is history."

Alice and her mother stormed out of the station. Although I felt relief, I felt sorry for Alice. *Like mother, like daughter*, I thought.

(Years later, I ran into Alice on a street corner. She remembered me, but I didn't recognize her at first. She had become a prostitute.)

Regardless of the difficulties we had encountered, we had learned more than we ever imagined from the young people. They'd challenged us to look inside and explore the depths of our souls. There was no question in anyone's mind that we had achieved what we set out to do. And that we proved we were capable of helping the performers behave like professionals.

That sentiment couldn't have been more apparent than during the last day of shows. They crackled with electricity. Everything went smoothly—the piano, the candelabra, the musical notes, and the Liberace puppet. We ended our last performance with applause and whistles from the audience, including two standing ovations. As we stood on stage, with tears streaming down our faces, Fred whispered in my ear, "Diane, that's showbiz."

Just as rewarding were the parents' reactions. Greg's mother gave me a silver charm of a piano bench. When I looked at it, the leg was bent. How appropriate, after all Greg and I had been through. Most of the other parents told me how proud and grateful they were for their children's experience.

As we loaded the props and puppet box into Mom's station wagon for the last time, I couldn't help thinking about how the grant and my dream were fading away. Ron and Ann were talking about returning to university—Ann wanted to get a degree in psychology and Ron in art. I had to file the final grant papers to rate the success of the program. But this wasn't where my dream ended.

While the fireworks exploded over the CNE grounds, we walked, arms around each other, not glancing back, but moving forward. This was not the end…but the beginning.

CHAPTER FOUR

Building Team Spirit

I stretched my leg over Bernard, as he slept soundly in bed, and looked up at the ceiling. It felt strange not to get up and go to work. I thought about the performers going back to the Haney Centre that morning. I felt empty. How could I keep the Famous PEOPLE Players going? How could I ignite the dream?

Bernard started to wake up. "Is the coffee on?"

I started to get out of bed slowly to do my 'spousal duties'—something I had not done since the day we had exchanged our wedding vows. I was walking on the cold kitchen floor, sniffling. I reached up to the cupboard to get the coffee.

"So, Dupuy," I turned to see Bernard standing at the kitchen doorway, "what's the problem?"

"No problem," I snapped.

"Oh, no problem. You just tossed and turned all night long."

"I did not."

"Oh yes, you did. Then you were grinding your teeth when you went to sleep." (A bad habit I've had since I was a child.)

"Well, if you want to know—"

"I already know, Mademoiselle." (This is his affectionate term for me.)

"Oh, you think so, do you!" I started to make the coffee. "Yes, it's the Famous PEOPLE Players. No grant, no money and no job. And no company!"

"I have an idea for you. I think I know how you can keep the company going."

"How?" I watched the water come to a boil.

"The money we have for a down payment on a house, you can have for the company."

"You're joking." I was shocked.

"No, I'm not. I think you should do it."

"But our house…"

"Ah, we'll get a house another time. If my promotion comes through, I'll be earning more money and if we stay in this apartment and sacrifice a little, then we can make it."

I threw my arms around him, gave him a big kiss, and then rushed to the bedroom to get dressed.

"Wait! What about my coffee?" he called.

"I have to go see Dr. Roeher." I, Superwoman, flew out of the apartment, leaving my Super Husband behind.

When I arrived at the institute, I ran up the winding stairs, skipping each step. All the secretaries stood up to applaud me.

"Congratulations!" they cheered.

I gave a quick bow and ran over to Dr. Roeher's office, where I found him chatting on the phone. He waved me in with a big smile, cutting his conversation short.

"Congratulations. You did it."

"We did it! All of us, and I couldn't have done it without you."

He laughed, "Don't underestimate yourself, but thanks anyway. I thought, knowing you, you would have felt post-natal blues."

"Well I did, but not for long, thanks to my very special husband."

"Oh? What did he do?"

"He's allowing me to use our down payment for a house to invest in the Famous PEOPLE Players, so I can keep the company going."

"He *what*?" Dr. Roeher looked shocked.

"Yes! And I'm going to make it an even greater success. I have hundreds of ideas. I'm going to get Liberace to see us if it kills me. I'm going to start right after school with the group, at my apartment, until I can get more funding and have a rehearsal hall with a new sound system."

"Now, Diane, calm down a bit." I sat down in the chair he pointed at. "The space here at the institute is no longer available. It's now being used by a…"

I cut him off: "Oh, Dr. Roeher, how could you? After we were such a success!"

"Diane, stop it! It was too small for you and your group, and you know it. With your ideas getting bigger and bigger, you need to find another place."

I sank in my chair, feeling rejected.

"Now, now, Diane. Knowing you, you'll find a better place, and you'll be happier."

"I suppose you're right," I twirled around in the leather chair with my feet off the floor.

"You're proud of me, Dr. Roeher?"

"Very proud of you, Diane. What you did this summer at the EX opened the eyes of so many of us who are committed to this cause. And, without realizing it, you changed our direction. You brought normalization out in the open when before it was just on paper."

"Thank you."

"Now get going to fulfill that dream, and remember—we are all rooting for you."

I hugged him. It felt like a final goodbye. Walking out the door, I ran into one of the bureaucrats from the Toronto Association for the Mentally Retarded who was visiting the building.

"Diane."

"Oh hi, doctor."

"I understand everything went well."

"Went *well*? It was a great success!"

"Yes, but Diane, please be realistic. This will never be a long-term occupation for them," he said condescendingly. "The project is over. They have all gone back to school. Where does that leave you?"

"I'll tell you where it leaves me. It leaves me with new sponsors. The accolades were great, doctor, but perhaps you don't read the papers. We were a raving success and, well, the money keeps rolling in." (I crossed my fingers behind my back.) "I just came to tell Dr. Roeher goodbye because that place is much too small for Famous PEOPLE Players. I have to find a theatrical space out there that is larger and more appropriate for professional work."

He looked startled. "You're still mad at me for not supporting the project."

"Mad? Not me. You're the one who should be mad."

"Why should I be mad?"

"Because you couldn't do it yourself. I'm sorry for you."

I brushed past him as the head secretary leaned over the top of the stairway and said, "Diane, the rug in the office needs to be cleaned. The fluorescent paint won't come off."

"Call a rug cleaner," I yelled back, "and have them send me the bill."

The bus ride back home gave me some time to cool off. The nerve of that man! *He's just jealous*, I thought.

My apartment soon became my office. The first thing I bought was a reel-to-reel tape recorder with speakers. I installed a second phone and bought an electric pencil sharpener. Ron came over to visit one day.

"You bought an electric pencil sharpener. What for?"

"I am going to need it for all the work I'm going to have, writing. Besides, it looks neat." His eyes rolled. "My second bedroom is now the prop department. The performers come here every day after work and we brainstorm and rehearse in the living room. We move the couch and chairs into the hallway so that we have space."

"What about Bernard?"

"As long as I put everything back before he gets home and he gets to have dinner on the table, I'm safe."

Then the phone rang. "Famous PEOPLE Players!" I answered energetically. "Sybil, how great to hear from you!" Ron watched me pace the floor with the cord tangling around my legs. "Thanks, I'll see you tomorrow. Oh, and Sybil, thank you for all your wonderful help." I hung up. "Guess what?" I looked at Ron. "There's another grant program available. It starts in December. It's six months long and she said because of the success of the last project, I'm a shoe-in."

Rehearsing in the living room was fun but we needed more space. I stored the props in our locker in the basement of the apartment building until we could move them somewhere else. During the day, while everyone was at school, I looked for rehearsal space that could accommodate our dream.

On a cold, windy day, I found the perfect place. St. Mary the Virgin Church. The priest in charge, Father Creighton, proudly showed me around the church basement, which had a lovely small stage. The stage area was bigger than the one we'd performed on at the EX and I was thrilled. There was a washroom and a kitchen facility, even a little room off to the side of the stage that we could use to build props.

"You can move in starting December," he said with a smile. "And because you're doing God's work, I will not charge you rent."

I thought to myself, *God closes a door, then opens a window*. Dr. Roeher was right—I had found a bigger place and it was better. The commute was within walking distance of my place. And the performers could get to it a lot easier by subway.

When I told the performers about the new grant program, they were excited about coming back to work full time. "We start December first," I told them.

"Just in time for Christmas," said Kevin.

"We'll earn money for presents," said Mike.

But Eleanor wouldn't be coming back. No one was willing to tell me why, not the school, not her parents, no one. Eleanor also stopped attending the Haney Centre. I tried calling her home repeatedly and finally got hold of her father, but all he said was, "Don't call here anymore. Eleanor is not coming back to school or to Famous PEOPLE Players." SLAM went the phone on my heart!

Just the same, I couldn't show the troupe that I was down about it. "We need to get back in front of an audience!" I said with enthusiasm. Everyone was gung-ho as they sat cross-legged on the floor, eating hamburgers and French fries. "For our next project I'm going to rent the St. Lawrence Centre."

"The St. Lawrence Centre—what's that?" Fred asked.

"It's one of the best theatres in Toronto. We'll have a huge stage and we can sell tickets and make some money. "We're going to invite Liberace," I added.

"Liberace!" Everyone screamed at the sound of his name.

I called the theatre and rented it for one night at $300, which was all we could afford if we were going to host a successful fundraiser to benefit our company. In fact, it would cost about $3,000 a night these days. I booked it the next day after rehearsal.

We couldn't wait to get back into rehearsing. The experience at the CNE had given the players the confidence they needed to continue, and now they would get to perform in the city's most prestigious theatre. Philip jumped up, spilling his Coke on my rug.

"Hey Philip, slow down—Bernard's going to be mad." Mike ran to the kitchen to get a cloth to clean it up. Then it was back to one, two, three and "Aruba Liberace."

It was hard to work leading rehearsals without Ann and Ron, who were back at school. But the rehearsals were going smoothly and the team seemed really united, which is what I was counting on to make this work. I even got calls from parents who were excited that their children would be continuing in Famous PEOPLE Players.

"Brian is really looking forward to coming back," his mother said. "He was so lonely after the CNE was over, staring at the walls, and grumbling as he walked out the door in the morning to go to school," she sighed.

Greg's mother was also thrilled. "Greg will probably be there first thing in the morning. I hear him down in the kitchen at around 4 a.m., getting ready. I have to tell him to go back to bed," she laughed. I was really starting to feel the emphasis on *people* in Famous PEOPLE Players.

A few weeks into rehearsals, things we're going smoothly when I received some wonderful news about a gift that I was about to receive in my life. "Hi Diane, it's Dr. Turner (my family physician)."

"Oh hi, Doc."

"You sound really upbeat answering the phone. Do you want to come into my office and teach my secretary how to answer the phone?" he laughed. "Anyway, do you have a moment?"

"Yes, sure! Is everything all right with my tests?" I had gone for a physical and did the usual gamut of tests, including blood and urine tests.

"You and Bernard are going to be parents. You're expecting."

I screamed. "I can't believe it! I'm going to be a mommy!"

"Congratulations!" he said. "I'll pass you to my secretary and she'll book an appointment for next week."

I couldn't believe that I was going to have a baby. Me, the Lone Ranger, having a baby. I was so busy with rehearsals that I hadn't stopped to think about me or a baby. I was overjoyed.

Is this what my mother felt like when she was given the news? She was just as stunned about the news as I was; after all it seemed like yesterday that she was changing my diapers, she said to me. As soon as I hung up, I called Bernard at work and yelled into the phone, "We're having a baby!" He was yelling with excitement, too, and all of the mechanics and secretaries heard him.

"Pass the cigars," I heard one of the workers behind him say.

"I'll be home soon and we can celebrate."

"Funny, I feel a craving for ice cream. Pick me up some butterscotch ripple."

The rest of the day I was on the phone calling everyone I knew to give them the good news.

Father Creighton called when he heard the good news and he also wanted to tell me that we could start holding rehearsals at the church at anytime. I took him up on his generous offer. We gathered up the props immediately, loaded them into my mom's station wagon and headed over to the church.

I called Ann to give her the news. It convinced her, and Ron, to come work part time for me. *Better than nothing*, I thought. In the meantime, I called an old friend of mine, Lisa, who was between jobs. I needed someone with puppeteer experience and Lisa fit the description.

"Once the grant is confirmed, would you join the group?" I was hoping that she'd be excited to work with the players and become a sort-of role model.

"I'd love to, thanks for asking," she replied. "That's great! I've got a job!"

It was an exciting time for me: the pregnancy, the new rehearsal space, and then Sybil Powell called. The timing couldn't have been better. She told me the grant got a green light. "You're on!" she said.

Everyone showed up for work at St. Mary's every day from Day One. As I entered the church, I felt like Ingrid Bergman in *The Bells of St. Mary's* who, with Bing Crosby, was committed to putting together a choir made up of kids from the wrong side of the tracks. There was something very special about working in the church. *We're all sacred people and we must treat others and ourselves as sacred*, I prayed. It brought me even closer to God and the church, and it gave me even more spirit and passion.

Mike continued to show real leadership qualities, so I put him in charge of the group. I could hear him running through "Aruba" over and over until it was perfect. I stationed myself from the nearby office, where I sold tickets for the St. Lawrence Centre performance. But I needed help to bring in a large audience. I called CNE general manager Dave Garrick and asked him to lend his name to the invitation. I was hoping that by having a respected person to do the inviting, I would be guaranteed a sellout. And I planned to invite as many important people as I could think of from the city of Toronto.

Once the invitations were printed, everyone pitched in to stuff the envelopes, lick the stamps and mail them out. One, which was given a blessing from Father Creighton, was addressed to Seymour Heller, Liberace's personal manager. He has got to come, I thought. The invitation would be too tempting for him to pass up:

David Garrick
General Manager of the CNE
Invites You to
'A Tribute to Liberace'
Performed by the Famous PEOPLE Players

My plan worked. It didn't take long before the phones started ringing with numerous RSVPs. With some reassurance we had a sizeable audience, I focused on the show. I started to add more variety to the numbers, including Liberace's "Boogie Woogie" and Barbra Streisand's "The Way We Were."

Now that the players were getting the hang of black light, the rest of the performance was easier to learn, although musical cues were still hit-and-miss, and the rhythm still needed some work. Brenda, who was the sweetest-looking girl, was all over the place during rehearsals. When she was good, she was very, very good and when she was bad, she was horrid. Yet, at the same time, she was one of the better performers, who could learn a part easily and had wonderful rhythm.

Brian, the quiet young man with the bent shoulders, was developing some strange problems. From time to time, he would start punching the walls for no apparent reason. I called Dr. Turner, who by now had agreed to become our company doctor.

He told me: "You may not realize it, but Brian has developed a major crush on you and he gets jealous when you ignore him, or spend more time with the other members of the troupe."

I decided to watch myself carefully to make sure I didn't arouse any anger in him. All the other players worked hard and did their best to be professional.

Everything seemed to be in place. Tickets were almost sold out. And then we got a call from the St. Lawrence Centre. Apparently the centre had received a letter from Seymour Heller, who was very concerned about the invitation. The letter said something like: "As personal manager for Liberace, please advise me what this is about. It appears that someone has put together some sort of performance, which might be a spoof."

"Are you planning something slanderous?" asked the general manager of the St. Lawrence Centre on the phone.

"No, I'm not. We're just doing a puppet of him."

"Well, you'd better get this straightened out. I don't want any lawsuit against the St. Lawrence Centre and you may have to cancel your show."

I slumped into my chair with the music of "Aruba Liberace" playing in the background. I hadn't realized all the pitfalls of show business. I picked up the phone and called Mr. Heller directly.

"Hello, Seymour Heller's office. Who's calling?"

"It's Diane Dupuy. I would like to speak to Mr. Heller."

"One moment please..." I waited on hold. "Sorry, Miss Dupuy, what company are you with?"

"I'm with the Famous PEOPLE Players."

"One moment please." Hold...hold... "Is there anything I can do for you? Mr. Heller is engaged in an overseas call."

I was nervous. "Yes, I wanted Mr. Heller to know that the invitation he received is a wonderful performance in honour of Liberace, and we hope that he would be the guest of honour."

"One moment, please." Hold....hold...hold.

"Hello, Ms. Dupuy, may I take your number? Mr. Heller will call you back, and may I have your address as well?"

"Yes it's..." (I paused for a moment. I couldn't give a church address.) "... it's 720 Spadina Avenue, Suite 1207."

"Thank you, he will get back to you."

Click.

I was scared. *What if he says we can't do the show?* The day went by and there was no phone call from Mr. Heller. A week went by and a letter arrived, addressed to me. His letter was brief: "Liberace is not available to attend. Best wishes, Seymour Heller."

I dashed the letter over to the St. Lawrence Centre and gave it to the much-relieved general manager. Back to rehearsals and back to the drawing board.

The St. Lawrence Centre fundraiser was three weeks away. The new show numbers were starting to take shape. I rehearsed with Ann, who worked the hands of Liberace, while performing Liberace's song, "Me and My Shadow." She would wear the top hat, cane and shoes and dance with the puppet.

I was getting more excited as the date neared. Somehow, I knew the show was going to be a hit before it was even finished. We had so much fun putting it together. We were especially proud of the creative concept for our invisible man. We'd laugh as Ann would sneak around in black, then pop up wearing just the hat, then the hands would appear from behind, and the shoes walked on to join the rest of them. It was everyone's favourite part in the show.

Mike came into work one morning and started rambling on about Renato.

"Renato? Who's Renato?" I asked, as I composed another letter to Seymour Heller.

"He is up at the Haney Centre. He doesn't go anywhere, 'cause he has this face."

"What do you mean 'this face'?"

"Well, it's ugly."

"Mike, that is a terrible thing to say."

"I know what you're thinking Diane, but it's not that way; that's not what I mean."

"You say someone's face is ugly and that is not what you mean?"

"Well, it's purple."

"Purple?"

"Yeah, it's huge and his hands spread out wide. He lives in his bedroom. He even has a towel over the mirror so he doesn't have to look at himself. I wish he could join the company. He's my very best friend," he smiled.

"He's real nice," Brenda interrupted.

All the group started to gather around me.

"Can he join?" asked Greg.

"I don't think he can perform," Mike said, looking at Greg.

"Look who's talking, the *expert*," I interrupted. "Is that the best you can do? Say 'I don't think he can perform.' From the greatest, the best performers in the world: Mr. Piano Bench, Mr. Candelabra and My Piano, with its perfect musical notes!" I joked, reminding them about their horrible performances when we first formed as a group.

Everyone backed off. How quickly we forget.

"I didn't mean that," Mike said. "I just think he'd be afraid to perform and wouldn't like it."

"Maybe he can help with props," Fred suggested.

"I need someone to answer the phone during the day at my apartment and take messages. Do you think he could do that?"

"He can answer the phone. His voice is nice," Brenda said.

"Bring him in to see me." I hurried them back to rehearsal.

"I don't know if he'll come," Mike said, "but I'll try. He doesn't take the subway, 'cause people stare."

"How does he get to school?"

"He comes by taxi."

"Taxi! That's expensive."

"His mother is afraid that he will be taken by a circus."

"Circus! Oh, come on, you guys. You're pulling my leg."

"No!" said Brian. "It's true."

Sandra mumbled, "He's never been on the subway."

I pushed the button on the tape machine, and it was back to Liberace's "Boogie Woogie." Every performer was performing some kind of bug: Philip and Fred were the spiders with top hats; Mike and Brenda were lady-bugs. Kevin and Greg moved the worms. The green-eyed monster came out when Liberace said, "Now I'm going to play boogie-woogie 16 to the bar." The monster would chase all the other bugs away. We worked really hard on this part of the show.

The harder we worked, the more impressed I became with my players. Philip was getting to be really creative. One day, he said, "Diane, I have a big announcement to make."

We all stopped to hear what he had to say. "I was thinking, when I got my paycheque…" His head started to move and his eyes rolled up to the ceiling. "I cashed my paycheque and went to Sam the Record Man on Yonge Street and bought Hagood Hardy's "The Homecoming." Then I went home and opened my mother's drawer, and took out two of her silk scarves and moved them to the music. I want to do it for you."

I was impressed as he walked toward my stereo and took out a 45 record from his coat pocket. Placing the needle on the record carefully, he picked up his mother's scarves and moved them to the music.

I was taken by surprise. He was amazing to watch. Perfect rhythm, right to every beat of the music. I was even more amazed because he moved his head around so fast—I couldn't figure out how he managed not to get himself tangled with the scarves. It was a miracle. Something I could never understand when Philip performed. We applauded until our hands hurt.

"Philip, it's in the show. You have your own number."

He clutched both his hands tightly together and moving his head toward the sky, he started to cry.

A few days later, I was rehearsing with the group when I saw a man with a scarf wrapped around his head and a hat pulled down over his ears.

Mike whispered to me, "Don't stare. It's Renato."

"He'll run away if you look at him," Brenda said.

We kept on rehearsing. I noticed, as I turned to walk toward the sound system, that he was watching my mother spray paint the puppets. Thank God I was able to convince my mom to help out with the props on a full-time basis. We needed her. After all, she also made the costumes for the Hamilton Opera Company and had all that wonderful experience with paints from my dad's sign shop.

An hour later, Renato crept through the door and walked toward the prop shop, to the side of the stage. Mike yelled out, "Hey, Renato, we won't be long. We have to do this one more time."

"Do you want to watch?" Brenda added.

He never said a word. He just waved his hand and sat on a wooden chair that faced the rehearsal area.

"Okay," Kevin said, "let's make this one a good one. Renato, the man, is watching," he giggled.

I hit the button on the sound system and we all started to perform "Boogie Woogie." Renato was watching us, but kept turning to look at my mother in the props department. At the end of the run-through, he waved goodbye and left.

The next day, just as I was getting ready to walk out the door to go to the church, the phone rang.

"Hello...Mrs. Dupuy?"

"Speaking."

"My name is Renato."

I was surprised at how clear his voice sounded.

"Yes, Renato, I believe we almost met yesterday when you came to the church."

"I'd like to help," he said softly.

"Then come to the church and we'll get you in the show."

"No, no...I don't want to go to the church. Is there anything else I can do?" he sounded anxious.

I pondered for a moment. Not wanting to lose him, I said, "How would you like to mind my apartment and answer the phone for Famous PEOPLE Players? I have a problem, as the church won't let me use their phone. I run home at lunch to pick up the messages off the answering machine and return calls. I really could use the help. Besides, your voice sounds like a radio announcer."

"Oh, thank you, Mrs. Dupuy. Where do you live?" He sounded confident and took down my address.

"Have the taxi bring you here by 8 a.m. I'll have to leave to go to the church."

As soon as I hung up, I called Ann. I wanted to catch her before she left for school.

"He didn't sound like he was handicapped," I said.

"Did you see his face when he came by yesterday?"

"No, he was bundled up tightly."

"I'll see you at the church this afternoon. I have an exam and then I'll be right over."

I wished her luck, and then dashed out of the apartment.

The next morning, there was a faint knock at my door. I glanced at the clock. It was exactly 8 a.m. When I opened the door, there stood a man with a hat over his ears and a scarf bundled tightly up to his eyes. I could tell he was really nervous, so I pretended to be in a big hurry.

"Here, let me show you where everything is." I quickly showed him around the apartment. "The phone is right here. The answering service clicks on after four rings. Here's a pencil and paper for you to write messages down. I'll come back with some of the performers for lunch." *That will put him at ease*, I thought. "You can hang up your coat here." I slid the closet door open.

"It's okay, Mrs. Dupuy. I'm still cold from being outside."

I made a mad dash to the door. I told him I was late, and left.

When I arrived at the church, the performers were already in their jumpsuits, raring to go.

"Renato is at my apartment. He is going to be the company's receptionist."

Everyone cheered. "Did you see his face?" Mike jumped down from the stage.

"No, he kept his hat and scarf on. I did promise him we would join him for lunch at the apartment."

At lunchtime, we headed to my apartment. Renato was still wearing his hat and scarf, as the performers fussed all over him. He proudly gave me all my messages.

"Your mother called three times and you have to call Dr. Turner." He seemed very much at ease as Mike gave him a big slap on the back. He handed me a piece of paper with the phone numbers on it. I noticed his handwriting was big, with long strokes. By this time, he took off his scarf but still kept his hat on. I returned my calls, and then went back to the church for rehearsal with Ann, who had just finished her exam.

"We have our first Famous PEOPLE Players reception-ist," I told her, "and he's great."

We worked feverishly, up to the 11th hour, putting the new show together for our fundraiser at the St. Lawrence Centre. The house was going to be packed. I wish Robert could have been there to share this moment with me, but he just too busy falling in love with a young woman who he had just met. To stretch out the evening, I invited the minister for job creation to speak after our performance about job opportunities and job creation.

On the big night, we were all nervous as we got ready to put on our black hoods and leap on to the stage. Then the music began and we were off and running. The applause was unlike anything I had ever heard before. People were screaming in delight when they saw the spiders wearing their top hats. When Liberace said, "Now I want the ladies to shout 'Hey!' the whole audience went 'HEY!'"

During the excitement, I noticed the candelabra had stopped moving.

"Pssst, Fred," I kept whispering. No response.

During the rest of the numbers that followed, Fred wasn't performing his parts. I couldn't figure out what he was up to. At the end of our show, we all came out on stage for a bow. As we took our hoods off before the audience, I saw Fred sitting in the front row applauding and cheering us on. Then he quickly jumped up on the stage, hugged us and took a bow. As soon as we got off the stage and into the dressing room, I let him have it.

"How *dare* you watch the show? How *dare* you leave us in the middle of a performance!? What on *earth* were you thinking?"

He started to cry. "When I heard all the applause, I thought to myself, this show must be so good...I've just got to see it."

Just then, I looked up and saw Victor Polley, the general manager of the St. Lawrence Centre, standing at the dressing room door.

"Sorry to interrupt. The show was wonderful. The audience is waiting for the rest of it."

"The rest of it?"

"Yes," he looked at his watch.

"That was all we've learned." My face sank.

"Ten minutes," he said.

I'd never realized it was only 10 minutes. We'd worked all day long rehearsing and it seemed like hours to us.

"That's all we could learn," I whispered with tears in my eyes.

"Diane, the audience didn't pay to hear the minister of job creation speak, they came to see Famous PEOPLE Players."

"Well I'm sure he'll fill the time on stage, and next time we come back, I promise you we'll have a longer show."

Victor Polley's eyes moved across the faces of all the performers and said, "I'll try to explain to the audience that there is no second half."

The door closed and I collapsed back into my chair, wondering how we would ever learn more numbers. I looked up and there was Fred, sniffling away.

"I thought you were so good," he mumbled. I handed him a Kleenex. As for the audience, I wanted to go out and meet them but Victor explained that the show was over. We started to pack up and leave because I felt we must have embarrassed ourselves. I was nervous that I might have upset Victor and that he'd never rent to me again. Instead, he turned out to be a gentleman, with empathy. He understood my predicament and did his best to appease the audience.

The next day we returned to our humble rehearsal hall in the basement of St. Mary's. Father Creighton watched us all arrive in a sombre mood.

"I thought you were good last night," he said, "but may I make a suggestion?" Embarrassed, we looked up at him.

"The show needs to be much longer, like about an hour more."

"An hour more?" The very thought was too exhausting to contemplate. How were we ever going to do anything an hour long? We started hanging up our coats, changing into our black jumpsuits, and plugging in the record player.

"And, a one, two, three—GO!"

The music began, and everyone started to rehearse with their musical notes. Then Brenda started pushing Brian and he started to push Fred.

"Stop it!" I yelled.

Brian threw his note down and started screaming. He picked up a sandbag and started chasing me around the church. I ran and just before I reached the washroom, he took the sandbag and hit me in the back. Renato, who was working at the church hall that day, grabbed him and pinned him to the wall. Father Creighton came to calm him down. It was an awful moment. Then, I noticed I was bleeding. I quickly called Dr. Turner, who told me to lie flat in bed because I could miscarry.

"What made Brian so mad? Especially when we get along so well?" I cried to Dr. Turner.

"He has a crush on you, Diane. You're pregnant, married, the other performers love you—it's a combination of all those things."

The performers accompanied me home by subway and put me to bed. Bernard was out of town on business for a week. I didn't want to tell him what had happened. I wanted to keep the baby, and resting, I thought, would fix every-thing. The players were wonderful—they kept me company that day and even cooked up an eggplant, which was awful tasting, but I smiled to disguise my real reaction. Then I let Mike open my purse and take out some money to buy hamburgers for everyone from the restaurant downstairs.

As I lay in bed, I began to feel painful cramps. When I called Dr. Turner back, he said I was in danger of losing the baby. We called an ambulance and the performers all competed to help me get onto the stretcher.

"I can do it!" screamed Brenda to the ambulance driver.

"Me too," Mike said.

They all came with me to the hospital. In the meantime, Bernard raced home to be with me. We held hands while I lay in the hospital bed and I cried uncontrollably. The performers all sat out in the waiting room, pacing back and forth. Renato was at home when Mike called him from the hospital.

"What happened?" he asked.

"She's losing the baby," Mike was sobbing. "We're all at the hospital."

"I'll be right there!" he yelled into the phone. Renato was so devastated that he hopped on a bus, instead of taking his usual taxi.

When I miscarried, Bernard and I both cried. The doctor came into the room to console us both, and the performers came to the side of my bed in tears. Now Bernard and the doctor were trying to calm them all down. Brian was hiding behind them, with his eyes swollen from crying.

I asked Brian to come closer. "Please Brian, don't cry, we all love you and Bernard and I forgive you."

"I'm so sorry Diane, I didn't mean to do what I did."

"I know you didn't."

Bernard put his hand on Brian's shoulder to give him some reassurance.

"Okay, guys," the nurse said, "time's up. No more visitors, she needs to rest. You can go home and come back tomorrow."

As they walked out the door, Mike turned back and said, "Diane, we're gonna get that show up to an hour— you wait and see. You'll really be surprised."

Lying in bed, staring at the ceiling, I started to pray for an answer: *why—why—why?*

Suddenly, the drapes around my bed were pulled back and there was Renato, huffing and puffing. "I found you! I found you! I got on the bus, I asked the driver how to get to the hospital. He told me to get on the subway. I asked everyone for directions. I went to the wrong floor of the hospital. The nurses were telling me to take the elevator and leave because no visitors were allowed. I couldn't wait, so I took the stairs," he continued. "Look! I stopped at a grocery store and bought you this plant." He handed me a half-dead spider plant.

I took the plant. At that moment I realized that the child I lost had been born in Renato. He had taken on a new life. He was not afraid to leave his house and to face the world, to show his face, to talk to people, and to ask for directions.

I couldn't help thinking how everything in life happens for a reason, and this reason helped me to appreciate that life has meaning, no matter what the circumstances are. As my dear friend, the psychiatrist, Victor Frankl would say, "The answer awaits us in the future."

Returning to work wasn't easy. It was now early December and it was extremely cold. Snowstorms made walking to work next to impossible and the subway was often delayed. Besides the weather, memories of that awful day in the church made me even more depressed as I hung up my coat, waiting for the group to arrive. Ann and Ron wouldn't be coming in to work this morning. Ann was writing her final exams over the next two weeks and Ron was busy with school. The first one to come into work that cold morning was Lisa. I heard her banging her boots against the wall to get the snow off.

"Are you okay?" She said as she took her coat off.

"Just a little down, but I'm okay. The doctor said we could still have children and that it is not unusual to lose the first. Not to worry, so I won't."

"Well, what do we start with?" she asked.

I reached into the cupboard to take the sound system out. "We, my dear friend, are going to get this show of ours to be one hour long."

"Oh, my God," she responded. "How are we going to do that?"

"We will do whatever it takes, but we'll do it. After all, nothing is impossible!"

At that very moment, the entire gang came storming through the doors. As usual, all of them were hollering at each other.

"Look at them—" I said to Lisa. "One minute they're a together group, the next, they're all over the place. Not working together. What's really missing is the team spirit. They keep saying we're a family, but sometimes I don't know what's going on with them.

"Okay, guys, everyone ready?" I hollered.

"We're raring to go," Kevin blurted out.

"This is what's happening," I pulled up my wooden chair, and turned it around to face me. I sat down with my arms over the back of the chair. "First, we are going to get this show to be an hour long."

Everyone started whistling and hooting. Brian even joked around with Kevin, giving him a friendly punch, and Kevin punched him back, giggling.

"STOP IT and LISTEN, please."

They stopped and looked at me.

"You know how when we started this company, everyone said it couldn't be done? That you could never do what you are doing? They said we couldn't be integrated, that you belong in a sheltered workshop."

Everyone looked at the floor.

"We proved them wrong. We went to the CNE and we were a success."

The hollering began again and the performers started to jump around.

"Well, guess what? We have to prove them wrong again! We have to get this show to an hour if it kills us. Unfortunately, we are going to have to keep proving ourselves. You're only as good as your last performance. Remember that. Now let's get up and start rocking and rolling.

"We will start with Philip on the ribbons." Philip was beaming and turning red. He pressed his hands tightly together, and his head started moving around.

"While Lisa is working with you, I'm going to try to get Liberace on the phone." The screaming started again. Only this time, it was louder.

"QUIET! He will only come if the show is one hour long. Not a minute shorter."

I called the O'Keefe Centre, where Liberace usually played when he came to Toronto, and asked the box office when he was expected to return.

"He will be returning in April. Tickets are not on sale yet," an efficient young woman told me.

April. That gives me December, January, February and March to work on getting him to see the Famous PEOPLE Players, I thought to myself. *This time—no more letters. Phone calls—that's all I'll do,* I mumbled to myself. The shotgun approach.

Behind me, the performers were working noisily, when, all of a sudden, I heard a *CRASH!*

I ran over to the performers and saw them all standing around, looking at a black-light tube that had smashed to bits on the floor.

"What happened?"

"I don't know," Lisa looked stunned. "I was in the washroom when I heard the crash."

"All right, who did this?" Silence.

"I'm asking you a question and I expect an answer!"

Silence.

"This black-light tube is expensive; you have five minutes to tell me who broke the light!" Silence.

Greg piped up, "What happens to the guy who broke the tube?"

"He or she is fired!"

Silence.

I then stormed out of the rehearsal area and went to the back, where we hung our coats, to wait for an answer.

Five minutes later, everyone came looking for me and said, "We aren't telling!"

"You're not telling me who broke the black light?"

"Nope!" said Kevin.

"No way!" said Mike.

All their heads were shaking.

Silence.

"Then do you know what I'm gonna do to all of you?"

Silence...

"I'm going to treat you to pizza at lunchtime!"

"What!" There was a buzz among them.

"You heard me, we're going for pizza! Do you know why?"

Everyone looked at each other in wonder.

"Because you are now officially a team!"

They all started to applaud and pat each other on the shoulder.

"A team, just like the Toronto Argonauts!" Brian yelled out.

"No, like the Maple Leafs," Greg interjected.

"This is exactly what we needed—" I said to Lisa. "A team. They stick by each other. They help each other. Once that happens, working in the dark and reaching out to each other on stage will be much easier."

The team spirit helped make that morning's rehearsal really smooth. We started to work on Barbra Streisand's "The Way We Were," then it was Elvis Presley's "Viva Las Vegas." Somewhere inside, I had the feeling that Liberace would discover our dream one day and that we'd be opening for him in Las Vegas.

The pizza lunch was the best party we ever had as a company. It was better than the Swiss Chalet dinners at my apartment or the burger lunches. It was the first time everyone seemed to be friendly and good-natured with each other without incident.

"Here's to the Famous PEOPLE Players!" Mike yelled as he stood on a chair.

"Hip hip hooray!"

We had finally become a TEAM!

CHAPTER FIVE

Our Father Who Art in Las Vegas

"Hello, is Seymour Heller there?"
"Who's calling, please?"
"Diane Dupuy."
"Company name?"
"Famous PEOPLE Players."
"One moment, please."

As I waited for someone to pick up the line, I heard a tape of Liberace playing the piano.

"Sorry, Mr. Heller is in conference. Please call back."
"When?"

"In about an hour. I don't know how long he'll be. He has Australia waiting on line two, and another call on line three. In fact, he'll be busy most of the day."

An hour later, I called back.

"Is Seymour Heller there?"
"Who's calling, please?"
"Diane Dupuy."
"Company?"

"Famous PEOPLE Players."

"One moment, please."

More music. "Sorry, he's just stepped out for lunch. Please call back."

Business card or no business card, this wasn't going to be easy. What I needed was to be someone else. Someone important! Someone who Seymour's staff would pay attention to. But who? I couldn't be Liza Minnelli or a famous star—they'd catch on too quickly. I kept mulling the idea over and over in my mind.

During one of my many phone calls to Seymour Heller, a beautiful piece of music was playing while I was on hold. It was Liberace doing a rendition of "The Impossible Dream." *This is the impossible dream*, I thought, *and I'm going to reach for that star!* It proved to be a motivator not just for our one-hour show but in helping me reach my dream. So much so that "The Impossible Dream" became the next number we worked on as a company.

Our Liberace played at the piano while stars appeared and eventually covered the stage. Philip performed with his ribbons at the beginning of the number during the instrumental part of the music. At the end of the number, which was also the end of our show, a small star appeared and turned into a big star. Dreaming the impossible dream was our creed and the star was what we reached for when times got tough.

As we worked hard to lengthen the show, Dr. Roeher proposed my next challenge. "Do you want to do something great?" Dr. Roeher asked. "Why don't you perform for the annual meeting of the Toronto Association for the Mentally

Retarded? It's high-profile—about 500 people will be there and it would be a great opportunity for you to show them what you have accomplished."

"What *we've* accomplished," I answered. "Why would I want to perform for an association that didn't support the project?"

"Because Diane, you don't burn bridges. If you want to change attitudes, then this is the place to do it."

I thought about what he said and, as much as it made me burn inside to give the association a free show, I couldn't forget his words. My mother had always said the same thing. Don't burn bridges. Turn the other cheek. To err is human, to forgive is divine.

I went to see Helen Honickman, the chairperson for the annual luncheon, which was being held at the Inn on the Park in Toronto. She was a gracious lady who volunteered her time and effort to help raise funds for the association. I believe that there are two kinds of volunteers: those who do it for themselves (most people) and those who do it for others (a rare few). She was in the latter category.

"You're one of the first to receive this invitation for the luncheon," she smiled. I noticed the date on the invitation —April 10. It was the same day that Liberace would be in town performing at the O'Keefe Centre. I had decided that he was going to be my guest of honour and I would guarantee his presence. I decided right then and there how wonderful it would be to have Liberace as the guest of honour for the April 10 luncheon and I was going to get him to come.

I picked up the phone and called Seymour Heller's office again.

"Is Seymour there?" *(Now, I'm on a first name basis. Hey, it's worth a try.)*

"Who's calling?"

"Mrs. Goldbaum."

"One moment, please."

I waited.

"Seymour is wondering if I can help you?"

"I'm hosting a social function for the visiting Emperor of Japan and I would like to book the Liberace puppet to perform."

"The what?"

"The puppet of the master of showmanship. I saw the group perform. They were unique. And I want something unique."

"You mean you want Liberace?"

"No, the puppet."

"One moment."

I waited while the music played.

"Hello, this is Seymour."

"Oh Seymour, darling," (I tried to sound really snooty and uppity, like Mrs. Society from La-di-da Avenue) "I need the Liberace puppet. It's for the Emperor of Japan's dinner and I've just got to have it."

"I believe I've heard about this before. Let me call you back. I'll have to find out more information."

"Look, darling, I'll call you next week, once I return from my trip to Japan with my husband. I promise to get

back to you. But darling, don't let me down. It's a must—
the puppet will be a big hit at the dinner."

A few days later, I called back.

"Good morning," I said, in a stiff English accent, "is
Mr. Heller there?"

"Who's calling?"

"I'm calling from the office of the Prime Minister of
Canada, the Right Honourable Pierre Elliot Trudeau."

"One moment, please."

Nothing fazes this woman!

"Seymour here!"

"Good morning, Mr. Heller. My name is Mrs. Bradshaw.
I'm the personal assistant to Prime Minister Trudeau."

"Liberace is a big fan of Mr. Trudeau!"

"Thank you, I will pass that on. I'm calling because
the prime minister saw a wonderful performance of a
puppet of Liberace. He couldn't remember the name of
the theatre troupe that did such an excellent, moving
performance of the Liberace character. He thought it
would be perfect for a gala affair he is having for the
Emperor of Japan."

"Really? I believe I've heard about this before. By the
way, is Mr. Trudeau still dating Barbra Streisand? Did you
know Liberace discovered her?"

"No, I didn't know that. Mr. Trudeau's personal life is
not my concern." I tried to sound official.

"Sorry! I was just curious," he said humbly.

"Not at all, I get questions like that all the time," I
continued smoothly. "Now back to the Liberace puppet—"

"Oh yes, let me see, I think…I have something here… about this…" I could hear him ruffling papers. "May I call you back?"

"No, I'm on my way into the House of Commons with the Prime Minister. I will call you back."

"Please tell Mr. Trudeau—Liberace thinks he is one of the world's greatest leaders."

"He'll be pleased to hear that."

I hung up.

The plan was working and it was time to give Mr. Heller a call, only this time as Diane Dupuy of Famous PEOPLE Players. I waited a day before I called back.

"Hello, is Seymour Heller there?"

"Who's calling?"

"Diane Dupuy of Famous PEOPLE Players."

"One moment, please, I believe Seymour is anxious to talk to you, Ms. Dupuy."

I listened, heart thumping, to Liberace playing "Tea for Two."

"Ms. Dupuy, would you please hold? Seymour is just wrapping up a long-distance call and he'll be right with you."

My heart skipped three beats.

"Hi! It's Seymour here. Where have you been? Everyone is looking for you."

"They are?"

"Stick with me, kid. We're going to do some very good business together."

"We are?"

"Yes, this is Seymour you're talking to, and Liberace is dying to see that puppet of yours."

"Well, that's why I was calling. There is a prestigious event happening in Toronto on April 10 when Liberace comes here to perform. It is a gala dinner to support the Association for the Mentally Retarded. Everyone is going to be there, the mayor of Toronto, the premier of Ontario and the prime minister himself."

"Pierre Trudeau?" he sounded excited.

"Yes, Pierre Trudeau."

"His office called me just yesterday," a proud Seymour said.

"They did?"

"Yes, they wanted to book the Liberace puppet for the Emperor of Japan."

"Oh wow!" I acted surprised.

"I don't know the date," he sounded puzzled. "Come to think of it, she never mentioned it."

"Did you get her number? I'll call her," I offered, trying to distract him.

"No, I didn't get her number, but her name was Mrs. Bradshaw."

"Mrs. Bradshaw called you? Why, she's the most important lady next to the Prime Minister."

"Everyone calls Seymour," he said, laughing. "I can find her number and I'll try to get in touch with her."

"Oh, don't worry, I can do that," I said hastily, "but Mr. Heller…"

"Seymour."

"I mean, Seymour…Is April 10th okay?"

"April 10th—for what?"

"For a gala luncheon in honour of Liberace, to pay tribute to his career."

"I don't know, I'll have to speak to Lee—[short for Liberace]. Send me an invitation and I promise to get back to you."

"Thank you, I will."

"And please keep in touch, we're in this together," he laughed.

Little did he know how true that really was. I got off the phone and started to laugh so hysterically that my eyes were watering.

"What's the matter, Mrs. Dupuy?" Renato, who was sitting in the chair in front of the stage, sounded alarmed. "You look like you're in pain. Are you all right?"

I was back at the church still practicing *Aruba Liberace*. Once I came up for air, I gathered the company and told them the good news; "The plan is working! We're going to conquer Liberace. We're going to make our impossible dream come true!"

Everyone was as excited as I was. "We're gonna get Liberace, we're getting Liberace," Brenda was running around shaking her maracas.

"Let's get a calendar and mark off each day that goes by, Mrs. Dupuy," suggested Renato.

"Stop calling me Mrs. Dupuy, Renato."

"Sorry, Mrs. Dupuy."

Ann and Ron walked through the door as we were rejoicing. They were happy to have their exams behind them. And Lisa was the happiest of all. Now she would have more help to make rehearsals go a lot smoother.

"You know what?" I grabbed a wooden chair and sat on it facing the group. "I'm fired." Everyone stopped dead in their tracks.

Mike, Kevin, and Fred started laughing really hard.

"You're fired?" Brenda pointed to me with one of her maracas.

"Yes, I'm fired." I looked so serious that everyone could tell I wasn't joking.

"Who fired you? You're the boss," said Renato. "Nobody can fire the boss."

"I did. I fired the boss. Me," I pointed at my chest.

"You're not staying in the Famous PEOPLE Players? You're quitting?" Lisa moved closer to me.

"I'm waiting for the explanation," said Ron.

"Look, performing on stage, going after Liberace, coming up with ideas and running the business end of things from my apartment makes it difficult for me to be in the show. You need a performer who can be here for rehearsal all the time."

"But it won't be any fun without you on stage," said Mike.

"Yeah, we need you," Brian straightened his shoulders.

"Thank you for the encouragement, but it's not like I'm leaving the company."

Everyone let out a sigh of relief. "I'll still come up with the ideas for the new numbers, direct the show and when I can't be here, Lisa or Ann and Ron will take over. This frees me up to organize the performance for Liberace when he comes on April 10. You know how important that is."

At that point I got up from my chair and felt like a big weight had been lifted off my shoulders. Everyone gathered around me and gave me a big hug.

"If there is an accident on stage and we can't 'form," said Greg, "then you jump in."

"Yes, I will jump in, but there will be *no accidents*, do you hear me?"

"Oh oh, Mrs. Dupuy is still the boss," Renato saluted me, as he reminded the group.

The luncheon was less than a month away. The snow had melted and the tree branches were starting to bud. Everyone's enthusiasm was still up, and we kept marking big and bold X's on the calendar. There were no incidents at rehearsals, but our progress was slow. The full length of the show, after five months of rehearsals, was now 30 minutes.

"At this rate, it will be two years before we can do an hour-long performance," I said to Ann over coffee one morning at the coffee shop down the street from the church. "Why can't they learn faster?" I started to cry.

Ann lifted her eyes to the ceiling and let out a big sigh. "The good news is that the Barbra Streisand puppet is looking good. I like the way you thought of bringing her out with a harp," she laughed.

"She does look good in her arabesque pose." I lifted my arms like a ballerina. "Very Streisand, wouldn't you say?" I winked. "Liberace is going to love it. Did you know he discovered her and gave her her first break?"

"Where did you hear that?"

"From Seymour. But I'm waiting for him to call back. There are so many ups and downs in this business and I still don't have confirmation of Liberace's attendance at the luncheon."

"You *told* them he was confirmed," Ann looked horrified.

"I know."

"Diane, they sent out the invitations with his *name* on them."

"I know, you don't have to tell me about it."

"But I don't get it. Why did you tell them he was confirmed? Don't answer," she opened her wallet to pay for the coffee. "There is never any sense in your thinking. I just close my eyes and follow and don't ask questions. But let me tell you something," as she waved a dollar bill in my face, "you're going to be in deep caca if he is not there."

I looked at her sheepishly and said quietly, "Especially when they think he is the keynote speaker for the luncheon."

"*The keynote speaker!*" she gasped. "This is one time I'm glad to be up on stage dressed in black—invisible to the audience. They can't find me, but they will find you; you're sitting at the head table."

Ann helped bring back that uneasy queasy feeling in my gut, but I would never let anyone, including Ann, know I was scared that Liberace might not show up. We headed back to the church to start rehearsals. As we came in, we could hear the banging from the tiny prop shop that was no bigger than six feet by five feet. Mom was already hard at work and Ron assisted whenever he could.

I rolled up my sleeves to get rehearsal going with my usual opening line. "Okay guys, three more weeks before Liberace arrives, so let's work hard and keep improving the show." Ann pulled her hood over her face and gave me the evil eye.

The next few days, I was trading calls with Seymour from the church and my apartment. He'd leave me a message on my answering service, but when I tried calling him back I'd be going through the same routine.

"Seymour is busy..."

"Seymour is on another line..."

"Seymour is out for lunch..."

"Seymour is out of town..."

"...He'll call back."

One night, I was lying on the couch watching TV when the phone rang. It was Seymour, finally.

"Sorry, Diane, I can't do it. Liberace is busy that day doing interviews and talking to the press. He can't make the luncheon."

"*What*!" I screamed. "What press? All the press will be at the dinner. We need him! He is the guest of honour and the show—the show is going to be great!" I was almost crying. "Surely you're not going to miss an opportunity of a lifetime with the press...well, are you?"

"Diane, Lee is tired after the show, you know what it's like—it's too much. Besides, everybody honours him all over the world."

I was starting to hyperventilate at this point. "Please Seymour, talk to him one more time. Tell him Trudeau will be very disappointed."

Oh, what a tangled web I'm weaving. I couldn't tell anyone, not one person—not even Ann—how many lies I was telling to lure Liberace to our show. I left the apartment and went to the only place I could turn—to church, where I lit a candle. In a panicked whisper as I kneeled, I called for help. "Dear God, help me! I need you! The Famous PEOPLE Players need you badly. Drop whatever it is you're doing. We have an emergency!"

I can almost hear God answering back. *"You always have an emergency."*

"I know, I know," I agreed, as if he was staring right at me.

"And you created it yourself."

"Well help me undo what's been done—make it better."

"Why do you lie, Diane?"

"I'm just stretching the truth."

"The truth? Pierre Trudeau, Mrs. Goldbaum—what next?"

"I'm sorry, I'm so sorry—honestly, I am. Please forgive me. Don't let anything hurt Famous PEOPLE Players."

"Yes, I forgive you, but I can't help you this time. You'll just have to learn how to get out of this mess by yourself. If you stop lying—even though it's for a good cause—and just have faith, everything will fall into place."

I looked at the statue of Mary in front of me.

"Mother Mary—talk to *Him*! Convince Him—you've got pull!"

I could almost feel her praying for me. Just the same, I had no choice but to listen to what my inner voice was telling me. The next morning, I stood before Famous PEOPLE Players, eyeing each member one by one. Their bright smiles, the sparkle in their eyes—it was a perfect Kodak moment, only I was about to ruin it.

"I have to tell you something."

"Go ahead, dearie," said Greg. "The stage is all yours."

Kevin giggled, as usual. Everyone was staring, except Renato, who was trying to pick the adhesive glue off his fingers.

"I received a call from Seymour last night."
Everyone started to jump up and down.

"Wait," I cried. Silence.

"He said no. Liberace is not coming—finito—never! He's never going to see Famous PEOPLE Players. Understood? The dream is a nightmare, and I created it...and... I'm sorry. I lied about everything—and, well, he doesn't care. Seymour says that Liberace gets honoured all over the world and besides, he is tired after his show."

I walked away, leaving everyone in shock and dismay. Several performers were in tears. Next, I had to face the chairperson of the luncheon, Helen Honickman, and tell her the truth.

"I know," she said.

"You *do*? How do you know?"

"I'm a mother," she responded. "I'm older...I've been around. Besides, when you run a luncheon like this, you don't put all your eggs in one basket. Just make sure you perform well that day."

"You can count on it."

The show was still on, but there would be no Liberace. I kept praying and leading rehearsals with the group, who were now full of doom and gloom. The "oomph" in "Aruba" sounded more like a balloon letting out air. And there wasn't the typical banter from the performers after each set.

Liberace's absence was taking a toll on all of us. Ron thought I looked white as a sheet when I arrived at work each morning. I just chalked it up to the blues of losing Liberace. I felt sick to my stomach every time I saw one of the ads for his performance at the O'Keefe Centre. But we had a job to do and "the show must go on," I reminded the troupe. We started making our preparations for our performance; organizing the sound, lights and props to be transported to the Inn on the Park Hotel.

On our first day organizing our props, I heard the yelling start up in the distance. "That's my musical note!" Brenda screamed to Fred.

"No, it's mine—you're the candelabra!"

"But it's my note after I dance with the candelabra."

"I packed mine and you bent it—YOU BENT IT!"

"STOP IT!" Fred screamed.

"Shut up!" Brenda screamed back. "It's my note, I want my note!" Her face was reddening with anger, and her saliva was spraying everyone around her.

"Calm down," Ron tried to intervene. "We love you, Brenda, let us help you." She picked up a wooden chair and threw it in the air. Then another.

"So there!" she said. "Take that!" Then she hurled a chair and just missed the light fixture. Suddenly, she stopped, shook and started to howl. It was as if a dam had opened up.

Everyone froze. Ron calmly walked toward her and put his arms around her.

"I'm sorry," she said, "I'm so sorry." Her hair was wet with sweat. I watched as Lisa got a cold cloth to rub her down.

"In some way, it's a good thing that this Liberace thing didn't pan out," Ann whispered in my ear.

Before I had a chance to respond, I heard the phone ring. I rushed toward the office, leaving Brenda whimpering behind me.

"Yeah?"

"Is Diane Dupuy there, please?"

"This is Diane."

"Hi, it's Seymour."

I fell onto my chair. "*Seymour?*"

"You don't sound happy to hear from me."

"No—I'm happy!" My voice jumped with excitement.

"Liberace is coming."

My heart started to thump. "Really? Truly? You're not kidding me?"

"Nah, why would I kid you?"

"Well after the last time we spoke, you sounded so firm."

"Liberace doesn't want to let you down, and now the bad news—"

Bad news? My heart jumped again.

"—I won't be attending. I'm going to leave you in the hands of my client. You're to pick him up at the Royal York Hotel at 11:30. Meet him in front of the elevators at the mezzanine level. Please make sure the limo is directly at the front of the main entrance to the hotel."

"Yes, sir!"

"You don't sound very disappointed that I won't be there."

"Oh, I am, I am! Why can't you come?"

"I'm very busy in Hollywood. I also represent Debbie Reynolds, Ginger Rogers—everyone loves Seymour!" he gave me his trademark laugh.

"We all love you, too. Thank you so much. You have no idea how much this means to us!"

As soon as I got off the phone, I flew into the rehearsal hall, screaming louder than Brenda ever could!

"HE'S COMING! HE'S COMING!" No one could make out what I was saying because I was so hysterical.

"What?"

"Who?"

"Calm down."

"What's she saying?"

The performers were all looking at each other. I started to catch my breath.

"*LIBERACE...IS...COMING,*" I said slowly, before collapsing on the floor.

As I looked up, I could see everyone dancing around me, screaming, cheering and laughing. Even Brenda had transformed herself back into the happy girl we had all come to love.

"I don't believe it," Ann bent down to talk to me in my ear so I could hear her over all the loud noise.

"He said he's sent a letter confirming it, but I haven't received it yet...Ann, I get to pick him up—OH MY GOD!" I screamed. "I need a new dress! Wait, just wait till everyone sees me walk in with Liberace, they'll die! They'll just die!" I was hyperventilating again.

"What's she doing that for?" Sandra asked. "She can't breathe."

Ann helped me calm down. I got so excited that my emotions kicked into high gear. When I finally got up, I joined everyone running around the room, hollering, "Liberace is coming! Liberace is coming!" Brian put on "Aruba Liberace" and we all started to mambo. "Aruba Liberace—OOMPH! He's coming, OOMPH."

The news brought a much-needed spark in our rehearsals. I could feel the electricity lifting me up in the air as the weeks flew by, even though the show had still not reached our projected one-hour length. I had arranged the limousine and I bought a new dress—a gorgeous, silk chiffon number I could barely afford, which crowned the excitement. The excitement also made me hungry—I was eating perogies and sour cream, which I craved first thing in the morning.

"Be careful," Ann said, "you won't fit into your dress."

On the night before our big date with Liberace—after we had set up the stage at the Inn on the Park—everyone slept over at my place. I wanted to make sure we were all up early to prepare for our make-or-break performance. But, it was a long night for all of us. During the night, the toilet kept flushing. I could hear whispers throughout the house as the group kept passed each other in the hallway back and forth from the washroom.

"Liberace's coming."

"Man, I can't sleep." Kevin whispered.

Neither can I, I thought to myself. The one person who seemed to have no problem sleeping was Bernard. He snored away all night long.

I must have dozed off just as it was time to wake up. I was awakened not by an alarm clock but by the bellowing of the name "LIBERACE" as everyone folded blankets and dashed to the bathroom.

"Wait!" I stopped them. "Bernard's gotta go first—he has to get to work."

As quickly as possible everyone scrubbed up, got dressed and rushed out the door, each with a piece of toast in hand. I grabbed my gown, which was neatly pressed, before I made our exit.

We got to the Inn and double-checked that everything was in its place in record time. Then we stared at the stage in silence. "God bless our stage," I whispered.

"It's time," a reassuring hand rested on my shoulder. I turned to see Ron smiling at me. "Your limo awaits."

I felt like Cinderella off to the ball, waving to all my helpers as I drove off. When we pulled up to the Royal York Hotel, the driver jumped out to open the door.

"You look beautiful, Madame."

"Thank you. I'm so nervous."

"Don't be, everything's going to be wonderful. I feel it in the air."

I walked toward the mezzanine level and waited. There were eight elevators. Every time one of the doors opened, I spun around to see if it was the one that would bring Liberace. People were getting off, bumping into me, asking me to move out of the way. I was spinning around from left to right, standing on my toes, trying to look for Liberace above the crowd.

It sounded like my heart was thumping louder than the elevator doors opening and closing before me. Then everything went quiet. I waited for what seemed like forever. I stood between the two banks of elevators, not knowing which one was going to open first. Then the door opened, and it was like a bright ray of sunshine hit me in the face. There he was, standing in front of me. I couldn't speak as Liberace walked out, smiling, that huge smile he was famous for.

Oh my God, I said in my mind, *his puppet doesn't look anything like this man at all!*

"Are you Diane?" He took my hand.

"Yes," I said.

"Well, let's go."

I walked with him outside. I was so in awe that I didn't realize everyone was staring at us as we held hands getting inside the limo. All I can remember about the ride is how everything seemed like it was moving in slow motion. Liberace talked to me all the way there and I suppose I must have replied, but I can only remember his rings as he moved his hands gracefully and his teeth as he smiled.

We arrived at our venue, still in slow motion. My feet didn't feel like they were touching the ground. The doors opened to the ballroom and I felt just like a princess with Liberace by my side. Five hundred people, mostly members from the Toronto Association for the Mentally Retarded, stood applauding and smiling. Cameras flashed in front of our faces from the time we entered the ballroom to the time we took our seats. The ballroom chandelier dimmed and everyone sat quietly as the show began. Then the curtain opened and the magic of Famous PEOPLE Players began to spill over from the stage. I thought I could see guardian angels everywhere.

Throughout the show, I kept hearing that voice inside me say I loved the show. *I loved the show! I loved the show! They were great! Unbelievable!* From time to time, I glanced over at Liberace and I could tell he was enjoying every minute.

I laughed when Liberace's puppet played the piano with his feet and cried when Philip performed with his ribbons to the beat of the music. I didn't realize it at the time, but I kept grabbing Liberace's hands, squeezing them tighter and tighter. In fact, I think I still have his candelabra ring imprinted in the palm of my hand. Then, my performers were on the final number—Liberace's rendition of "The Impossible Dream." It was perfect. The whole stage lit up in fluorescent stars, and only I knew the number of performers who held those stars. The Liberace puppet looked like he was floating in space, and on the last note he stood up and reached for the unreachable star. *To dream the impossible dream; to reach the unreachable star*—that was what we were all about.

Everyone stood up, clapping and crying out "Bravo!" "Fantastic!" "Wonderful!" Before I realized it, Liberace had let go of my hand and was heading to the podium. He began to talk as if he was the keynote speaker that I had promised.

"Isn't this wonderful, ladies and gentlemen? I'm deeply touched and deeply honoured. I'm always looking for a new talent to promote and I would love to showcase Famous PEOPLE Players in my show in Las Vegas."

The room went nuts. People started screaming and whistling. My eyes scanned the room to get a better view of everyone's facial expressions. Judi was standing on a chair, whistling, next to my mother, who was wearing the biggest flowered hat in the room. I could see her telling the lady next to her: "That's my daughter."

I felt so proud that the people I loved could be there to share in this moment. I felt a little pang that Robert was missing. *Oh why couldn't he be here*, I thought. He'd be bawling. He was there from the very beginning when the seed of intention was planted that later bloomed into Famous PEOPLE Players. He was now off creating his own dream with a great job to take over the business world and planning a wedding.

Then before I could say anything, and just as we had rehearsed it, the performers came out from behind the dark, taking off their hoods and revealing themselves to the audience. They each stepped forward, holding a rose. Then they came down from the stage to meet their dream star—Liberace.

"Liberace," I spoke into the microphone, "Greg Kozak."

Greg gave Lee a rose and a big hug.

"Kevin Morris."

"Brenda Woods."

"Brian..."

As each player walked offstage and toward Lee, audience members applauded and patted each of them on the back.

Philip was crying. Ann and Ron were deeply touched by the miracle before them. Tears streamed down their cheeks and the audience showed their praise. Then Liberace looked at the performers closely, realizing for the first time the miracle that had actually unfolded. He picked up his program on the table, which read, "Metro Toronto Community Association for the Mentally Retarded Annual Luncheon. April 10. Guest of Honour, Liberace."

He moved back toward the podium and asked the audience to please sit down. He then quietly looked at us and said, "It's not who you are that makes people laugh or cry. It's because you're truly talented people who have every right to share the same stage with me. And I'd be honoured to take you to Las Vegas."

That night, Liberace invited everyone to see his show. We felt like real stars as we entered the O'Keefe Centre for the Performing Arts. It was just as I had envisioned it. When Liberace walked out on stage before his show, he introduced the audience to the Famous PEOPLE Players. We all stood and Sandra tripped over the hem of the long dress she was wearing. We all felt like we had met and fallen in love with our Prince Charming, who was going to take us away to his kingdom.

Then it was midnight and I took the bus back home. There was no limousine on the ride back.

I hung up my dress in the closet. Funny, I had just bought it two weeks ago and it was already too tight.

That night, I slept soundly, but not before I looked up at the sky from my apartment balcony and thanked God for Our Father Who Art in Las Vegas!

CHAPTER SIX

Hallelujah Hollywood

"Who the hell is calling at four o'clock in the morning?" Bernard grumbled, as he pulled the pillow over his head. I scrambled for the receiver, which was on my side of the bed. *Clonk*! I hit it against the night table. I bent down, lopsided, to pick it up from the floor.

"Hello?"

"It's Seymour."

"Seymour, it's 4 a.m."

"I'm in Vegas. Lee just called me to tell me the news. Congratulations…." (I couldn't get a word in edgewise.) "I'm coming to Canada next week. Lee's playing at Hamilton Place and I want you and the kids to come and perform for me like you did for Lee. I have to see it and approve it before you come to Vegas."

I shot up straight in bed. "*Approve it!*"

"Yes, I'm Lee's personal manager and I have to see your show."

I swallowed hard. *I'm Cinderella*, I thought. *I have to make the glass slipper fit*. I sorted out some of the details with Seymour and hung up. I couldn't believe that it was only hours ago that we were savouring our incredible victory and now we'd have to work harder than ever to prove we deserved a chance in the big time.

"God, don't do this to me. Can't you let me sleep one night without worrying and sobbing?" I whispered to myself.

"*Goodnight*," he replied.

"I've got an exam that day," Ron said. "I can't do Hamilton Place."

"You have to do it!"

"I want to, but I can't. This time it's impossible."

"There is nobody else who can do the head and body of the Liberace puppet," I told him.

"Can't be done, Diane."

I was desperate. "I'll call your professor—give me his phone number."

"You must be joking. He won't allow the exam to be moved. I'm in university, remember? Don't you get it?"

"Let me try."

Ron wrote his professor's name and number on the back of his bus transfer. Within a couple of hours, I was able to reach Ron's professor. I cried on the phone. "*Please*," I begged, "change his exam—I promise he won't cheat. You have no idea how important this show is. Why, it's a major breakthrough in the treatment of mentally retarded people and you will be responsible for making it happen.

You will be! You're the one man in the world that will enable all of us to go to Las Vegas, *please!*"

"Okay, okay, I will reschedule. Have Ron call me."

"I can't believe it," Ron said in shock. "You got my exam changed!?"

During our rehearsals that week, I pushed everyone to do a better job than ever before. I wanted to make an even greater impression. I just knew in my hearts of hearts that everyone was going to hit their mark again.

We chartered a bus to get to Hamilton Place. Seymour had arranged for us to set up our stage in the Studio Theatre for a private performance in front of Liberace's crew. "Then Lee and I are taking you all to lunch after your presentation," he told us.

All the people who had performed with Lee on stage in Toronto took up the seats in the theatre. The musical director, musicians and others (who I would later come to know as the wardrobe people, stage manager and producer) were all watching, now, as the audience. I was nervous, sitting between Seymour and Lee.

I kept praying and wondered, *Is the magic still going to be there?* Then I would tell myself, *Don't lose faith, Diane,* as I continuously wrapped and unwrapped a Kleenex around my fingers.

The show was a blur to me. All I remember is the audience's laughter and standing ovation afterward. Lee beamed like a proud parent and Seymour kept saying, "I found her! She was like a bulldog, Lee; she had her teeth in the seat of my pants and didn't let go until I said, yes, you can have Liberace!"

The next thing I knew, I was being invited to see Lee's Vegas show, "...which is different from the show you saw in Canada," said Ray Arnett, Lee's stage manager and producer. "You need to see this so you know how to prepare your children."

"They're not children," I said.

Ignoring me, he kept talking. "There are cars to go with every outfit. He never walks on stage. He is a star— he is driven on. The stage at the Las Vegas Hilton is long and deep, not like the ones you're used to working with. There are rules to be followed, as the stage can be danger- ous. We have a fly system to bring in the sets, dancing waters, and a 60-piece orchestra on stage. Everything moves, so I want your children to be prepared. See you in Reno next month." He walked off, shutting the door behind him, and left me looking at a sign that read Backstage.

"They're not children," I said to the closed door. When I turned around, the group was saying goodbye to Liberace.

"It's gonna be a challenge," I said to Ron on the drive back. "A huge challenge. Everything has to be bigger— speaking of bigger, I can't wear this dress anymore. I need to go on a diet."

The next morning I couldn't lift my head off my pillow. I was sick and figured I had a bad case of the flu. Besides, all the stress I had endured over the last few months surely took its toll on my body. Just to be sure, I went to see Dr. Turner.

"It's not the flu, it's morning sickness," he told me. "You're pregnant again."

Although I was nervous about the pregnancy after what had happened the last time, both Bernard and I were just as thrilled. This time I was determined to do everything right. I was careful not to overexert myself physically during rehearsals, but I still had the habit of shouting cues.

"You're pushing them too hard," my mom kept saying, as she barged into the rehearsal hall. "Be careful," she sat me down.

"I'm not treating these performers like they're handicapped. They're professionals—and that means hard work."

My values hadn't changed. I never let people think that because my performers are "retarded" they need to be treated differently. In real life nobody's going to let them off easily. The working (and show business) world expects the best—and that has nothing to do with IQ.

In July, now five months pregnant, I flew alone to Nevada to see Liberace's show and discuss how Famous PEOPLE Players could be a part of it. The hot air hit me as the plane door opened and the flight attendant escorted me to a limousine that awaited me on the runway. The hour-long drive along winding roads to Lake Tahoe was incredibly beautiful. With my nose pressed to the window, I felt like a little kid in Wonderland. The experience was overwhelming, especially the slot machines that lined the first floor of the hotel where I was staying. I had never been in a casino before that day.

"Diane!" I turned to see Ray Arnett, wearing a denim jacket covered in rhinestones, with matching pants and sunglasses. "Follow me."

We walked through the back kitchen, which was engulfed by the deafening sound of plates and glasses clattering, food sizzling, doors swinging, and people rushing back and forth. We kept walking down the corridor, to the backstage area of the theatre.

"Good evening, Mr. Arnett," said the security guards as they moved aside to open the door for us.

"This is it, Diane—backstage. The most dangerous place in the world. Move aside, move aside," he kept saying as he waved his hands. "Watch over here, move this way," he directed me. "Here is car number one, for the first entrance…Car number two, second entrance… There is three, four. Dancing waters are behind the orchestra, and these are the pianos—DON'T TOUCH THEM!"

I jumped back.

"Don't *ever* touch them," he warned.

Then we walked in front of the orchestra, centre stage. "See how big it is? Your children have to get from right to left. See the exits and entrances? When they're finished their number, they go back down to the dressing room until I call them on the intercom. I don't want them getting in the way during Lee's performance."

"They're not children," I muttered stubbornly. That night I watched in awe as Liberace performed at the Hilton. *Wow! If only my mom could see this*, I thought, *she wouldn't believe it!*

After the show, I was escorted to Lee's private dressing room, where we'd be sitting down to talk about how we would integrate our show into Liberace's grand performance. When I entered Lee's dressing room, I noticed it was bigger than my apartment back home. Seymour and Ray made a grand entrance, applauding Liberace, who followed closely behind.

The dressing room had a gorgeous wrap-around couch, with matching chair, that could easily sit eight comfortably, a beautiful glass coffee table and a gorgeous bar with six stools. Mirrors were everywhere, and from the ceiling hung a stunning chandelier that lit up the whole room. The dressing room had a separate space for a bedroom and ensuite bathroom with a sunken tub. It was home sweet home and I could live there with no problem. I took my place on the couch in front of the hors d'oeuvres that were on the coffee table.

"She eats like a horse," Seymour told Lee.

"I'm still hungry. Can I have some of those hors d'oeuvres that were on the bar?" Ray got up quickly and put them in front of me. "I'm eating for two."

"Oh," Liberace smiled, "we have a mommy. How nice."

"Now down to business," began Ray, taking the lead. "We want you to open the show, but we need to think about what you will do."

"What about letters?" I suggested. "Spelling out Liberace's name, followed by the candelabra, the piano—"

"—and when I say Liberace," Ray added, "Liberace will make his grand entrance…Liberace!" he announced, making Liberace's name sound very long and ending it with a kick, just the way we perform *Aruba Liberace!*

Liberace smiled. "Diane darling, we need another puppet of a famous personality."

"As a matter of fact, we're introducing Elvis Presley," I told him.

"Elvis? Perfect! Elvis is a friend," Seymour said, while I continued to wolf down hors d'oeuvres.

"The letters, darling, need to be really big so everyone can read them. Timing is important," Ray was taking charge of the meeting again. "You will have a six-second blackout before Lee makes his entrance."

I almost choked on a caviar canapé. In truth, I was thinking about those six seconds. *How were the performers ever going to move that quickly?*

"Is something wrong?" Seymour looked at me.

"No, I'm fine, I just ate too fast."

"Let's talk about the Liberace puppet head," said Lee. "I think we need a new one, something that has a bigger smile that can read well from the big stage to the audience."

"I know just the place," I interrupted, telling him about a sculptor in Hollywood by the name of Bob Baker, who was internationally known for his work. "He apparently can create exactly what you want."

Liberace was sold on my suggestion. "You'll take Diane and go to L.A. tomorrow and get everything set up," he said to Seymour. "And I will personally supervise the likeness of my head and while you're at it, get a new one done of Elvis," he said with a chuckle.

By the time I got back to Toronto, my head was spinning with ideas. I envisioned giant dice props and dollar signs for Elvis's "Viva Las Vegas," among a host of other possibilities. But I was worried about how my performers were going to clear the stage in six seconds. The stage was

65 feet wide and we had only six seconds to exit stage left, in the dark.

Rehearsals shifted into overdrive. We had to teach everyone how to run in the dark, a challenging feat. We tried running with the lights out, while my mother and Renato laboured over new costumes for the puppets. Within a week we were down to a 22-second exit, and we had no more ideas on how we were going to shave off 16 seconds. In four months, we would be opening in September for six weeks, with two shows a day everyday, one at the 8 p.m dinner show and the other at midnight.

If I didn't know it already, the next few weeks taught me a valuable lesson in this business. No matter how good we got at performing, repetition would never go away. We had to consistently practice our routine. And I had to learn patience—just as the performers had to master the six-second exit.

Lesson two: always expect the unexpected. The following week into rehearsals, I got an unpleasant surprise. "Diane?" Lisa came in and closed the door to my office. "I don't want the others to hear." She was crying. "I can't go. Mark said no. I'm engaged to him and I love him and I don't want to lose him—please."

A jealous fiancé. How insecure is that, I thought.

"Don't say anything to me," she cried. "I can see by the look on your face that you're upset."

"I can't believe you're going to turn down an opportunity like this," I huffed

"I can't go. You know how hard this is for me. I love the kids, I adore Famous PEOPLE Players—this is killing me. I promise with my whole heart I will be here for you when you return. I'm so proud of you. But I just can't go." Then the door closed and she left.

As much as I was devastated by Lisa's news, I didn't waste any time holding auditions and interviews to replace her. Sure, there were plenty of talented performers around, but black-light performers don't grow on trees and I needed to find some special talents to work in the dark. In fact, I had my work cut out for me. Seymour called days later to tell me he wanted me to hire three extra performers in case of an accident or sickness, so the show could go on. I wasn't very happy about this, mainly because this was our dream and I didn't want to share it with strangers. And I had to make sure that whoever came on board would not only be dedicated and committed, but would make the others feel comfortable. It was an important ingredient in our tight unit.

When I finally agreed on the extra people, I found them—or should I say, they found us. As soon as people hear the words 'Las Vegas' and 'Liberace', everyone finds you, and quickly. Bringing in new people required hard work from the group too. They had to practice rhythm with the new players, and rhythm is key in our line of our work, along with trust.

The players operating the Elvis puppet had the most difficulty. Three people had to synchronize Elvis' swiveling hips, legs and guitar-strumming fingers. Added to the frustration of moving in sync were the extra props in his numbers—dice, playing cards, a slot machine and roulette wheels. The roulette wheels were a particular headache because they kept breaking. First my mother and Renato made them out of Styrofoam, but they split apart. Then they tried wood, and although they were too heavy, wood wheels would survive the trip to Las Vegas.

Our departure date to Las Vegas was weeks away and we hit another stumbling block. We would be losing another valuable member of our troupe—Renato's mother refused to let her son go to Vegas despite my mother's pleas in eloquent Italian. She'd be sick with worry and couldn't bear him leaving home for six weeks.

On the day I was leaving (my performers would arrive the day after), Renato and I sat on the front steps of the church, waiting for my cab. We sat quietly and shared a few tears while I held his hand. "To think this was to be the happiest day of my life—leaving for Las Vegas, a dream come true—but you're not by my side."

"Well, Mrs. Dupuy," he finally said, "I did get to meet Liberace." Then the cab pulled up to take me to the airport.

After checking into the Las Vegas Hilton, I rushed to the backstage area. I was relieved to find that our props had been delivered safely without being damaged. There on stage, all of them were laid out neatly in a very 'Ray Arnett' manner. "Are you going to join us for the Cosby show?" I turned to find Ray standing behind me, holding a clipboard.

"*Bill Cosby?*"

"Who else?" He smiled. "The reservation is under Lee's name," he said as he ushered me out.

As I tried to keep up with his energetic pace, he told me, "Exercise, diet, great for the heart—focus! When I worked with Judy—Judy Garland, that is—"

"You worked with *Judy*?" My eyes lit up.

"I was a hoofer," he said. (Hoofer is show-business speak for professional dancer.) He opened the stage door to let me through as he kept on talking: "I loved dancing. Wait till you see Ann-Margret, Diane. She moves in when Lee moves out."

"Ann-Margret! My favourite."

"You ain't seen nothing yet. She flies in the air. Male hoofers pick her up and carry her across the stage." He acted it out as we walked into the casino. I thought at one point that he was actually going to lift me up and fly me to the elevator. "You gotta see it. Those children too."

The elevator came, he got on, and the doors closed. "They're not children," I said to the doors.

During Bill Cosby's show, I was determined to go backstage and meet Mr. Cosby. After all these years, I wanted to tell him about the last time I had met him. I wanted to tell him that I had taken his advice about black light, and let him know that I was now in Las Vegas, performing with Liberace.

I stood in the wings, waiting for him to finish. As he walked toward me, I waved at him enthusiastically. "Hi there! Remember me, Mr. Cosby?" I was six-and-a-half months pregnant now and when Bill Cosby took one look at my stomach, he started to walk the other way. I chased after him, explaining what I was doing—black light, meeting Liberace, and now Las Vegas. A much-relieved Bill Cosby looked at me and said, "Did you ever hear the expression, 'You can lead a horse to water'? Don't thank me, thank yourself. Congratulations and have a great run."

The next morning, still in a wonderful daze from the night before, I pulled back the drapes from my hotel window and looked out. To my amazement, I saw a huge marquee that read LIBERACE AND THE FAMOUS PEOPLE PLAYERS. At night, it lit the Vegas sky along with other large marquees. I got ready to greet my players, who had arrived safely, led by my mother, Mary. It felt like something was missing when I saw my mother without Renato by her side. I imagined him saying, "Gambling machines at the airport? Oh my God, Mrs. Dupuy, I'm gonna have a heart attack!"

It wasn't long before we encountered our first crisis in Las Vegas: the Hilton Hotel had a policy that every guest had to sign in. While it sounds like simple thing, it was a huge challenge for the performers. Many of them couldn't read or write, let alone sign their name. I offered to sign on behalf of them, but the hotel refused. Looking at me strangely, the desk clerk repeated, "Everyone must sign their own name." An hour-and-a-half later, we all managed to sign our own names.

There were other challenges that had nothing to do with performing on stage. For example, we had to teach the players that they couldn't take the money that sat on the table in the hotel's coffee shop because it belonged to the server. It was often about details, details, details—and it took time to deal with.

After the troupe checked in, we made a mad dash to our first rehearsal with Liberace. But there were distractions along the way. For one, Sandra gazed at all the slot machines in awe.

"There are no clocks in our hotel," Mike quickly noticed.

"How do we tell time?" asked Brenda.

"They don't have clocks in Las Vegas because it's open for 24 hours. All they want you to do is gamble and not be aware of the time," I told them, sounding like a full-fledged Las Vegas pro.

Then Philip was lured. I saw him walking backward and his eyes peering in one direction. All the performers followed him and I ran ahead to see what was happening. "This is a black lace chiffon negligee I'm wearing and it may be purchased in the Va-Va-Voom Boutique on the mezzanine level," announced a scantily clad young woman.

"How much is it?" Mike asked her, as she eyed the guys up and down. I reached out and moved them in the other direction.

"Oh my God," Brenda said to Ron, "they're wearing their underwear in public. I can't believe it!"

Ron had a big grin on his face, as he started to move toward backstage. I had to remind him that we needed everyone focused on rehearsal and not on negligees.

When we made it to our dressing room, which was one floor down from the main stage level, the performers were understandably impressed. "Stop admiring yourself in the mirror," I said to Kevin.

"I'm gonna put my stuff here," said Sandra. "Don't touch anything."

"Look at the bathrooms," Kevin was awestruck. "Do you think Liberace uses the toilet?" he asked.

"His is made outta mink," said Brian.

"How do you know?" asked Greg.

"I know, I know. His piano bench is made outta mink."

"It's time. Focus, guys, focus. This rehearsal is serious. No talking about negligees, mink toilets, or slot machines —hear me?"

"Yes, Diane."

"Now let's give it all we've got."

The troops were rallied and off we went. We ran up the stairs to meet with Ray Arnett. The stage was already set.

"Please sit on the boxes, children. We will rehearse when Lee arrives."

"They're not children," I said automatically.

Mike laughed. "I don't know about you, but I like being called that."

"I think he wants to be our father," Brenda said.

"Yeah," Mike said, laughing, "and we're his babies."

"Hey, Daddy-O, buy me dinner with the lady with the negligee," Kevin perked up.

"Kevin, stop that!" I started to get angry.

"That's all right," said Ray, "I'd love to buy you dinner."

"See, I told you," Kevin giggled.

"What are your names again?" Ray asked. "I'm sorry, I can't remember."

One by one they rhymed off their names, followed by Ann and Ray.

"I want you to have fun—enjoy yourselves," Ray confirmed his acceptance of them. "But first we have work to do. So please sit down on your boxes and I'll call you when I need you."

Ray started pacing back and forth on the stage, looking at his watch, "Where is Lee? He's late!" He continued to pace. "We can't start without him," he called out to the lighting man, "and I'll kill him when he gets here!" Everyone at Famous PEOPLE Players was shocked to hear that Ray was going to kill the star of the show; they adored Liberace.

We sat on the black boxes used as steps for the performance and waited and waited as Ray paced back and forth. Two hours later, as Kevin was dozing on Ann's shoulder, Liberace made a grand entrance with dozens of shopping bags. We all stood at attention.

"LEE, WHERE HAVE YOU BEEN?" bellowed Ray. "You're two hours late. You're rude and inconsiderate to the performers, musicians, the stagehands and to me. I want you to personally apologize to all the children."

Liberace put down his shopping bags and went up to each of us and said sorry. Then he turned to Ray and said, "Ray, I'm truly sorry for putting you out." He had incredible respect for Ray and his workers admired him for it. I was starting to learn that the biggest stars in the business are those who take their professionalism most seriously.

Ray was determined to get rehearsals going and asked everyone to take their places. The orchestra played the overture—it would be the first time my performers were working with live music and it was difficult. But Bo Ayars, Liberace's conductor and musical arranger, made the transition easier by speeding up the tempo to sound like the taped music that we were accustomed to hearing. We ran through the letters four times until we had mastered the rhythm and the size of the stage.

"Now for the transition to the car," Ray bellowed. "Remember what I told you, Diane. They have six seconds to get off the stage in the dark. When there's a blackout, GO!"

We performed the letters set and then came the blackout—GO!

One...two...three...four...five...six...seven... eight...nine...

We're going to be fired, I thought.

"Do it again, Diane. I need six seconds," Ray said. "Blackout—GO!"

One...two...three...four...five...six...seven... eight...nine...ten...eleven...

"What's the problem?" Ray walked on stage.

Shaking, I replied, "I don't know. I tried to teach them to run in the dark, but we had trouble getting it to six seconds."

"You, dear, are going to learn something about directing from me. Children, please take your places. In the next blackout, Vince will drive the car on stage."

The music played. Blackout.

"VINCE, BRING ON THE CAR!"

When everyone saw the car coming toward them in the dark, they were off that stage in four seconds!

"See, a little dose of reality was all they needed," said Ray with a proud smile.

September 23. Opening night. Being nervous was an understatement. Our combined perspiration was enough to flood the dressing room. We all sat quietly before the show, waiting for our call.

Bang! Bang! There was a knock on our dressing room door. "Come on in!" everyone said.

Seymour entered, holding a gold Styrofoam guitar with flowers coming out of it. "It's from Elvis," he said, "wishing you well for the opening."

"Elvis!" we all shouted in disbelief.

"Who else?"

"You know *Elvis*?" Kevin's eyes were wide.

"I know everybody," Seymour laughed.

Lee entered the dressing room, wearing his bathrobe and white knee-high boots, followed by Ray, who was wearing a form-fitting black leather suit.

"Is everyone getting ready for the big opening?" Liberace was beaming. The performers all took turns hugging him, trying to ease their stage fright.

Once Liberace and his handlers left, it was time to give my team a pep talk. I felt like a hockey coach pumping up his players before they hit the ice in a Stanley Cup final game. "I know you can do this," I said to the team. "I love you." We all got up and hugged each tightly. Brenda started to cry.

"Don't cry. Please don't cry. We all need you." I hugged her.

"I can't. I'm afraid."

"Afraid of what?"

"The audience. What if they hate us?"

"They won't hate us, because we're good, Brenda, we're all good. And no matter what happens, remember, Liberace comes after us. Just concentrate on the letters and getting off in the dark."

Kevin looked up at me. "What if I can't make it? I don't want to get run over by Liberace's car."

"You won't. I'll grab your hand and pull you off," Ron assured him.

"Me too, I'm here for you." Ann rubbed Brenda's back.

"ATTENTION FAMOUS PEOPLE PLAYERS. This is Ray Arnett speaking. Please take your places stage right, in front of Liberace's limousine. Don't touch the car—I don't want any fingerprints on it."

"Yes, Ray," everyone looked at the intercom.

"I betcha he can see us through that box," Philip said.

"He's got eyes in the back of his head," Mike agreed.

Everyone ran up the flight of stairs and walked carefully around the limousine where Vince Cardell, Liberace's stage chauffeur and protégé, was standing dressed in a white rhinestone chauffeur suit.

"Wow, you look handsome," Brenda told him.

Vince was as nice as they come. He was always bringing treats to everyone in the dressing room and making sure we were all having a good time. He smiled and gave us all a thumbs up just before we went on stage. "You'll be great!"

After one final hug for the group, I ran out to sit in the sound booth, where I would be watching the show. The beautiful gold lamé curtain rose on Bo Ayars's overture. I watched the letters dance, float and move across the stage. They spelled LEE, then ACE, then LIBBY, and finally

LIBERACE. Then Ray Arnett's voice boomed over the speakers. "The Las Vegas Hilton is proud to present the Liberace show, produced and directed by Ray Arnett!"

Boom, boom went the drums. "Now the man who's famous throughout the world for his candelabra—"

Poof—Philip spun the candelabra on stage.

"And his piano—"

Kevin wheeled the piano to the centre stage mark (thank God!) with Greg following behind with his bench, right side up.

During a long drum roll, Ray Arnett stretched the name, "L-I-B-E-R-A-C-E!"

Boom, boom went the drums and—BLACKOUT!

One...two...three...four...five...six...

The spotlight hit stage right and the limousine purred onto the stage. Then, to my horror, I saw Kevin wrapped around the curtain on stage left! Ron's black arm reached around the curtain, pulling Kevin off.

We're fired, I thought. I ran backstage and hugged each performer after the first number; then I ran back out to see our Elvis, Streisand and Liberace numbers.

Elvis was clumsy, with his legs going one way and arms going another. However, the roulette wheels, as heavy as they were, spun beautifully, and Streisand made a graceful entrance, her legs and arms in sync.

At the end, Liberace called the performers on stage. "From Toronto, Canada, the Famous PEOPLE Players." Everyone came running out, each one bowing awkwardly, up and down, sideways. Sandra stood with her back to the audience as she bowed backwards and Brenda and Mike were holding hands. *Fired!* I thought. *Now I know what it feels like to open and close in one night. Thank God nobody knows we're here!*

I made my way to the dressing room, ready to tell them what I thought. I pointed my finger in Brian's face. "Don't you ever touch your crotch while taking your bow again."

"The bows," Ron piped up, "we forgot to rehearse the bows."

"The legs of Elvis have to go in the same direction as the arms. The roulette wheels, dice and violins—that was great! Letters, wonderful. But the exit—Kevin, what happened? You were wrapped around the curtain."

"How embarrassing," Brenda said, her voice rising. "We bombed. We're going to get fired! And it's all your fault!" she pointed at Kevin. We grabbed her quickly, before she threw a tantrum and the Las Vegas police came to our dressing room.

"Happy New Year!" Seymour said as he entered the room.

"New Year?" I said. "It's not New Year."

"We're celebrating early. I brought my client here to meet you. She loved your show. Boys and girls, Ginger Rogers."

"Ginger Rogers!" There was a stampede as the performers ran for their autograph books.

"I saw you dance with Fred Astaire," Brenda said, breathlessly.

Liberace entered wearing a bathrobe and white socks to his knees, beaming with pride, followed by Ray Arnett and Bo Ayars. "K-E-V-I-N," Lee said, stretching the name out, beckoning Kevin with his index finger toward him.

"We've got a great idea for you," said Ray. "When we do the blackout, just drop to the floor. Bo will pull you under the curtain and the musicians will pull you off."

"You want me to fall down?"

"Hit the dirt behind the boxes," Ray smiled.

"I'll be there to pull you through," reassured Bo.

"The show was terrific," Lee said, beaming with pride. "Don't worry about the bows. There weren't supposed to be bows, but we decided to do it anyway." Lee looked at Ray and said, "Let each one of the players hold a letter, and that way everyone will look more professional for their bows. I want *both* hands on the letters."

I went red, knowing full well what he meant about the wandering hands.

Liberace lifted our spirits with his compliments. Now I was thinking that maybe the show wasn't as bad as I had imagined.

Our next show was at midnight—we had never performed that late before and I was worried about my group's energy level. But we were all flying higher than a kite from our first performance, so it didn't become an issue, at least not that night. Once again we had to prep the stage and the orchestra its instruments. The piano tuner arrived after the first show just as we were setting up our props. That's when we found out we had even more supporters among the professionals we worked with. Ralph Enriquez, Liberace's bass player, was immediately drawn to the performers.

"Nice man," said Greg.

Then there was James Moody, a jazz saxophone player, who worked for many years with the great Dizzy Gillespie. "Wanna chew?" He offered a stick of gum to everyone.

Ralph said, "I'm having trouble remembering everyone's name. Wait, I got it, Small Bird for Greg cause you're so small."

"Me love birds," Greg said, grinning.

"You I'm calling Ketchup," Ralph told Sandra.

"How come?" Sandra gave a big smile for the attention she was receiving.

"I saw you pour all that ketchup on your chicken," he said.

"What about me?" Brenda stepped in.

"Blondie—I'll call ya Blondie."

"Then Mike's Dagwood," she laughed, referring to the cartoon strip Dagwood & Blondie.

"No, he's Paysan."

Naturally, I had to step in and spoil the moment to get all the performers back to business, finishing the set-up of their props. The musicians all went back to tuning their instruments. I paced the floor.

When midnight came, Ray's voice spoke to us over the microphone. Everyone acknowledged his direction as if he could see and hear us.

Drum roll…One…two…three…four…five…six…

"Hit the dirt!" yelled Bo.

Limo, lights, Liberace—and no Kevin. Great! Problem solved.

Kevin felt like a star, rolling under the black backdrop with the musicians pulling him along to find his way into the backstage wings. I was worried that the curtain would rise to reveal the orchestra with Kevin sitting inside a tuba.

"Don't worry," Bo said, "I'm ahead of you. I had an empty chair in the orchestra—he could pretend he was playing a violin."

I was always worried, but more so about the reviews about our performance. The next day, the syndicated columnist, Forest Duke, "The Duke of Las Vegas," wrote:

The company of eleven inspired and gifted young people is sure to be listed among Lee's most illustrious discoveries. Working in black-light, the players perform with life-size puppets; huge, brilliantly colored letters, spelling out the showman's name, a heart, musical notes and little creatures floating and cavorting in mid-air. The captivating act by Famous PEOPLE Players is an ideal complement for Liberace!

Even the show business magazine, *Variety*, had nothing but praise for us:

Octet opens the show with funny anthropomorphic figures shaped in letters to spell out Liberace's name, dancing around on a ghostly white grand piano...

Group does leave off Liberace long enough to include a shot at Barbra Streisand and another towards Elvis Presley, complete with dancing designs moving around the central figures.

The players' last depiction of Liberace takes his usual boogie-woogie sesh from the repertoire and places it, imaginatively, with the group. They have fun with the rhythms, bringing forth still more odd characters to bounce around the piano.

Altogether, the players are a strong addition to the Liberace show and could be showcased exceedingly well in other environments.

I couldn't wait to read out the reviews in the dressing room.

"What's e-n-v-i-r-o-n-m-e-n-t?" Sandra asked, saying the word slowly.

"It means we can perform anywhere we want—Europe, wherever."

"There is no stopping the Famous PEOPLE Players!" Seymour came up from behind me. "I'm proud of you. You did a great job for me and Liberace."

Brenda curtsied. He put his arm around her and drew us all together in a huddle.

"I have been in the business for many years. I represent the world's greatest stars—Debbie Reynolds, Ginger Rogers, Frankie Lane—"

"Frankie Lane!" Mike gasped.

"You mean *Rawhide?*" said Philip, referring to the TV series.

"Yes, *Rawhide*, and none of them, when they weren't performing, laid out in the hot, Las Vegas sun all day by the pool and got sunburned. I'm telling you this because I noticed that you were all at the pool today. I'm reminding you that you're here to do a show. This is serious business, show business, and you're here to do a good job all the time. If you lie by the pool all day, you'll be drained by the hot Vegas sun—and believe me, I know this desert sun."

"We can't go swimming?" Brenda said.

"Yes, you can go swimming, but don't lie in the sun. Be careful—or else."

When he left the dressing room, I reminded them about the ground rules. Then, I suggested what they could do in their spare time.

"We can't go to the casino, it's against the rules. Besides, we don't have money to gamble, and Liberace doesn't want us gambling," I told them.

"But there is nothing else to do in Vegas."

"We can't go to any shows," Ron said. "They perform the same time we do."

"It's boring, sitting in our rooms all day," Ann jumped in.

"Look, this is only for six weeks—make a sacrifice. We swim one hour a day, eat for one hour, go for a walk for one hour, rest, eat supper, get ready for the show—it's not like you're up early. With the midnight show ending around 3 a.m., then eating at the coffee shop, you're not even in bed until 5 a.m."

"Yeah, but we have to be at the buffet in the dining room by noon or we'll miss brunch," one of the new understudies said sarcastically.

"Your contract gives you lunch and dinner—it's up to you to be there, then you can go back to bed," I snapped back. "If you don't want to do anything in the afternoon, go back to bed—or read a book."

"This is unfair," he said.

"If you don't like the rules, leave. I can understudy in your place."

Everyone laughed. "You're pregnant!" they yelled.

I was so adamant about the rules that I forgot there was only so much I could do to remedy a situation. Just the same, I was angry by the lack of respect in the room. Now, I wished Bernard had been there to advise me and support me. His very presence would have calmed me down. I was learning that negativity is contagious and when one person has a negative attitude, it spreads like wildfire, as it was starting to do in our camp. There were squabbles among the performers; the understudies continued to keep to themselves; members were sometimes late when we met for brunch and the mood of the group was unstable and edgy.

I was much too young to run a company that was involved in a show as big as Liberace's. I made mistakes. I pushed, and I pushed hard. I kept nagging the group about rules. "Don't use the elevator, use the stairs to get to the stage," I told them.

"Liberace uses the elevator—so we can too," Brenda responded.

"Use the elevator *and there's no going to the coffee shop between shows*," I warned.

Brenda screamed and threw a chair across the dressing room. Ron and Ann jumped on her to calm her down. Thank God Liberace didn't hear or we would have all been fired.

"We can't work like this," the understudies complained.

"What's the trouble, Dora Doom?" Ray Arnett snuck up beside me with his trademark clipboard.

I went red. I didn't want him to know about my own problems.

"Come with me, Dora."

I followed him nervously into Liberace's dressing room.

"Dora—you worry too much. I'm going to call you Dora Doom. You worry about the show, the children, your understudies. Haven't you noticed?"

I stared at the floor.

"You're always crying, broody and hysterical. Your understudies will be history in five weeks," he reassured me. "Don't worry about the children, the show is good. You're having a baby and you need your husband."

"I know. I miss him a lot."

"Then call him to come down and see the town."

"I want my company to work like a family," I said.

"It will. Just give it time." Ray patted my shoulder.

I took his advice and called Bernard to come down on a weekend junket.

But there were incidences I had to deal with before Bernard made it down. Philip left his room in his pajamas and became lost in the hallways of the hotel. Dick Lane, the entertainment director, called me when they found Philip and warned it had better not happen again.

"What happened, Philip?" I questioned him.

"I was sleeping and I woke up because I heard a funny noise in the bathroom. The door was locked, so I said, 'Hello? Is anybody there?' Nobody answered and I got scared. I looked under the door and there were green under-pants on the floor. Then I looked in the keyhole and saw two people." He started to cry.

"It's okay, Philip. I'll find out what happened." I went over to the bathroom and opened the door. "They're not

there now." I got him to look inside. "See, they're not there."
As I reassured Philip, I noticed that the understudy who
slept in his room was not in his bed and it hadn't been
slept in. "Go to sleep, you're dreaming. Next time, if you
have the same dream, call me in my room and I'll come
right away."

"I love you, Diane."

"Me too, Philip."

"I'll be real good with the candelabra."

"I know you will, Philip, I know you will."

He went back to bed. But I went up and down the
corridors, knocking on doors, looking for those understudies. Finally I saw the two of them get off the elevator.

"I really don't give a damn what you do when you're at
home—but here we have an obligation to offer our
support, love and respect to the Famous PEOPLE Players."

They squirmed in embarrassment.

"You should be ashamed of yourselves," I continued.
"You talk about how you offer them support, but instead
your support is screwing each other in the washroom."

Walking back to their designated rooms, I looked at
the female understudy. "What would happen if you had
walked into your room and found Brenda missing? Then
what?"

She looked scared, and for a few moments, I felt better.

It was peaceful for the next couple of days, until
Brian ordered $800 worth of Heineken beer to his room.
"You don't even like beer," Ron said to him. "Why would
you order all this beer?"

"I felt like it," he said.

"Well, you'll just have to send it back." Ron was adamant.

"I won't." Brian was defiant.

"Are you going to drink all this?" Ron questioned him.

"I'm taking it home as a souvenir."

"How are you going to pay for this beer?"

"I'll find money."

"Where?"

"In the casino," Brian responded.

"You can't go in the casino—Seymour said no one is to go in the casino. Where is the money your parents gave you?"

"I spent it," he said.

"You spent the money they gave you on beer?"

"No, I charged the beer to my room and I lost the money gambling."

Ron was upset. He forced Brian to call room service and return the beer. During these troubled times, it was Ray Arnett's vote of confidence that helped me get through it all. I managed to stay calm with the performers, but I wound up fighting with my mother to ease my frustration. We fought about the props—I wanted them brighter. Or we fought about the costumes—I wanted her to work faster to mend the hems, or glue back the spider's leg.

"I've had it," she said one day. "I'm going home."

On the day she flew out, Bernard flew in.

"Go see *Tits and Feathers*—my treat. Go to the MGM and see it. I know you'll love it," offered Liberace.

I didn't want to go see a show that was called *Tits and Feathers*. I was too embarrassed. I didn't want to offend

Lee, so I made the excuse that I couldn't leave the performers.

"What are you going to do if something goes wrong on stage—run up and fix it? It's final, you're to take Bernard and go see *Tits and Feathers* and that's an order. Seymour," Lee called over to him, "buy her a dress to wear. She can't go to the show in her company uniform."

I accepted the offer. All the dresses I tried on were so beautiful that I couldn't make a decision on which one to choose.

"We'll take all three," Seymour said to the saleslady.

"Three? I can't take three," I protested.

"It's either that or nothing, and you'll hurt Lee's feelings if you don't take them."

"I'll take them." I gave him a big hug and kiss.

Liberace called a cab and sent us off to the MGM to see the famous *Tits and Feathers*. When we arrived at the hotel, we didn't see a posting for the show on its marquee. "Go to the showroom over there, through the casino," the concierge pointed.

The sound of slots, with change falling out, bells ringing and players screaming echoed through the casino. It was too tempting for Bernard to pass up. "Wait," he said, "I want to try my luck." He put in a quarter and pulled the arm but he lost it. One try was enough, so we made our way to see the maitre d'.

"Are you here for dinner?" he smiled.

"Yes, for the show *Tits and Feathers*."

"Sorry there's no show called *Tits and Feathers* playing here. Only *Hallelujah Hollywood*."

221

"No, no, we were distinctly told by Liberace that *Tits and Feathers* was playing here."

"Are you sure it was this hotel?" the maitre d' looked at us strangely.

"Positive. Liberace told the cab driver to come here." We turned around and left. Beckoning another cab, we instructed the driver to take us to the Riviera. We went to every hotel in Las Vegas—Caesar's, Flamingo, and the Frontier, but there was no show called *Tits and Feathers* playing at any of them.

When we got back to the Hilton, I went into Liberace's dressing room and tried to explain how we couldn't find the hotel that had our reservation for *Tits and Feathers*. Liberace and Ray looked at each other and burst out laughing. "That's just an expression," Ray fell into the couch in Lee's dressing room, gasping with laughter. "You were supposed to see *Hallelujah Hollywood*." When I realized how naïve I was, I grabbed Bernard by the hand and ran out of the room to catch a cab back to the MGM.

I was starting to sense a shift in our group, a positive one. Together with Lee, Ray, Seymour, Bo, Vince and Ralph, we were becoming a family. Lee and his group were incredibly caring and affectionate, and always watched out for the Famous PEOPLE Players performers. The performers, in turn, were getting more comfortable with the master showman. Even the musicians pitched in when they could—like the time Philip kept sending his tea back because the milk curdled. "He sent it back three times," Ralph slapped his forehead, "only to find out that he'd ordered tea with lemon."

Liberace adored the performers, and it showed. "You're a pretty popular guy, Liberace," Kevin told Liberace one day, as he was putting on his make-up.

"I'd like to think so. Thank you, Kevin," he said as he pulled on his bathrobe.

"I'm telling you, Liberace, you're pretty popular," Kevin said emphatically, as if to convince Liberace. "You know that couple?"

"What couple?"

"You know, every night you tell the audience there's a couple who just got married, and she's 68 and he's 72 and it's the second time around for both of them?"

"Oh yeah—that couple," he winked over to Vince, who was admiring his face in the mirror as he adjusted his chauffeur's hat.

"Every night they come to both shows—eight o'clock and midnight. And every night they ask you to play their favourite song."

" 'It's Impossible,' " Lee responded.

"You're a pretty popular guy."

That night, as Liberace sat down to play the song, Kevin was standing in the wings, watching him like a hawk. When Liberace announced the couple, Kevin screamed, "I knew it! I knew they'd be here!"

When Liberace came offstage, Kevin patted him on the back and said, "You're one popular guy."

"Thank you, Kevin, and I'll let you in on a little secret. They follow me everywhere. When I perform in Florida, they're there. Canada, England, for every single show."

On another night, as the performers were getting ready to take their bows, Liberace was standing up in his convertible while getting ready to make his entrance. As he chatted with the performers who were holding up their letters, he looked at Brenda who was standing by with a serious face. "How do you like Las Vegas?" he smiled.

No response. She seemed frozen, still holding onto her letter L.

"Are you enjoying working for me?"

Silence. Her letter didn't even quiver.

"Are you happy?"

Nothing.

After the bows, Liberace walked over to me with his feathered cape dragging across the stage. "I don't think they like me." He looked worried.

"Who?" I was confused.

"The children—I tried talking to Brenda and she had such a serious look on her face."

I started to say something when Brenda stormed over to Liberace. "Liberace, how unprofessional to talk in the wings. You might miss your cue if you don't concentrate."

Liberace laughed for a good five minutes. Three nights later, he did miss his cue while talking in the wings. After the show Brenda said, "See, I told you so."

"I promise it won't happen again," Liberace said solemnly.

The trip was now coming to an end and we knew that we were going to miss being with Liberace. Ann-Margret was already booked to do the next show. On our last day, as I walked backstage, I heard singing coming from the back corner. There, sitting at one of Liberace's pianos, was a beautiful redhead, practicing her music.

It was Ann-Margret and my heart skipped a beat. She looked up at me and said, "Hi, am I in your way?"

"No, I'm Diane Dupuy, with the Liberace show."

"Let me guess, you're with the Famous PEOPLE Players."

I was astonished she had heard of us.

"My husband, Roger, and I are coming to the show tonight and we're dying to see your group perform."

"Can I call my performers to have them take a picture with you?"

"Yes, you can," she smiled.

I ran and I called everyone. They quickly flew back-stage and were greeted by a warm and gracious Ann-Margret. What a night to remember as we'd be performing for another of my favourite actresses. As a young girl in Hamilton, I had seen her in *Bye Bye Birdie* about 70 times. I even had my mother make me the same outfit—pink hipsters, with a frilly top—she wore when she danced with Conrad Birdie. There was only one difference—I didn't have Ann-Margret's body, certainly not now.

At our last show, Ray came over, teary-eyed, to hug everyone. He looked at the understudies and said, "We didn't need you after all." It gave me a sense of relief.

As the performers stood on stage, taking their last curtain call, with tears streaming down their faces, Lee asked them to take a second curtain call. After the show, Ann-Margret and her husband, Roger, joined the entire Liberace company in presenting Famous PEOPLE Players with a farewell cake and a big surprise.

"We want you back in February," said Seymour.

Boarding that flight home, I witnessed for the first time the confidence that each of the performers had gained. Philip asked the steward if he could move to another seat to get him more leg room, and Greg was telling the pilot how to fly a plane. And Brenda, who was upset to be leaving, didn't tear the seats out of the plane.

Hallelujah Hollywood!

CHAPTER SEVEN

Feet First

We arrived home, leaving behind a world like no other place we had ever seen. For most of the performers, this was the first time in their lives that they had been away from home, and the first time they were challenged to write their own names and make change for a dollar. But they stood on stage and performed with one of the greatest entertainers in the world—and on one of the most incredible stages. Against all odds, we'd taken on the challenge and risen to the occasion, surprising even ourselves. Our work, however, didn't end there. It would be just one stage in our long journey of stages and audiences. We knew, just as the piano tuner would say, we needed to practice to make things perfect. We had to get better at our craft and become stronger people. After all, PEOPLE is our middle name.

Soon I wasn't the only one hollering the words *"We have to rehearse."* The performers themselves would often be heard in the hallways of the church basement echoing the very same phrase to motivate themselves. We were always practicing to make things perfect because everyone had a terrible tendency to forget their parts if they didn't rehearse them every day. There were constant reminders to everyone—don't black out, enter from this wing, lift the Liberace puppet up.

Months passed quickly, and I was sporting quite the tummy. I received a call one morning from Brenda's mom telling me that all the parents wanted to see me as soon as possible at her house the following night. I was caught off guard, so I just agreed without asking questions. I worried all day about it—*maybe they were upset at me for the way I speak to the performers, or maybe because I work them too hard,* I thought.

I didn't like yelling at them, but I needed to be heard over the music. I needed to be heard over their yelling. And it wasn't until I yelled that they actually stopped and listened. But that was not the way I wanted to run a company. We were adults and we had to behave accordingly, and that included me.

"Surprise!" everyone screamed as I walked into Brenda's mother's house the next day.

"Surprise for what?" I asked, as I looked around and saw everyone staring at me.

"Your baby shower!" said Brenda.

I looked stunned.

"*Baby*. Remember? You're having a baby!" laughed Brenda's mother.

229

"You'll never have to buy diapers—we bought them all," said Ann.

The last few months had been such a whirlwind that I hadn't really had time to think about my baby. Thank God for my mother, who had everything organized: the crib, the supplies and even the stuffed toys.

A few weeks later, on November 23, 1975, Bernard and I had some friends over for dinner. Bernard prepared bouillabaisse—the worst dish he had ever made—and I started to feel funny. Just looking at the fish made me feel queasy. I called Dr. Turner.

"Diane, it's time."

"No, it's not," I replied.

"You're having a baby!"

"No, I'm not. It's going to be born in December. Remember? They deliver the baby in a Christmas stocking."

"Diane, who is with you right now?"

"Bernard and a couple of friends. We've just had this awful bouillabaisse and—"

"Please ask Bernard to come to the phone," Dr. Turner insisted.

The next thing I knew, I was being forced into our car and taken on an Indy-500 trip to the hospital. "I'm not having a baby!" I screamed, as Bernard kept his foot on the accelerator and swerved around corners. Because of construction on many downtown streets, we had to take a detour and we ended up somewhere near the incomplete CN Tower. As we looked around at the dark construction site, wondering how we were going to get to the hospital, I yelled out, "I'm not having a baby!"

We finally got to the hospital but I was still in denial, even after lying down on a gurney, my stomach as big as a house. While I was being wheeled into the delivery room, you could still hear me screaming, "I'm not having a baby!" Reality finally hit. As I started pushing, the doctor noticed that the baby was coming out feet first and instructed me to push even harder. The entire staff was now singing "Aruba Liberace" and on every "Oomph" I gave a push.

"Aruba Liberace, they mambo for me," sang the nurses.

"Oomph!" And out came Jeannine Lynn Marie—a gorgeous baby who rolled her head toward me and stuck out her tongue when she first met me face to face. I had no idea what an amazing miracle it was to give life.

And yet, I couldn't take my mind off work. From my hospital bed, I started selling two-dollar tickets for our show at the St. Lawrence Centre, where we'd be performing our Liberace show. Mike picked up all the tickets from the box office and we divided them up on my bedside table to sell to all our friends.

During my hospital stay, I got a call from Lorraine Thomson at the CBC. "I'm the story researcher for *Front Page Challenge*," she told me. "I read a great review of Famous PEOPLE Players in *Variety*, and we'd like to feature you on the show."

Wow. *Front Page Challenge* was one of the most popular Canadian shows on television at the time. It was a quiz show with a panel of mostly journalists, who guessed the identity of a mystery guest (me) that was connected to recent front-page news.

"I'd love to."

"I'll call you back next week to discuss details," she said. "Is this the number I can reach you at?"

"No, I'm at the hospital right now. I just had a baby."

The same day I brought Jeannine home, I was leaving her behind to appear on the live CBC-TV show. I had to sit on a rubber donut because I had broken my tailbone on the last "Oomph" while delivering Jeannine. Liberace called in while I was on the show to surprise me and I started crying, mainly because of the pain in my tailbone.

While Las Vegas gave us the confidence to forge ahead, the appearance on CBC helped propel our company to new heights. Soon, Famous PEOPLE Players was on every TV show across Canada—CBC's *Good Company* with Hana Gartner, the noonday show on the CTV network, and more. Everyone who had a radio show requested an interview with me about the company's accomplishments.

We were becoming more and more confident. And it showed in every aspect of our show—Philip and his ribbons were mesmerizing to watch and everyone's transitions from one scene to the next were perfect. The experience in Vegas had really sharpened the group's skills, and I was a proud mother to boot.

"*Don't get too confident,*" I often heard Seymour's words ringing in my ears, but I didn't plan for a potential fall-out just the same. I should have listened more closely. The St. Lawrence Centre show was a disaster and we paid a heavy price for it. Philip, who was anxious about his solo entrance, stood in the wings and blocked the other performers and their props. When "Boogie Woogie" started, the performers were pushing and shouting for Philip to get out of the way.

"Your spider, Philip, comes first—not your ribbons!" yelled Brenda.

Philip, realizing his mistake, ran to get his spider, and knocked down a black flat. It prompted a series of other mishaps. The other flats collapsed on top of it and the rest of the set, including the ants and bugs, all hit the deck. Philip retrieved his spider to make his grand entrance while the flats around him toppled with a resounding C-R-A-S-H! Victor Polly, the general manager, got up on stage to fix the flats while 300 people watched from the audience. We were so embarrassed that we waited until everyone in the audience had left the building before we went out to the lobby.

Before we left Las Vegas, Lee told us he wanted us back to perform the same show, although we added a new number—Streisand's "Evergreen." So, in February, we were on our way back to Vegas for six weeks. This time there were no understudies, but one new addition—Jeannine Dupuy. Once again we were leaving behind Renato in tears because his mother wouldn't let him go.

"Where are you going?" the customs officer asked Greg.

"Las Vegas," Greg said.

"What is the purpose of your trip?"

"Perform with Liberace."

"Liberace?" The officer looked at Greg's mom. June Kozak began to speak for Greg, but the officer interrupted her, "He can speak for himself, thank you."

"What's in the box you're carrying?"

"Spider," Greg grinned.

"Okay, lady." He looked at Mrs. Kozak. "Have your son open his box." June helped Greg open up the box and out came a spider puppet. One by one, the company filed through, each performer holding a box full of puppet worms, ladybugs, spiders, dice, ribbons, letters, butterflies, and finally Liberace himself.

"Stop! Don't go anywhere. Where's your work permit?"

"Work permit? We're performing with Liberace. We were there in September."

"I don't care about what you do. I need your permits before you can cross. You're not boarding the plane without them."

"But we're opening tonight in Vegas. You have to let us through."

"I will when I see the permits."

It was the first time I heard we needed permits and we had just one hour before the plane took off. I woke up Seymour in Las Vegas.

"Help!" I screamed into the phone.

"What, what?" he sounded disoriented. "Your permits? I have them—I sent them to you."

"Well, I didn't receive them," I said.

"I didn't know," he sounded out of it.

"Look, I've got an idea. Give me the information on the permits, the office where they were issued. I'm calling the White House!"

"The White House!" Seymour suddenly snapped awake.

"You heard me—the White House."

I got off the phone with Seymour and made another call.

"Hello, may I speak to the president of the United States?"

"Just a moment, please."

The phone rang through to another line.

"Hello, may I speak to the president of the United States?"

"Just a moment, please."

I was put on hold and transferred several more times, until I finally got through to a secretary who listened to my story as I cried my tale of woe into the phone. Then another person came on the line and I explained, yet again, how the Famous PEOPLE Players were stranded at the Toronto international airport, and that a major break-through in mental retardation would be jeopardized if we didn't cross the border. Then she asked for the number of the pay phone. "Someone will call you back."

"Please," I begged, "our plane leaves in an hour and it's the last flight."

"I promise," she said.

After a long and worrisome 20 minutes, a woman called and identified herself as a special assistant to President Jimmy Carter. "What is the phone number and the custom officer's name?" I dropped the receiver and ran across the hall to the immigration office. The lineup was now so long that it snaked several metres in front of the officers' desks. I cut in front of everyone, jumping ropes and waving while I yelled, "I've got the president of the United States on the phone! What's your phone number?"

The officer, in a state of shock, wrote the number down on a piece of paper. I raced back to the phone booth, hopping over the rope barriers like an Olympic hurdler. Out of breath, I told the woman the number.

"I'm going to call back and have you cleared through the President's Office," Jimmy Carter's assistant said.

"I LOVE YOU!"

"Let me go," she said, "so I can call him—I've got to go to a meeting."

I gathered the group and we ran with our spiders, worms, ladybugs, ants, Liberace, Elvis, and Streisand heads to the lineup.

We arrived in front of the customs officer, who had just hung up the phone. He looked even more dumbfounded than the last time I'd talked to him. He stamped our boarding passes and watched as Brian and Kevin got tangled in the rope with their ants.

"Move, Brian!" yelled Kevin. Brian yelled back at him.

"Stop fighting—you'll miss your plane!" I yelled over to them. They picked themselves up and presented their boarding passes.

With the last stamp, the customs officer looked at Brian and Kevin, shaking his head in disbelief. "I've never seen anyone put through Immigration by request of the president of the United States. You must have one powerful friend."

Our second trip to Vegas had fewer hurdles to overcome. For one, we didn't have to deal with the understudies. Signing in at the front desk wasn't such a big ordeal either, since everyone had learned how to write their own names in a lot less time. Although I had more work with a baby accompanying me, Sandra was a great help. She looked after Jeannine, changing her diapers and dressing her every morning and night. Sandra also bought daily surprises for Jeannine, who was making quite an impression. One day, when my mom, who thankfully also made the trip, went to change Jeannine, she saw Sandra's latest present—baby underpants that read, "I hit the 750 Jackpot." No kidding, Jeannine sure could fill her diapers!

Besides Sandra there were other doting aunts and uncles. Mike would often push a baby carriage through the casino, and the gamblers would throw chips at it. "What a killing!" Mike would say. "Take Jeannine through the casino and we get $100 worth of chips." Brenda, who thought Mike had a great scheme for a fundraiser, would push Jeannine slowly in her stroller with Tony by her side so people could easily throw their chips in it.

"Stop spoiling her!" I'd tell them.

"We love her," they told me.

The players weren't the only ones spoiling Jeannine. Liberace would take Jeannine in between shows and feed her. One night, the inevitable thing happened—Jeannine spit up on his stunning red brocade costume. "It must have been the dancing waters in my show that did it," he said calmly.

Besides the dry-cleaning requirements on some costumes, this run was going smoothly. During rehearsals one day, the stagehands told my performers that Tony Orlando—the big star who had his own TV show following the success of his hit song "Tie a Yellow Ribbon Round the Old Oak Tree"—would be performing at the Riviera, and he was coming to see our show! The welcome news spurred an idea in my mind to create a Tony Orlando puppet. In between shows, I gathered the group and started to rehearse the Tony Orlando number for a future performance. "We'll have lots of yellow ribbons on stage and three giant oak trees. The one in the centre will split open and there will be a Tony Orlando puppet dressed in a prison uniform." We had so much fun improvising our parts.

Just before Tony opened his show, he came to see ours. Lee walked out onto the stage and welcomed Tony Orlando. "Tony, the Famous PEOPLE Players tell me they want to do a Tony Orlando puppet. I think you would make a great puppet." The audience, including Tony, burst out laughing as Liberace introduced the Famous PEOPLE Players. Some time later, Tony would see our puppet creation and fall in love with it.

I couldn't be happier with how things were going during this run. But I think the overconfidence may have clouded my judgment and caused me to make one of the biggest mistakes I've made in the history of Famous PEOPLE Players. I had always shared Lee's opinion that the show should stand on its own—there was no need to announce the performers' background or use the word "retarded." But at one point while we were there, I wanted the audience to know that the show they were applauding and standing on their feet for was even more remarkable than they imagined.

I spoke to the group—leaving Ron and Ann purposely out of the meeting—and told them how I felt. I thought if they approached Lee, he would respect their wishes. After a couple of them asked if he could address the audience that night, Lee, against his better judgment, agreed, to our detriment.

When he stood before the audience and made the announcement, I could tell by the strain in his voice that he wished he had never done it in the first place. The performers cried under their hoods after seeing Ann and Ron in tears. But the audience didn't clap. They were uncomfortable with what Lee had said: that the group was made up of people who were *mentally retarded*. Nobody spoke to me after the show. When I went to my room, I got a letter from Bo Ayars, Lee's conductor, saying that Famous PEOPLE Players is a professional company that didn't deserve to be put through such a humiliating ordeal. Bo was obviously upset with my poor judgment. About an hour later, Liberace called to tell me that the manager at the Hilton was very distressed about the announcement.

I wasn't fired. There was no recrimination and the performers started talking to me by the end of the next day. But it was a painful lesson. I had founded the company for them so they could be looked upon as professionals and stand on their own merit. And I achieved my goal, only to tear it apart. It was so hard to believe I had done such a stupid thing.

The most wonderful thing about this embarrassing mess was that the performers were professionals. Our work had proven that. What was even more amazing was that the players continued to trust me and forgave me. Their gift of unconditional love kept me going.

A week later, nearing the end of our trip, my spirit was lifted. I was fortunate to be introduced to Natalie Wood and Robert Wagner, who had been spending a few days with Liberace. Natalie was terrific, babysitting Jeannine, along with her own girls. Ann-Margret was also back in town with her husband, and both of them continued to support the Famous PEOPLE Players.

My spirits soared even higher when Seymour came into our dressing room to make a special announcement: "Our Father Who Art in Las Vegas is here with a big present," he said. "We're going to Canada in spring '77— Montreal, Ottawa, Hamilton, and Toronto, then on to Lake Tahoe, ending up in Las Vegas. And you're all coming!"

I couldn't wait to get home to Bernard. And I couldn't wait to prepare for our next tour, with the addition of the Tony Orlando number.

In the months that followed, our success was sweet, but expensive. We earned good money when we were with Liberace, but at home we had no work for months at a time, relying only on the money from our work in Vegas to carry us over. There were no more grants—that finished the day Liberace discovered us. And our free rent ended when Reverend Creighton asked us to leave his church because our rehearsals were continually noisy—Tony Orlando's music, the yelling and door slamming and Brenda's outbursts. "Our parishioners can't pray," he said. "But, don't worry. When God closes a door, He always opens a window."

That window of opportunity came by way of a wonderful man named Wally Neil, who worked in Goodwill's development and marketing office. In exchange for free rent at the Goodwill building and a donation of black lights—a gift we needed to keep our show going—we had to perform free of charge for the Goodwill delegates a year later at the Sheraton Hotel. The rent-free room resembled like a bowling alley, long and narrow. Mom and Renato tried to make the long, narrow room work for us. They took a corner for props, but there was no stage. In fact, with a total area of 15 feet by 10 feet, there was not even room for flats, so we painted the walls black and created our stage. Though it was smaller than what we were used to at the church, we could still play our music and learn our cues.

Just as we settled in, Ron was telling me, "I can't stay. I have to finish school."

"You *have* to stay. I know we've had our differences, but we need you, Ron. You're like a big brother to all of us."

A few days later, our luck was starting to turn and our 'family' started to grow. Over a plate of fish and chips, Ron had a change of heart and whispered in my ear, "Okay, I'll stay!"

Even better, Lisa agreed to join the next tour. "The hell with my boyfriend—I want to be with all of you!"

Then I got a call from the Haney Centre: "We have a kid here called Benny D'Onofrio and he keeps asking to join your company," said the woman at the other end of the phone.

"I'll take him!" I answered, before she could finish.

The next day, a short, chubby kid with a round, friendly face and a beautiful smile showed up for work. He made us fall in love with him on the spot.

It felt good to have a new beginning, but I still had a lump in my throat when the last of our props left the church. It had been our home and it had many memories. As I looked back at its emptiness, I saw our ghosts running around; the times we rehearsed; the day I got Seymour on the phone; the room where Mom and Renato made our musical notes. So many miracles had come from that church basement. It was a place where we had cried, laughed and loved each other. The same place where we packed our props for Las Vegas. The day I saw myself running from Brian when he got angry and the accident when I lost my first child. I remembered the day when we got the news that Liberace was coming. And the time when we rehearsed in the dark and then turned on the lights to find Ken Bell—a famous Canadian photographer—had come to take professional shots of our props

"It's a miracle!" he said.

"Our show?"

"No, the church—I was an altar boy here," said Ken, who never charged us for the photographs he took. Later, he became one of the company's closest and dearest friends.

Now we had a new space, a place where we would make new memories and we could call home. It was at this new home that we began our most challenging project to date—*Carnival of the Animals*. It originated when we got a phone call in the early hours of the morning while we were in Las Vegas. It was Richard Owen, stage manager for Boris Brott and the Hamilton Philharmonic Orchestra.

"Did I wake you?"

"No. Well. Yes," I tried to sound alert.

"Have you ever thought of doing something other than famous people with the Famous PEOPLE Players?"

"Not so far. Why?"

"We'd like you and the Famous PEOPLE Players to perform Saint-Saëns' "Carnival of the Animals" with the Hamilton Philharmonic Orchestra.

I wasn't familiar with the piece, but I was intrigued because I was raised on opera, Glenn Miller, big band music and jazz. So when I returned home from Vegas, I bought the recording of "Carnival of the Animals." Immediately, I had my own ideas for performing with this children's classical music. I met with Boris Brott, one of Canada's finest conductors, and described my vision.

"'March of the Lion'—imagine a huge lion with a wild mane of hair that little baby chicks are brushing and combing. They'll even manicure his nails and place a crown on his head as one chick is fanning him on his throne. For the 'Hens and Cocks' number—picture a mother hen running on stage to collect her chicks while she pecks the lion off…"

Boris was laughing, "Funny, very funny."

"…with the rooster claiming the crown that the lion wore."

"How would you portray the 'Dying Swan'?" he inquired.

"It would be sad, lonely and graceful as she folds her wings to cover her face," I continued. "And 'Aquarium' will be really awesome—the highlight of the piece, as the whole stage will transform itself into a tropical aquarium of fish. Angelfish will be kissing and a mermaid will retrieve a pearl from an oyster. It will end up looking like Halloween when the fish exit and fossils appear—with a giant dinosaur skeleton for the human skeleton to play its bones like an xylophone in the music."

As I listened to "Carnival of the Animals" over and over again, I knew this was going to be the most ambitious undertaking of our history. Fourteen scenes—all to premiere at Hamilton Place in January 1977.

With Liberace, we had worked with recorded music—except for Bo's overture during our letters performance. *Carnival* would be an exciting opportunity to work with live music. But it had an expensive price tag and we had to find creative ways to come up with the money.

Our expenses kept mounting, including the salaries we would have to pay out over the next six months to build new props for the *Carnival* production. I was at my wit's end trying to make ends meet. Our new family at Goodwill offered to issue tax receipts to anyone who wanted to make a donation to our company. Goodwill was there anytime we needed help.

While I was gazing despairingly at the accounts one day, I heard shouting from the prop area. "Get the f— out!" Brenda screamed at Mike. "I hate you. You're fooling around with Lisa!"

"No I'm not!" He was defensive.

"Yes you are!"

The lights in the ceiling started to shake as I ran from my cubbyhole office behind the prop area. Brenda was foaming at the mouth with rage. She went to pick up the Liberace head to smash it on the floor when Ron grabbed it from her and ran.

"I hate you, Ron. I hate all of you!" She ran to the washroom and with all of her strength, tore the sink right out of the wall. I grabbed her and slapped her across the face.

Silence.

Then she started to whimper like a dog that had been hit by a car. She flung herself in my arms. I was scared. I wasn't thinking when I slapped Brenda, but I didn't know how else to stop her tantrums. That night when I returned home, her mother called me while I was feeding Jeannine mashed carrots and peas.

"I'm going to sue you for slapping my daughter." She slammed the phone down.

I stood stunned, while holding the phone and shaking with fear. Two minutes later, the phone rang. It was Brenda's mother again.

"I can't take it," she cried. "My life is hell. She's violent, breaking things—my dining room table, the chairs, vases, everything...I'm afraid she's going to kill someone. I'm sorry, Diane, I don't blame you for what you did. What else were you to do?"

Bernard leapt up from the couch to hug me. Sobbing over the terrible threat I had received, he tried to offer some reason. "She's just frustrated and doesn't know what to do with a kid like that." I continued crying as Bernard admitted, "They both need professional help. This is now out of our hands."

My mother, who was in the kitchen, stepped in to offer more reassurance. "Bernard is right."

I felt a sense of responsibility for Brenda's well-being so I took her to see a female psychiatrist. The doctor, who specialized in people like Brenda with violent behaviour, was wonderful. She prescribed medication that would stop Brenda from having temper tantrums. In the weeks that followed, Brenda was quiet and calm. Her mother slept better. But there was a price to pay for her muted behaviour: the pills made Brenda listless and lethargic, unable to lift her puppets with the same energy she had before. After a month, she went off the drugs and she seemed to get better.

Rehearsal resumed and everyone came to them with high hopes for the future and lots of excitement. In the meantime, I was developing the most important technique in my role as a director—incorporating the performers' personalities into each of the characters on stage. For example, Philip was notorious for bumping into things and pushing his way around, so I gave him the part of the mother hen. Lisa, a natural dancer, became the legs of the dying swan. Mike, a sensitive guy, was the kissing angelfish. Kevin was the lion's throne, and Brian, Greg and Kevin together made up the dinosaur. Brenda was one of the chicks, a turtle and the mermaid chasing after the oyster. We laughed a lot in rehearsal, learning to act like the animals and getting familiar with the classical music by Saint-Saëns. And we didn't have the stress of worrying about transitions because Maestro Brott recited Ogden Nash's poetic verses to give us time to set up for the next set.

Everyday, for more than eight hours a day, we went over and over and over every number. In the meantime, Mom built the props, adding months of additional work for the players to properly use them and develop their characters.

When summer came, I found I was pregnant again—or should I say the company found out that *they* were pregnant. "We're having a baby!" yelled Brenda. Everyone was enthusiastic, except for Benny. He was very shy and seldom spoke. He sat on the floor, still afraid to get up and perform after being with the company for two months.

"Come on, Benny, you can do the little baby fish," I would direct him daily.

He tried, but the process of training in black light made him confused and anxious.

"Don't stand here."

"Duck."

"Squeeze."

"Sit."

I was determined that Benny would work out. I knew it in my heart. It would just require time, and besides, once I make up my mind, there is no changing it. I was not going to fail as a director because I couldn't make Benny a performer.

I also wanted Renato to have more responsibility in Famous PEOPLE Players and feel more integrated into the company especially since he had missed being with us while we performed in Vegas. So, I had arranged for him to pick me up every morning and help me get to work with Jeannine. It wasn't easy for Renato, however. Everyone stared at us on the subway—with me pregnant while Jeannine held hands with Renato and I.

"I just can't take it, Mrs. Dupuy. Everyone's staring," he would say.

But I insisted. "Help me, Renato. I need you to watch Jeannine when I get my hair done. Come with me to the beauty salon."

It was getting harder to carry Jeannine, now a bouncing year-and-a-half toddler. To lighten my load, I decided to buy a double stroller, and dragged Renato shopping with me. At the last minute, I also bought a high chair and decided we would lug it with us on the subway during rush hour, where we stood shoulder-to-shoulder with other passengers. I pushed Jeannine in the carriage, while Renato carried the high chair.

As I pushed the carriage onto the escalator, I accidentally stopped it. A man halfway up the escalator shouted down to me, "Get that goddamned carriage off the escalator, you dumb bitch!"

Renato, who had little interaction with the outside world, found it difficult to control his emotions. He was near the top, and plunked down the high chair and said, "You'd better apologize to the lady right now or I'm waiting for you up here."

Silence. The man saw how big Renato was compared to him, so he turned to me and mumbled an apology. When we got out of the subway, I told Renato that he was never to do that again. But he shook his head and said, "I'm sorry, Mrs. Dupuy. I respect you like my mother and I don't let no one speak to my mother like that."

Eventually Renato learned to control himself, especially when he was wearing his Famous PEOPLE Players uniform.

He got used to the stares and even volunteered to go on errands.

If it wasn't people who were my next challenge, it was money. We needed lots of it to build props for our upcoming show. Sculpting the menagerie of wild animals for *Carnival* from foam was a costly venture.

"The cost alone will kill us!" I often complained to my mother when I received an invoice in the mail. Then one day I reminded her: "We don't get grants anymore, remember?"

"Look, stop barking at me like it's my fault—you're the one who wants to do *Carnival*," she said. "Stop treating me disrespectfully—I'm not cleaning up your elephant poop."

"Sorry," I said, "but can't we do this cheaper?"

"Cheaper? I'm not getting paid, remember?"

Suddenly, out of nowhere, a young man appeared beside us. "Hello, am I interrupting anything?"

"No." Mom extended her hand to greet him. "You must be Fred Kay."

"Yes, reporting for duty."

Mom then looked at me with an I-told-you-so look of satisfaction.

"This is Fred, Diane. He is now on the payroll. He'll be helping us build the props and set for *Carnival*."

With the pressure of finances mounting, I turned to my faith and often prayed to St. Anthony for help. And I prayed about poor little Benny, who couldn't seem to learn anything, not even the lion's throne. I was getting exasperated.

"He just can't do it," Ron kept saying every day over lunch. "We're keeping him for what? To sit in the corner like Little Jack Horner?"

I was exhausted at the end of the day, but I kept reminding myself, *when God closes a door, He opens a window*. In this case it was two windows. I hope St. Anthony was getting overtime.

The first window was an anonymous donation for $20,000 dollars! *Now the bills can be paid*, I thought.

The second one came in the form of an unusual phone call that would expose Famous PEOPLE Players to a world we never had imagined.

"Hello, is this Diane Dupuy?"

"Speaking."

"My name is Marc Daniels. I'm in town making a movie called *Emily Emily*, about the father of a girl who is retarded. I understand that you work with a number of people who might be interested in being in a movie— that's if they can play the characters we're looking for."

I suggested that he show up at our Goodwill location and meet everyone. I didn't take his project too seriously. I thought he was filming something closer to a short documentary rather than a Hollywood movie.

Marc arrived a few days later while we were in the middle of rehearsing the scene with lion, chicks, fish and swan. He was an older gentleman wearing a black cap and a noticeable hearing aid and he sat quietly during our entire rehearsal. Then he asked if Brenda and Mike could appear in *Emily Emily*.

"It would be for two weeks," he said quietly, "and I can have them here for your afternoon rehearsals every day."

Each day, Brenda and Mike would come back to work and talk about John and James. "They're real neat guys," they often told the group.

"I get to dance with James," Brenda said.

"Yes, yes, that's all very well, but let's get back to work," I would say, ignoring their conversation.

When the made-for-TV movie premiered on CBS I could have died—it was John Forsythe and James Farentino they'd been talking about! Marc Daniels turned out to be the legendary TV director of *I Love Lucy*—my favourite show! And the director of such blockbusters as *Star Trek* and *Gunsmoke*, my crew reminded me. Marc took a great interest in Famous PEOPLE Players, calling at least once a week for several months to see how everyone was doing.

Boris Brott took control of his orchestra like no other conductor I know. He walked with a strong, confident presence that made every musician sit up and take notice. It made him perfect for the Ogden Nash verses he recited in rehearsal:

"The lion is the king of beasts and husband of the lioness; gazelles and things on which he feasts address him as Your Highoness.

"There are those who admire that roar of his in the African jungle and velts—but I think wherever a lion is— I'd rather be somewhere else."

When *Carnival* premiered that February evening, the audience of 2,000 screamed with delight. Even I was overwhelmed watching the production on such a gorgeous stage like Hamilton Place. I was used to watching the show in the long, narrow room, where the puppets were right in front of my face.

I could see from a distance that the lion puppet was pompous. But what surprised me was how ridiculous the dying swan turned out to be. Because I was on top of the puppets in our rehearsal hall, I had never noticed her ungainly comical figure with bony legs. She was the most hilarious scene in our *Carnival* and the audience especially loved the three silly-looking cygnets that accompanied her during the set. At the end of the show, Boris came flying into the dressing room. "It's the best *Carnival* I have ever seen!" he said proudly. "You should do more symphonic pieces."

I had decided that same night to take on "The Sorcerer's Apprentice" for my next production after we finished touring with Liberace in the coming spring. I enlisted Boris's help.

"Too ambitious," Boris replied.

"I like ambitious projects." I began to create the production in my head, connecting all the puppets with the accompanying music.

March came in like the roar of the lion from *Carnival*, and in the wee hours of March 6, 1977, I was in another car race to the hospital with Bernard 'Mario Andretti' Dupuy. This time I wasn't in denial, but was anxious to get to the hospital. Bernard turned the corners so fast that I thought I was going to fall out of the car. We arrived at the hospital and, once again, it was a breech birth. The little bum that first wiggled out belonged to Joanne Dupuy— who came into the world farting butterflies! For a few days, Joanne was in intensive care with a badly twisted leg. One doctor thought she would have trouble walking, but her leg straightened out and she later became a dancer. Once Joanne started to come around, she gave us the first of many delightful smiles, while her big sister couldn't wait to hold her just like a doll.

Motherhood for the second time couldn't slow me down for the busy spring season ahead. Liberace's tour was on our heels and there were many preparations still to be made. We had to organize rehearsals for the Tony Orlando puppet, as well as plan fundraising luncheons in Hamilton and Toronto to support the work of Famous PEOPLE Players. Naturally, the guest of honour would be Liberace himself.

"Benny? He can't go on the tour!" Ron, Ann and Lisa all pleaded with me. "He makes too many mistakes."

"Benny, what's wrong?" I asked him every time he missed his cue. He was quiet, his head always looking down. "We need you to help us," I pleaded.

Ron never gave up because I was adamant that he succeed with Benny. Tirelessly, he worked on Benny's butterflies in the Barbra Streisand number. "Just hold them in your hands and flutter them," he said. "It's only six seconds. See? Flutter, flutter, flutter."

"When my violin disappears behind the box, you bring out the butterflies," said Brenda.

"It's like the violins turn into the butterflies," Kevin giggled.

Benny tried, shook his head, tried again—and again, and again. When Ron got tired, Lisa stepped in, then Ann, and then me. We worked to get him ready. Everyone did.

Sandra fed Jeannine while we worked late into the night. And I even breastfed while directing the butterflies with my other hand.

"Look, let's take Benny with us anyway," I said. "Besides, he's on the list to go—and it will all work out somehow," I said in the final hours before our departure.

We arrived at Place des Arts in Montreal. Liberace and his company ran to greet us. They were delighted to meet baby Joanne, who was dressed in a little pink dancing outfit. "Let's see your toes," Ray Arnett started to inspect them. "Yes, you're a ballerina—a *prima* ballerina," he laughed.

We were excited to be working with Liberace and his crew again, but we were nervous performing at Place des Arts with Benny in the cast. The night of the show, I was sitting in the audience when the Barbra Streisand character entered, accompanied by violins that played magically in the air. They disappeared behind the boxes and up came the butterflies! The butterflies graced the stage at first, but then they fell out of Benny's hand and got run over by the Streisand harp. I sank my head into my hands. When Liberace (not the puppet) made his entrance on stage, twirling around in his red sequined cape, he bent down to pick up the butterflies and handed them to Vince, who took the cape off Liberace's shoulders.

I knew we were in for it. After the show, there was a gentle knock on my dressing room door. "Dora, I know how much you love these children, but this one's got to go," Seymour said, with a serious look on his face. "Nice boy, but not for Lee's show."

"Seymour, I know if you give him one more chance, he won't let you down."

"We'll let him finish the run in Montreal, but if things don't improve, I'm sorry." He walked away.

That was my cue to run to the players' dressing room and talk to Benny.

"The butterflies—you left them on the floor! How *could* you?"

"I'm sorry," Benny whispered. "I was so scared, they fell out of my hands. Honest to God."

"Why didn't you pick them up?" I demanded.

"I saw the harp coming, then I waited and then I saw Liberace standing in the wings, looking at me."

"He can't see you in the dark, Benny!" I said.

Benny started to cry, "I'll do better next show. Promise."

But things didn't get better. Show after show at the Place des Arts was one fiasco after another. The butterflies either came out upside down, or they missed their cue. Each night Seymour reminded me...Benny had to go.

Our next stop on tour was the National Arts Centre in Ottawa. The dressing rooms were incredibly big with mirrors everywhere. They were even better than the Hilton's in Vegas. "It's the ballet corps' dressing room—that's why it's so big," Ray Arnett told me as he stood in the doorway. Meanwhile, Benny hid behind the costume rack, afraid to face Ray.

That night, as the performers took their places on stage, I reminded Benny. "Those butterflies must appear when the violins disappear. CONCENTRATE. They go down, you go up. Not before. Not two minutes after. Not upside down. Not lying on the floor for Liberace to pick up. *Hear me?*" I stared at him.

He nodded. As he started to walk away with the butterflies, I yelled, "And don't freeze them in the air like you did last night. Butterflies *move.*"

"We're right here," Ron assured Benny. "We're all together on stage." Everyone reinforced Ron's words by patting Benny on the back.

I ran out to watch the Streisand number. Music played. Violins appeared, playing right to the beat of the music. Streisand entered in an arabesque position. *Perfect*, I thought. Then the violins moved slowly down to disappear behind the boxes. I waited…no butterflies. Nothing. Not even a flutter. I ran backstage and flung open the dressing room door, bypassing all the players, and went directly to Benny.

"YOU'RE FIRED!" I yelled without thinking about Benny's feelings.

Then I ran into my dressing room, where Jeannine and Joanne were sound asleep, and cried by their crib. A minute later, there was a knock at the door and when I opened it, the whole company was standing there. "Benny wants to see you privately," Ron said.

I walked toward the ballet corps' dressing room. As I slowly opened the door, I was taken aback by the dozens of little Bennys crying in the mirrors. I looked around the room, mirror after mirror, until I found the real Benny. As I walked toward him slowly, Benny put his hand up before I could say anything and said, "Don't say anything. I was there, behind the boxes, crouched down with my butterflies in my hands. I heard the music and I saw Barbra Streisand enter on the harp with her leg up. I watched Brenda come up with her violin—" he paused to swallow, "Oh boy," he rubbed his eyes with his knuckles, "And I said to myself, 'Benny, you're not going to do these butterflies right, so why bother trying?'" He continued to rub his eyes. "Diane," he said, "I want you to give me another chance."

"Another chance? Why on earth do you want me to give you another chance after I yelled and screamed at you and fired you?"

"I got you figured out," he said with confidence. "You yell at us because you love us. Besides, I have to be in the show because my parents bought tickets for the Liberace show in Toronto and I just have to be in it."

I was at a loss for words. He stood up and we hugged each other, both crying like babies. With Seymour's support, I gave him another chance, and so did Liberace.

The next night, as I sat in the audience, I watched the show in amazement. A miracle was born. The butterflies appeared and floated beautifully across the stage. From that day on, Benny not only soared as a performer, but also began to open up as a person.

We came back to Toronto, to the O'Keefe Centre, the same theatre where I had leapt over the roped barrier to cut in on the lady dancing with Liberace. How far we had come—from sitting in the audience watching Liberace to performing with him on stage.

To celebrate the occasion, I hosted a luncheon as a fundraiser for Famous PEOPLE Players, right back where we had started, at the Inn on the Park Hotel. This would be our way to thank everyone who had meant so much to us. Naturally, history would repeat itself and Liberace would be our guest of honour. Just like the Academy Awards, I planned on giving out awards for people who had done their best. This ceremony would also include a very special award, named after Liberace, for the most improved performer. The Liberace Award was the beginning of a long tradition at Famous PEOPLE Players that would encourage the performers to strive to always do their best and reach for this special Oscar.

The first recipient was Greg Kozak. He had transformed from an awkward performer into one of the most professional members in our troupe—from always bringing the piano bench in upside down to bringing it right side up, on time, every night.

"Me?! Thank you," he said, wiping his tears with his sleeve.

Seymour Heller received the next award for being Our Father Who Art in Las Vegas. Another award went to Ray Arnett, who taught me how to be a better director. "Just give them a dose of reality," I said.

"In Hollywood, we have something called the Academy Awards," he said, accepting his award. "This is my Oscar."

After the Toronto run, we headed for Lake Tahoe—the place where I'd first seen Liberace's wild extravaganza, with his limousines and dancing waters. We would be performing there for more than six weeks.

While we were there, we reunited with Tony Orlando, who was closing his show just before we opened. He invited the company for dinner at his last show. When he came out on stage and sang, "Tie a Yellow Ribbon Round the Old Oak Tree," he introduced us to the audience, saying, "Stand up, guys—I love you. Ladies and gentlemen, meet our mentally retarded citizens of the world."

Everyone froze. No one knew where to look. Now I know how everyone must have felt when I got Liberace to make that awful introduction at the Hilton. Tony meant well. He was the honourary chairman for the National Association for the Mentally Retarded. He was proud of everyone and, like me, wanted everyone to know how much the performers had accomplished. The players reacted in shock, but with dignity. There was no screaming or crying—just silence. They were far from being retarded. They were truly professional, especially how they handled themselves backstage with Tony, congratulating him on a terrific show.

"You coming—you coming to see our show with your puppet?" Greg smiled.

"I'll be there—promise. Scout's honour," he winked.

Every now and then, our professionalism was tested with one of our performers. While we were practicing our numbers during rehearsals for Liberace's show in Lake Tahoe, we started having problems in the dressing room with Brenda. She was no longer taking the medication that controlled her temper and it was acting up again.

SLAM! Her fist went right through the dressing room table for no apparent reason. Everyone was afraid to go on stage with her. *What will she do next?* everyone wondered, as she mumbled under her breath and stomped her feet up the stairway. We were terrified that Liberace would find out about her behaviour.

Even after she cursed the others, I reminded Brenda how much we loved her. But she looked at me with an evil stare that was more frightening than her violence.

"Do you have any of her medication?" Ann whispered to me minutes from going on stage.

"I don't know. I don't know if it's in my room or back in Toronto." The overture began with Bo's masterful direction, while I watched from the wings, making sure that Brenda was all right. When the players started to come off stage, I noticed that Lisa and Mike were arm in arm. We were always very supportive and often hugged each other, but Mike was Brenda's boyfriend and she was notoriously jealous. We had barely reached the dressing room when Brenda exploded. Chairs went flying every-where and she threw the costume rack onto the floor.

"I hate you, Lisa!"

But there was no sense saying anything to her because it only made her angrier. After Brenda calmed down, Ann got a cold cloth and patted her head. You could only hear soft whimpers coming from the corner of the dressing room where she sat. I realized Brenda was in no position to perform the second show at midnight with Famous PEOPLE Players, so I got into a jumpsuit and quickly rehearsed her parts in my head. We left Brenda in the dressing room and headed to the stage.

After a two-year absence from performing, the blackness of our stage freaked me out. My heart was pounding.

Throughout the show, I was worried that my hood had become twisted and I had terrible trouble seeing. I heard Ann's reassuring voice behind me, "Make sure your hood is on straight—just breathe."

But it didn't take long for me to get my footing. By the time "Tie a Yellow Round the Old Oak Tree" started to play, I was in my element. I waved the yellow ribbons, loving every moment of it so much that I forgot about the blackout! The black lights went off and we had to run off the stage as Liberace entered in his limousine. Totally lost in the dark, I froze. I was too scared to move. Mike and Ron tried to push me toward the wings, but the more they pushed, the more frightened I became. I felt like I was in a horror movie where things were reaching for me in the dark. Then I tripped and went sprawling. I felt my legs being pulled as I slid along the floor with headlights coming at me, like a train coming in my direction. Ron pulled off my hood when I was safely in the wings.

"Are you okay?" he asked anxiously.

It was like waking up from a horrible nightmare.

"Why didn't you hit the dirt?" Kevin demanded.

"Did they see me—the audience, that is?"

"Maybe they saw your feet being swallowed up into the left wing—like the Wicked Witch when the house in Oz fell on her!" Ron laughed.

"Oh my God," I said over coffee, "I'd better choreograph the show more simply."

"No," Ann responded. "That's why it's so good—'cause you're not in it."

"Besides," Lisa smiled, "you're out of shape."

CHAPTER EIGHT

The Long and Winding Road

TRIUMPH 8000km

TRIALS 100K

TRIBULATION 200K

ADVERSITY 300km

It wasn't the same group that walked into rehearsal at our Goodwill location back in Toronto. We were still rehearsing in the same place, but everyone seemed to lack the same energy I once felt in rehearsals. Philip's head had swelled and he believed he deserved his own dressing room with a star on the door. Relationships were forming that were causing the chemistry in our group to change. Ron and Ann were becoming very close. Even the unthinkable was happening—Lisa and Mike seemed to be on their way to becoming a couple.

I noticed in Vegas that Lisa and Mike were always sitting together, but I never really thought much about it. Now that we were back home in Toronto, however, I could see the effect it was having on the rest of the group. I foresaw trouble ahead. One day I overheard a conversation between some of the male performers. "We've got to find normal girlfriends."

Sandra was upset in her own quiet way. And Brenda, who used to date Mike, was becoming very insecure and jealous and she became very vocal about it. "I saw the two of you walking down the street hand in hand," she howled one day at Mike, and threw a mug across the room, almost hitting Jeannine, who was sitting on her potty, while Sandra was trying to toilet-train her.

I decided enough was enough. I had to speak to Lisa to try and remedy the situation.

"It's none of your business," she snapped.

"But it becomes my business when I see the other performers regressing and not working as a team."

"He's not like the others. He's more normal than they are."

"That's a terrible thing to say."

"It's true. He doesn't deserve a girlfriend like Brenda. She's a crazy, violent nut—I'm afraid of her."

"Lisa, you always show favouritism. When I correct Mike on his parts, you jump in and protect him. Whenever you speak for him, he is not being allowed to grow or think or speak freely for himself."

"Mind your own business."

Maybe it wasn't my business, but I was worried about the consequences of this relationship—and it scared me. First, I feared that if Lisa found another boyfriend, as she inevitably would, Mike would be left high and dry and probably find it difficult to cope with a breakup. I knew Brenda wasn't right for him either, but it wasn't my place to judge the performers' personal lives.

When Lisa decided to move out of her house and move in with Mike, I spoke to Mike's father, who seemed happy about the relationship. I wanted Mike's dad to caution his son, and in part, help break up the relationship. I believed that when Lisa broke up with Mike, it would shatter his self-esteem. I was also concerned about the message it was sending every time Mike got a special part in the show—about the friction, the jealousy among the performers. But Mike's father didn't agree.

Neither did Mike, who saw my efforts as interference. He was furious. "You're trying to break up me and Lisa. You can't do that!"

"We've been through too much for you to say that to me," I said. "I'm worried about you. You've come a long way, Mike."

"I'm going further. She is teaching me to read and write."

"Mike, Lisa is not an experienced teacher. You should go to Surrey Place, where they specialize in teaching people with learning disabilities to read."

I then approached Lisa. "If you *really* care about this young man, you'll encourage him to go to Surrey Place."

With Lisa's support, Mike went to Surrey Place, where he worked with a wonderful teacher who was committed to helping him read and write. If it hadn't been for Lisa, that would have never have happened. However, the rift between Mike and the other performers was getting deeper and irreparable. When you work together on a three-person puppet, as Lisa did sometimes, you need to trust each other, but that wasn't happening anymore.

The already delicate balance of relationships was about to tip further with the addition of two new members from the Haney Centre joining the company. John Vass was one of those new members. His legs were so long that he seemed to leap when he walked, so fast, in fact, that he frequently crashed into walls! The other member, Harold, was an energetic, fast-talking 'Mickey Rooney' type, who didn't know when to stop talking. Every day I heard Sandra say, "Shut up, you're giving me a headache."

We faced the challenge of bringing John and Harold up to speed on the black-light technique. It was like starting all over again, trying to get them to move without bumping into each other or the other performers or standing in front of florescent props, which caused a black out. We decided to start them on the musical notes.

Training John for most sets was especially difficult. He moved too quickly and didn't know when to slow down, although it worked well for the Elvis number. The roulette wheel on stage with Elvis never spun so quickly! Even when John sat down, he couldn't stop himself from rocking back and forth, and he had an annoying habit that made the other performers uncomfortable. While talking to me, he'd look at his crotch, and then up at my face—up and down, up and down—crotch, face, crotch, face.

"John, stop. Don't do that!" I'd say over and over again.

"I know, I know, I know," he kept repeating.

Ironically, John lived with his mother across the street from my apartment, so I paid his mom a visit one day to learn more about John and see how I could help to understand him better. In a thick Hungarian accent, she pleaded, "Help my boy—he's a nice boy. Help him please!" He was a nice boy, but he needed help beyond just learning cues in our show.

"He's harmless," his teacher at the Haney Centre told me. "You just have to keep reminding him, that's all." I decided to keep working with John, but still I wondered why she emphasized "harmless."

In July 1977, Jack McAndrew, head of TV's *Variety* on CBC, called to invite Famous PEOPLE Players to perform as part of a TV special featuring André Gagnon, Quebec's beloved classical musician and composer. Jack requested we create a Gagnon puppet.

We started it immediately. It was a welcome distraction to keep some of us out of trouble and a way to avoid noticing others getting into trouble.

Mom, Fred and Renato started building a spectacular platform that would hold two pianos: one for the real André and one for his puppet. The idea was that they'd compete with each other to one of André's hits "Dueling in the Sun." Along the sides of the platform, I wanted oversized piano keys that would rotate as they played. Mom designed a big sun that was meant to split in two when the camera moved in closely. Kevin would take one side, Brian the other, and they would pull them apart to reveal the two Andrés in their duel at the pianos. The set, surrounded by balloons, looked fabulous.

Jack, who had first seen our performance at the Liberace luncheon, was very impressed with the company during the filming, especially since John and Harold had been with us for only a short time.

"You have all grown since the last time I saw you," he said. "You just get better and better."

"We rehearse all the time," Greg said.

"Never stop," Kevin laughed.

The company was looking better with every performance, but there were still rifts between our people. Mike,
for one, made sure he stood with Lisa, or Ann, or Ron and
never with the rest of the group when we huddled for a
talk or break.

During rehearsals for the variety show, Jack McAndrew
made an announcement that helped take our minds off our
own problems. He wanted to make *Carnival of the Animals*
into a TV special with the great Canadian actor Gordon
Pinsent reciting the Ogden Nash verses. Charles Dutoit
would conduct the Montreal Symphony. We left the CBC
studio that day on a high. We all had balloons in hand from
the shoot, and made a wish as we released them into the
air. We weren't aware of the crisis looming on the horizon.

Renato was always the first to start each workday. He was
proud of his little prop shop, where he made sure the
brushes, paint and any other tools to build the props were
ready for Mom and Fred when they arrived. One morning,
as he walked into the prop shop, he saw Brian with a huge
stack of silver coins on the prop table.

"What are you doing?" Renato said shocked.

"Nothing." Brian wouldn't look at him.

"Nothing, my ass—where did you get all this money?
Did you steal it?"

"No." Brian turned red.

"Then where did you get it?" Renato persisted.

"I got it from my mother's drawer." Brian kept piling
the coins on top of each other.

Renato left the room quietly. Brian was so preoccupied with counting his money that he didn't even notice Renato calling me at home.

Bernard suggested I quickly jet down to Goodwill and see what was really going on. "Sometimes it's not as bad as it sounds," he reassured me. "If he has the coins, as Renato claims, then call his parents. Whatever you do, don't handle this yourself." I quickly dressed Jeannine and Joanne and kissed him goodbye.

When I arrived, Brian was still counting his coins. I noticed his coins were old and probably very valuable. "Brian, you've got to take them home."

No answer.

"Brian, these belong to your mother."

He didn't respond, not even a blink of the eye. The only thing moving was his arm, counting and piling coins on top of each other over and over again. He reminded me of the man who lived on his own little planet, counting money, from the French story, *Le Petit Prince.*

"One, two, three, four, five, six…" When he got to 30, he'd tear it down and start all over again.

"One, two, three, four, five…"

I tiptoed out of the prop shop, recalling what Bernard had told me, to call Brian's mother. "Diane, oh my God, my coins. They were my dad's." She left the phone for a moment and ran to her bedroom. I heard her shriek when she discovered the drawer was open and the coins were missing. "Diane," she cried, "try to get them from him—they're very valuable. I'll be there as soon as possible."

I walked back into the prop room where Brian was still counting. "Brian—"

"—five, six, seven—"

"We need you to stop and put those coins away."

"—eight, nine, ten—"

"Brian, we love you and we want to help you."

"—eleven, twelve, thirteen—" his voice was getting louder.

I was too scared to cut in and grab the coins after what had happened when I was pregnant the first time. "Brian!" Renato's voice boomed. "Put those coins back in the bag now. They do not belong to you. They belong to your mother."

Brian turned to Renato and quickly gathered the coins and put them back into the bag.

Great, I thought, *he's coming around.*

Then he turned to us with his fist raised in the air, and put it right through the wall! I grabbed the children and ran into the Goodwill cafeteria to get help. When we came back, Renato was alone. Brian was gone—coins and all.

Later that morning, Brian's parents found him in the park. He had sold the valuable coins at a pawnshop for $15, to their horror. They were even more upset because they didn't know what to do with Brian's violent behaviour, which often occured without any reason.

"I can't keep him," I said, crying. "I wish I could, but today he scared me. There were knives on the prop table, he could have easily picked up one of them and stabbed us," I continued. "I'm sorry, I know Brenda has outbursts, but she doesn't steal. Stealing will not be tolerated at Famous PEOPLE Players."

It was a heartbreaking decision. Brian had been with us from the beginning, but when he went into a blind rage, I was frightened for everyone who worked at Famous PEOPLE Players. Brian's problems weren't new, but as he got older, the problems became more difficult to handle. I arranged for him to see the same doctor Brenda had been seeing.

That afternoon I called a meeting with the entire company. "Stealing will *not* be tolerated," I told them. "We work together; we are a family—a very special family that must have empathy for everyone. Yes, even for Brian. He needs professional help. Brenda, let Brian's incident today be a lesson to you because your violent outbursts are a danger to everyone," I looked right at her. "We have two children here (referring to my two girls)—and they could get hurt if you throw something and hit them by accident."

"I understand," she started to cry. "I'm sorry. I'm still going to the psychiatrist," she said.

I commended her for her efforts, but I still spoke in a stern voice because I wanted everyone to know I meant every word I said. A few months later, Brian's dad was transferred to Vancouver. Brian moved with his family and started his therapy there.

I was anxious to steer our company on a positive course after all we had been through. I decided we would begin rehearsals for a new production I called *The Gifts of André Gagnon*. Music has a wonderful way of igniting that flame in everyone, so I thought, why not a production based on it.

"The gifts of André Gagnon?" Everyone stared at me.

"Are we doing another special?" Greg asked.

"No, I just love André's music. I think we can make up a story about a man who receives gifts—gifts of music, love, humour and emotion."

When we were performing in Parry Sound, Ontario, an elderly lady named Marion Patterson came to our show and wrote to us after the performance. It was a heart-warming letter that read:

"I have a granddaughter who is handicapped. Your show lifted my spirits and gave our family hope for her future. I understand from watching shows about you on CBC that you are no longer subsidized by government grants. I want to help you in any way I can."

Enclosed was a cheque for $200, collected from the proceeds of a $2.50 chapbook called *Meditations from a Rocking Chair*. This kind gesture reminded me of something Mother Teresa once said: "It's not the amount that you give, but that you give with your whole heart, with love." That donation was a shot in the arm and the start of many more good things to come. Someone out there was sitting in the audience, watching our show, and had become a big fan of Famous PEOPLE Players. As Liberace would say, "You never know who's in the audience."

Marion became a great friend to our company. She continued to send us cheques, and in the following year send $600. "I am so happy to help in any way I can," she wrote.

The money helped subsidize our new production and Boris Brott agreed to premiere it, along with *Carnival of the Animals*, with the Hamilton Philharmonic Orchestra. Even TV director Marc Daniels arranged to get actor John Forsythe to narrate the piece in Hamilton.

As we got busier, many of the performers stepped up their responsibilities, especially Sandra, whom I was very proud of. She was, in her very quiet way, holding our show together. She was very organized, encouraged other performers to put away their props after rehearsal, and even helped keep me organized when it came to feeding Jeannine and Joanne. "She had beef at lunch. It's chicken tonight," she would say as she opened another jar of baby food. Jeannine and Joanne both adored her. When we arrived most mornings, Jeannine would run to Sandra and hug her. Then I'd notice Sandra slipping her a little red sucker. "For you, you little monkey!" Brenda, who was getting better at controlling her emotions, would come and prop the children up to watch rehearsal.

"Be good," Kevin winked. Then the show would begin with Jeannine clapping and Joanne fighting to get out of the carriage. She wanted to perform with the players.

Rehearsals, no matter how experienced we were becoming, took their toll on all of us. *Over and over. Repeat, repeat*—it never ended. Somehow, by the time Monday rolled around, everyone seemed to erase everything we had learned.

Working within our space wasn't helping either. The piano platform kept getting stuck every time Renato tried to move it and our props were bigger than our 10- by 15-foot rehearsal space, so we rented a high-school auditorium that was equipped to handle all our stuff. We worked hard, from early morning until as late as 11 p.m., trying to learn *The Gifts of André Gagnon* in time for its May 1978 performance.

We had big plans for this production, and thanks to John Forsythe, we had a great way to market the perform-ance too. John, whose voice TV viewers heard as the mysterious Charlie on *Charlie's Angels*, agreed to call a press conference with 'Charlie' while the press gathered around an intercom box, just the way the Angels did on the TV series that was a hit in North America at the time. 'Charlie' talked about how he would reveal himself for the first time for the Famous PEOPLE Players at Hamilton Place. Thanks to his publicity stunt, we were sold out—and what an event it was!

Everyone who was anyone attended. Jack McAndrew, our old friend from CBC's *Variety* was there; so were the stars of the show *Front Page Challenge*, as well as the lieutenant-governor of Ontario (who represents the Queen in the province). When the Honourable Pauline McGibbon entered the theatre and took her seat, a Scottish piper, wearing a kilt, played the bagpipes. After "God Save the Queen" the house went dark.

Boris Brott took his place at the podium to thunderous applause. The curtain rose to an empty stage—empty except for the stained-glass windows that Mom had designed. The gift of music, represented by a single musical note, appeared in the darkness. It was followed by a gift of love—a shining heart.

The fun really began when André performed on his platform, and the piano keys moved to the circus music. Clowns came to life, cavorting and rolling on the floor. Then came a fiddling contest between a rooster and a giant mouse, both dressed in overalls. This number was Gagnon's big hit, "Concertino for Carignon," and it later became one of the best-loved pieces of our repertoire.

Then John Forsythe surprised everyone as the man behind 'Charlie.' His narration for *Carnival* was hilarious and his hunky looks grabbed a lot of attention. It was nice to see John in person after seeing him in so many movies over the years. Later, at dinner, Marc and John discussed the possibility of making a movie based on our story.

Things were finally beginning to happen. And we were getting busier. Tours were being lined up and we were breaking even. With tours came traveling, which was difficult because there were more props than people and renting a big 47-seater coach bus became necessary even though it was costly. One day, just as we were about to board the bus to Guelph, Ontario, I received a phone call from Tony Orlando's manager.

"Tony has never forgotten your group and he would like you to open for him in Calgary," he said.

I was speechless for a second. All I could think of was, *wow we'd be performing for one of the greatest pop singers of our time!* As soon as I got my voice back, I accepted. We rehearsed "Tie a Yellow Ribbon Round the Old Oak Tree" so much that we almost warped the tape. When we arrived in Calgary at the Convention Centre, Tony's stage manager gave us a carefully choreographed routine. It showed who was entering or exiting and when. To make it easier for Famous PEOPLE Players, a separate stage was built at the south end, while Tony and his band performed on the north end of the ballroom. The audience was between the two stages. "All they have to do is turn to see your stage, then turn and look this way to see Tony," he smiled.

What I remember most about the show was the final number. Tony's closing act was the famous Beatles song "Hey Jude." Over a roaring audience, Tony made the mistake of inviting Famous PEOPLE Players on stage to join in the singing. I thought I was going to die of embarrassment when John jumped up like a hyena, cutting in front of Tony and screaming into a make-believe microphone. Tony tried to move to the front and politely move John to the back—only to find John bouncing in front of him. Eventually the number ended and everyone was bowing, except for John, who was still singing, "Hey Jude!"

We performed for Tony in Boston a month later. This time, we were not invited to sing with him, and for good reason.

Despite our success, there were stresses and strains behind the scenes. Ann, Ron and Lisa were getting fed up with the ongoing repetition of rehearsals, reminding the performers of their parts. Philip was spinning out of control and Mike didn't bother with anyone now that he had learned to read. He smirked and rolled his eyes whenever Kevin or Greg missed a cue or forgot their parts.

"He's forgotten his roots," I said to Ann one day over coffee. And he wasn't interested in building on them either. As quickly as Mike had come into our lives, he left us without a farewell party. He thought he could do better than Famous PEOPLE Players. I blamed Lisa, who had encouraged Mike to leave us. She kept telling him that he would be labeled as handicapped if he stayed with us. Soon after, Lisa left too: "The repetition just gets to me," she said, teary-eyed.

I missed them both a great deal. They had contributed to the company's success. Their departure left a void that affected everyone. Renato was depressed at losing his best friend at work. Sandra, Brenda, Philip, Kevin, Ann and Ron all felt the emptiness too.

About the same time, Goodwill's chairman, Gord Swayze, told us that our part of the building was being torn down and we had to move. "It's time," he said. "Look, you can't rehearse anymore. The props have taken over the place. You need something much larger and we will help you find another place," he smiled reassuringly.

He was right. Mom needed space to build the props for our *Carnival* TV special. She found a warehouse space in the west end of the city. In our new place, *Carnival of the Animals* became more alive than ever. It was Mom's special more than ours. Her designs—lions, elephants, swans, fish, birds, and turtles—were truly works of art. The colours were vivid and her painting created wonderful 3-D effects.

But everyone in the industry didn't always appreciate Mom's designs, at least not initially. Weeks before the special, Jack McAndrew flew me to Montreal to meet television producer Bernie Picard, who greeted me accompanied by a costume and prop designer. They showed me sketches of *Carnival* with the lion covered in a fleur-de-lis, and the rooster dressed in a 17th-century French costume. I lost my temper and told them both to leave my puppets alone. "If you start putting costumes on the puppets—like the ones you have in mind—you won't see their legs and they won't be able to move. Seeing them strut, run and crawl is the most endearing part of the act. You can't manipulate the puppets with all those costumes on."

"Let's work out these concerns, Diane," Bernie said.

"There is *no* working it out. I'm telling you, if you put too many clothes on them, you might as well do a fashion show." I burst into tears—and in anger told him to cancel the special. I cried all the way home, afraid that Jack McAndrew would not understand my point of view.

No sooner did I arrive than I got a call from Jack McAndrew, telling me that he had the sketches from Bernie Picard on his desk and they were awful. "You must have broken out laughing when you saw them," he said.

I was relieved and invited him to see Mom's creative work. "Don't worry," he said. "What I want to see on that special is what I saw in Hamilton. I'll straighten this out."

Mom was developing an exciting prop shop. One of her techniques was called 'flocking,' which is seldom used today in part because of the expense. She would spray enamel paint on her animal puppets, and while the paint was still wet, sift very fine lint (the same colour as the paint) through a sieve. The lint would stick to the paint, producing a velour effect that hid the seams on the puppet. The process, however, could be harmful to her lungs if the room wasn't well ventilated.

The mice, elephant, lion, peacocks, turtles and kangaroos Mom created for *Carnival* all looked stunning. She had only six weeks to complete everything and, on one occasion, she enlisted the help of the performers' parents to help sew the elephant's skirt. Night after night, Mom wouldn't fall asleep until everything was done to perfection.

The CBC studio where we were performing looked like a Hollywood studio. Gordon Pinsent, and even Bernie Picard, who initially had another vision for the props, were thrilled when Mom unveiled her work.

"Bravo," applauded Bernie. "You're a master."

Our TV special opened with actor Gordon Pinsent as master of ceremonies. Wearing a slinky ringmaster suit, he stood on a set designed as a circus while bellowing his introduction before the players appeared. (Gordon went beyond his duty as an actor on stage—whenever he sensed that Brenda was going to have a temper tantrum, he'd stop and do a soft-shoe dance with her to make her laugh.)

There were some new acts in our show too. Ann got into a foam penguin costume and was lifted 10 feet into the air by a crane to conduct the orchestra. She had to stay in a hot costume for two hours, doing retake after retake for the cameras, without ever complaining. When they brought her down and lifted off the penguin costume, sweat poured out like Niagara Falls.

The TV special was a big feather in our cap and, when it premiered, we became instant TV stars. In the meantime, Jack McAndrew continued to expose Famous PEOPLE Players with more TV coverage. It helped keep our profile high and, consequently, get us more touring work.

But show business is like a rollercoaster—it has its ups and downs. This time, the company would be facing many downs when it came to people. And it started when Ann came to talk to me one day shortly after the special. "I can't stay anymore," she told me. "I must go back to school and finish my education." I thought about begging her to stay, but I knew she had given me so much of herself over the years already. I didn't want to stop her from fulfilling her dream.

"I have to go, too," Ron said. But before I could say anything he assured me, "I will help train a new person and phase myself out gently. No sense upsetting the kids. We can't just think about ourselves, but about the company. It has to continue."

Finding the right people was going to be difficult—there were many people who could perform well, but I needed performers who also cared deeply and had empathy and compassion for their fellow players. I was just absorbing the implications of Ann and Ron's departures when I got another surprise.

"I'm quitting."

"What?" I looked up to find Philip standing beside me.

"Do I get a farewell party?" he asked.

"Philip, stay."

"I don't want to—I want a farewell party."

"What are you going to do?"

"I'm going to leave," he replied.

"Leave for where?"

"I'll make my announcement at my farewell party. I like Chinese, Diane."

Ron rolled his eyes in exasperation.

"What is he going to do?" Ron scratched his head.

I was at a loss but I had to think fast on filling the hole Philip would leave. So, I picked up the phone to call Lisa. "I know Lisa will come back to bail us out if we can't train people fast enough," I said to Ann and Ron while dialing.

I wondered if this was Philip's way of seeking attention, by being the guest of honour at a special event. Still, I went along with his announcement and ordered Chinese food for his farewell party. After dinner, Philip stood up and made his long-awaited announcement.

"I'm going to get a job cleaning the windows of the CN Tower."

"Philip, they don't clean the windows at the CN—," Ann hit Ron in the ribs before he could finish.

But Philip left to seek his dream and, in the end, opted for a sheltered workshop. "Tired of performing, Diane, just tired," he told me before he left.

There were other surprises. This time they were welcome ones. After his initial rocky start, Benny was growing quickly as a performer—he now even helped carry Mike and Philip's parts in the show. I was still down about losing several performers and people I had grown attached to. It was like seeing family members leave the nest. But, I started to realize that Famous PEOPLE Players was a stepping-stone to other things for many people. I had no choice but to accept it.

For all of the twists and turns during this period, I knew God had sent us a friend from heaven. A friend of ours, Father Tom McKillop (the founder of the Canadian

Youth Corps) recommended a man named Warren to replace Ron. When Warren came to the job interview, I could hardly see him behind his big scruffy beard.

"Don't worry," Ron said quietly, "I explained that we have a clean-cut image." With Ron's dedication and guidance, Warren went on to become the next big brother of Famous PEOPLE Players.

Ann's replacement ended up being a woman named Wendy, who was recommended by a teacher friend of mine. And, to make things even more complete, I hired the first administrator for Famous PEOPLE Players. Her name was Frances and she was a workaholic—a no-nonsense type who got things done. She was always running her fingers through her hair in exasperation.

"Hey Diane, get over here," she'd say with a jerk of her thumb. "Go upstairs and tell them to fix that pipe. It's leaking on my head." I obeyed. I let her boss me around because she worked so hard and diligently.

Before Ann and Ron left, they worked hard to train the new people for the Liberace Vegas show, which was a must for beginners if they were to learn the repertoire. We were introducing a new puppet character, Anne Murray. Her song "Everything Old is New Again" accompanied her when she appeared on stage, and it couldn't have been more appropriate, representing the very state of our company during this period.

Her character was difficult to improvise because it didn't move around the stage as naturally as the Liberace or Elvis puppets. Instead, Anne stood still while she sang. The challenge was to not make her look stiff. Everyone worked hard at this, including Warren and Wendy, who would be making their debut.

Soon we had an opportunity to show off our work with Anne. Gord Swayze held a gala in our honour where we would perform for his Goodwill delegates, with the Honourable Lieutenant-Governor Pauline McGibbon as the guest of honour. "You are invited to Queen's Park. I will host a reception for you in honour of your great work and accomplishments," she said, following our performance with the Goodwill delegates.

Greg ran home to tell his parents, "The Queen loves us! We're going to meet the Queen!"

On the day of our performance, we were all excited, maybe too excited. "The Queen, the Queen. There she is!" Greg was hollering as he pointed at the statue of Queen Victoria outside Queen's Park, confusing it for the Pauline.

When the lieutenant-governor walked in, the girls curtsied while the guys bowed, and Pauline laughed. Then Brenda pointed down the red carpet staircase. When I looked in that direction, I was astonished to see Anne Murray—not the puppet—coming toward us. One of the lieutenant-governor's aides said in a loud voice, "Announcing Anne Murray!" The applause was deafening. Then Anne Murray went to a microphone that had been discreetly placed in the corner of the room.

"You know, this year has really been good to me." (She had just won the Grammy for her song "You Needed Me.") "I was reminded of the way I felt when I was starting out, how I wished that someone had been there for me. Now I want to be here for you, so to celebrate 'You Needed Me'

I want to let you know that we need you. We need the Famous PEOPLE Players."

She called me over and presented me with a cheque for $10,000 for our company. The next day, everyone I owed money to in the city called for us to pay up!

Ever since Boris Brott had suggested that we do more symphonic pieces, I had had the idea of choreographing a stage production of "The Sorcerer's Apprentice." I didn't want to reinvent Disney's version. I wanted ours to be unique, where I would play the music over and over again, learning every cue inside out. I recited my ideas like a musician creating a symphonic masterpiece:

The story is going to be fast-paced with everything appearing, then disappearing quickly. Poof! It's there. Poof! It's gone.

The little apprentice gets the dirty job of cleaning up the mess left behind by the sorcerer. Envious of the sorcerer's magic, he waits until the sorcerer leaves and then picks up his magic wand—and goes on an adventurous ride that he wishes he never took.

First, he turns the sorcerer's ugly vulture into a bucket for his broom. Then he conjures up a kaleidoscope and ribbons that dance. He captures falling comets, makes stars appear, and flies on a half moon. He does all this while his broom is left to wash and clean the magic room.

Uh-oh! The moon suddenly appears, becoming a canoe and the little boy is paddling for his life as the water rises fast because the broom is overworking. The apprentice falls off the moon and swims among an octopus, shark and swordfish.

To stop the broom from creating a greater flood, he takes the sword off the swordfish's nose and cuts the broom in half. The water disappears, and everything goes back to normal.

Phew! He wipes his brow.

Uh-oh! The broom is coming back to life—not one, not two, not three, but six of them!

Help!

The brooms form a tournament, waving flags in the air as the lead broom gets on a white horse to joust with the apprentice on the other horse. It's a battleground and the brooms are winning!

Finally, the Sorcerer returns and puts everything back to normal. He gives his apprentice a well-deserved swat with his broom.

We started our first rehearsal of this production like a volcano in the fury of an eruption. There was no stopping the continuous flow of energy. Everyone seemed to fit their parts perfectly: Warren played the sorcerer and Wendy was the apprentice; Brenda was the vulture; Greg was the sorcerer's table, the vulture's perch and the bucket; and John was the horse. Benny, who had become a great performer, was one of the brooms.

Kevin, however, was not enjoying his part or the production. "It's out of my league," he said. "I quit."

"Quit!" everyone screamed.

"Not you," Sandra paced angrily.

"Yeah, I can't hit the dirt anymore. I want out."

"What are you going to do?" I asked him.

"I'm going on a long vacation."

"Where?"

"I'll think of a place," he said.

"Why Kev? What happened?" I asked in desperation.

"I'm tired."

"Does your mother know?"

"No," he shook his head. "I think I'll just go home and sleep."

"Take the day off, Kev. Think about it. We need you. You're an original."

"I know, but I want to—" he paused.

"You want to what?" I asked, waiting for an answer.

"Go fishing." He walked out the door and went fishing. He never returned as a performer. I think he missed Ron more than he could admit and didn't want to continue without him. But from time to time he would pop in and watch the gang at work.

"Boo! You guys stink," he'd say when he made his 'guest' appearance. Once he said, shaking his head: "The Maple Leafs [who had lost the night before] can play better than you guys." I was waiting for him to jump up, grab a broom and show us how it should be done, but he never did.

Kevin's mother was devastated to see him leave. As a single parent who was barely making ends meet, she worried about what would become of him. Eventually, he got a job working in a restaurant as a bus boy. Some time passed and he eventually forgot about Famous PEOPLE Players, Liberace and 'hitting the dirt.'

It was becoming a tradition that every time we started a new production, we had new people join us. Old members left through the back door while new members came in through the front. Training new performers wasn't just challenging because they had to know their part and cues, they also had to stay in rhythm with the other performers to ensure there was no danger on stage as players entered and exited in the dark. Every time a new production began, it seemed like we were taking a step backward. Or we faced other problems outside of work.

One very exhausting night, as I slept soundly, the phone rang. I looked blearily at the bedside clock. It was 3 a.m. Bernard picked it up.

"We have your son here," a police officer said.

"My son?"

"Yes, your son, John."

John, who seemed to be overcoming his fidgetiness and acting more responsibly, had been charged with intimidation and common assault. Bernard drove down to the police station to bail him out.

"How could you?" Bernard said.

"I know, I know, I know, I made a big mistake."

"Explain exactly what happened," Bernard said.

"I was on the subway, coming home from work, and I was being really good. I wasn't looking at my crotch or anything. I wasn't, Diane," he looked at me when Bernard brought him home. "Then this girl smiled at me, so I smiled back and then she *really* smiled at me. When she got off the subway, I got off to be with her. She wanted to be my friend."

"What made you think so?" Bernard kept looking for an answer.

"She smiled, Bernard. She kept smiling at me!"

"Then what happened, John?" Bernard was getting tired. It was now 5 a.m.

"I followed her home and when I got there, she slammed the door in my face. So I hit the door and started yelling."

"Yelling what?" Bernard was determined to get to the bottom of it.

"Bad words."

"What bad words?"

"Really bad."

"How bad? Tell me."

"I said, 'You f— bitch! I'm gonna screw your pants off!' So she called the police and they took me to the mental hospital and they did some tests to see if I was crazy. But I'm not crazy, so I went to the police station and they asked for my parents' phone number."

"So why did you give them ours?"

"'Cause if I gave them my mom's, she would've killed me."

He was probably right. I was afraid that his mother really *would* kill him because I had seen her chase him down the street and beat him with a broom.

Our company lawyer said that the woman intended to press charges and that it would be best if we let John go from the company. But I didn't want to do that. Who knew what would happen to him?

"Diane, I'm so sorry," John pleaded. "I would never hurt the lady. I learned my lesson, please don't let me go." It came back to me—now I knew why the Haney Centre said he was "harmless."

Over the short period of time John had been with the company, I felt that he had learned a great deal and that Famous PEOPLE Players could help him learn how to control his behaviour. The courts didn't send John to jail. Instead they agreed that our company was a good place for him. In fact, the busier we kept him, the better his temperament. His energy needed to be used up if he was to stay out of trouble. So he carried boxes, loaded and unloaded the truck, performed hard, and went for regular psychiatric treatment at Surrey Place. Over time, John became much more stable with all this intervention. Watching him was like seeing a miracle unfolding.

John's experience embodied what Famous PEOPLE Players stands for. I've always thought of our company as not just a place where people spend long hours preparing for performances, doing strenuous physical exercise and practicing precise artistry, but also a place that teaches people how to stretch their souls, as well as their minds and bodies. It's a place where they can depend on our help if they reach out to us. And a place where people need each other to grow.

While we dealt with trouble outside rehearsals, work continued on *The Sorcerer's Apprentice*, which was getting closer to its premiere. I rented the St. Lawrence Centre and decided we needed to dedicate the performance to someone very special in order to draw more attention. When I contacted Disney, they suggested James A. MacDonald, the voice of Mickey Mouse, and recommended the head of sound effects for Disney as the guest of honour since he had worked on the original *Fantasia*.

I flew to Disney to meet James, a white-haired, elderly gentleman with a handlebar mustache. He took me on a tour of the sound department, which was a mind-boggling experience. He showed me how he created the sound effects of birds, bears growling, car wheels coming off and going bump-a-dee-bump over a cliff, a mosquito buzzing in someone's ear, and a waterfall gracefully splashing in a river. We instantly became friends and I adored him.

After a great afternoon, he drove me back to Marc Daniels's house in his 1952 vintage automobile. When we pulled up at the house, I barged through the front door and said, "Look who I brought—Mickey Mouse!"

With Marc and James's help, *The Sorcerer's Apprentice* was going to have a great opening. James would do the sound effects, as he had for Fantasia. Marc wrote the narration, while Lorne Greene, whom Marc had directed for many years on Bonanza, would be the narrator.

"I can't believe you know Lorne Greene," I said.

"Heck, I grew up with him on *Bonanza*," Marc smiled.

Out-of-town practice runs were common for us before a big premiere. This time we were performing in London, Ontario. We needed a narrator there for *Carnival* and *Sorcerer's Apprentice*. We were thrilled when the prima ballerina and founder of the National Ballet of Canada, Celia Franca, accepted.

The stage was in an arena that could seat thousands, but only 300 people were in the audience and we were beside ourselves trying to get Kevin's new replacement, Albert, to stop talking in the wings. Albert was a gentle soul with lots of rhythm and a great musical ability. But he cried. He cried all the time. He cried when he was happy, he wailed when he was sad.

"How do we know if he is happy or not?" Benny laughed. "He's always crying. Boy, does he ever cry hard—look at the size of those tears." Benny was staring at him.

"Diane, they're dripping down his pants onto his shoes," Greg rolled his eyes up to his head.

"Please don't get him going," I told everyone. "If you're calm, he'll be calm. If you freak out, he'll freak out."

Celia Franca took the podium and started her narration. Following each Ogden Nash verse, she'd introduce one disastrous number after another. Number one, everyone missed their cues. Confusion set in. Turtles showed up for the lion number, birds for the turtles, kangaroos for birds. The trees in Tony Orlando's song fell apart. Three numbers later, Albert was still moving his turtle across the stage, causing chaos. "Get that turtle off stage!" Benny yelled to Albert.

Then, just as I thought it couldn't get much worse, Albert started to cry—so loud that everyone could hear his voice echo through the arena. Celia Franca was horrified. Warren and Wendy were appalled. By the time *The*

Sorcerer's Apprentice appeared, half the audience had left. I died a thousand deaths, hoping that at any moment Bernard would wake me up from this nightmare.

The next day, I took all of Famous PEOPLE Players to Varsity Stadium in Toronto, where I needed to vent. "You're nothing but a bunch of retards!" I screamed. "How dare you—each and every one of you! If Liberace could see you, he'd crawl into a hole with his candelabra and never come out again!"

Albert started crying. "Shut up!" I yelled at him. "If I *ever* see you cry like that again, I'm gonna take those tears, put them in a bucket, and then I'm gonna hold your head in the bucket!" I turned to John. "You, John! If you look at your crotch and then look at my face one more time, I'm gonna get the saw from the prop room and you'll never have anything to stare at again! Do you get my drift?"

(Those were such different times. Today, we would never speak like that; these days the emphasis is definitely on being professional, respectful and loving toward each other in all our dealings.)

"Yes, Diane, never again!"

"Now get back to work! That is, if there is anyone on the face of this earth left to hire us. Make a decision and make it right now. Do you want to stay in Famous PEOPLE Players or do you want to leave? If you want to leave, there's the bus stop. If you want to stay, the door to Famous PEOPLE Players is this way. Once you enter those doors, we will learn to become professionals all over again. We have fallen down the ladder and we have to climb it all over again to get to the top. We are all going to change for the better, and that includes me. So tell me, what's it gonna be?"

One by one, they looked up at me with tears in their eyes and said, "I'm staying."

"I won't screw up," said John.

"I won't cry," said Albert.

"I won't yell," said Brenda.

"I'll keep clean," said Sandra.

We headed back to our rehearsal hall. I opened the door and we went inside, walked up the flight of stairs and started all over again.

The players learned an important lesson that day. It would have been easier to turn their backs and walk away from a situation they found to be too challenging. Taking the easy way out is like being at the top of a mountain and sliding down where the ride doesn't last. Instead they chose to hang in, to climb that mountain where muscles get sore, legs start shaking, and hearts start pounding. They just need a constant reminder that reaching the top can be easier if they take the time to stop in between the milestones of their journey and say a little prayer of thanks. And when they finally make it to the top, then they can look around and see that the sky's the limit.

I'm the first one to admit that the climb to the top can be exhausting. In our company, it's an understatement. What players remember today, they easily forget tomorrow. The repetition is constant. The music and the motivation are the same. And every day, players must be reminded about the small things—Albert to stop crying and John to stop staring, which they did most of the time.

I called Ron, desperately in need of moral support.

"They can't do it," he said. "It's too much stress. A show that long is too difficult for them to remember. There are too many cues."

"But they *can* do it, Ron." I argued.

"Diane, they have trouble remembering simple things like, 'don't look at your crotch—no talking in the wings—where are your black gloves?' They keep saying, 'I forgot, I forgot, I forgot.'"

"Let's face it, I founded a zoo," I cried.

"Besides," he continued, "black light does not work for more than 15 minutes. Any show that is longer than 15 minutes will drive the audience cuckoo." He was adamant, and he wasn't much help.

But I wasn't about to give up, especially after making a contract for a future performance. I had to get the performers ready for the premiere with Lorne Greene and James MacDonald. The month went by fast and, thankfully, the premiere of *The Sorcerer's Apprentice* at the St. Lawrence Centre was a triumph. The *Globe and Mail*, Canada's only national newspaper at the time, said it best:

The Sorcerer's Apprentice *who thinks he can outdo his master was a perfect reproduction of his animated self. And animation is really what this black-light show is all about—animation that doesn't rely on celluloid tricks, or on complex systems of strings and pulleys. Getting his magic incantations mixed up, the Apprentice ends up being beaten by disembodied hands wielding brooms, paddling on the crescent of a moon, encountering barracudas and stars and capricious wash-buckets. The choreography, timing, costumes and puppets were all excellent.*

Just as I was beginning to relax a little, Wendy told me she'd decided to leave Famous PEOPLE Players to become a teacher. "I love it here—don't get me wrong. I learned a lot here and I gained the confidence to go out and fulfill my dream. You taught me that," she hugged me. It was hard to say goodbye to Wendy, but I felt comforted knowing we'd helped her get one step closer to her dream.

The ball kept rolling for us. We received an invitation to perform for the United States Presidents' Committee on Employment of the Handicapped in Washington, D.C. It was an honour and we all felt our spirits lift. I remembered how President Carter's office had helped us get out of that awful jam in the airport years earlier.

Ken Bell, our photographer, accompanied us to take pictures of the group at the Lincoln Memorial while we toured the city. The show was a success and glowing speeches followed: "From the standing ovation following your performance and the many people who spoke to you, I'm sure that you are well aware of the feelings of satisfaction and enjoyment we all share," said Bud Van Orden, head of the Committee for Employment of the Handicapped.

Back at home, Mom finally convinced Renato's mother to let him go on tour with us for five days to Calgary. Renato was beside himself with excitement. That's why I was shocked to receive a phone call at 6 a.m. on the day of our departure, telling me he wasn't coming.

"Why, what happened?" I asked.

"I just can't," he said, distressed.

"You have to—we are counting on you."

"I can't."

"You're a professional performer, you must come," I responded.

"I know, Mrs. Dupuy, but I can't."

"Why?" I demanded.

Silence. I could hear him breathing.

"Renato, are you still there?"

"Oh my God, I've had a stroke!" he screamed. "I can't go to Calgary."

Then Mom grabbed the phone from me.

"Feel your arm, legs, are they okay?" she asked.

"No, I can't move."

"Look Renato, don't worry about your stroke," she said. "We will be there in a taxi in 10 minutes—be ready, we will carry you on the plane if we have to."

"I can't go," he wailed.

"We're on our way," and she hung up.

When the cab pulled up at Renato's house, he stormed out the door, threw his suitcase in the trunk and got into the car. No one said a word.

"What next?" I wondered.

"Don't worry," my mother kept saying, "Lorne Greene will be there and the show is going to be great—just stay calm."

She was right. Lorne Greene was superb with the audience, ad-libbing to fill in the time so that Famous PEOPLE Players could be ready for the next number.

Transitions were still difficult for us, and we needed to fill in at least two to three minutes between each number. (Today, it only takes us three seconds to get from one scene to the next.)

One of Lorne's filler bits was to tell the audience about me. "Do you know what Diane Dupuy is like?" The audience listened attentively. "I'll tell you what she's like. Do you see this?" He pointed down at the stage. The spotlight followed his finger. The audience couldn't see anything.

"Don't you see it?"

The audience started to stand up, to see better.

Then Lorne bent down to pick up a piece of lint that only he could see.

"There, this is the kind of thing that Diane Dupuy worries about!"

After the show, I was always quick to tell the performers their mistakes. But Lorne was going to teach me an important lesson. He called me into his dressing room and in the baritone voice he's famous for, he said, "Don't scold a performer after a show. The audience had a great time. The group got a standing ovation and you—and I mean *only you*—know the mistakes. Give them their notes *before* they go on, that way they'll remember," he smiled.

"Dora Doom," Seymour said affectionately the next day on the telephone. "You haven't changed a bit." It was great to hear his voice. "We're bringing you back to do a benefit for Lee's scholarship fund for young artists."

Immediately following our brief Western Canada tour, we were on a plane back to Las Vegas—this time with

Renato and Lorne Greene. We felt like we were back home again to see old friends: Lee, Bo, Ray, Ralph and Seymour. Lee invited us to his house after our performance and made his famous stuffed pasta shells as we dipped our feet into his piano-shaped pool. He was the perfect host, indulging in Renato's fascination with his home.

"Slot machines? You have slot machines in your home?" Renato said with excitement.

"Oh yes, and everyone's a winner. They even get to keep the winnings," Lee explained, as his 12 puppy dogs followed him around from room to room.

Meanwhile, while I was dining at Lee's home, I didn't realize that James MacDonald was talking us up to Bob Jani, the president of Radio City Music Hall and creative consultant to Disneyland. Bob decided that after years of being closed to musicals, it was now time again to open Radio City to those performances, and he needed a unique act for this historic opening. Taking James's recommendation, he sent two of his choreographers and his musical director to check out our show.

Toronto's Ryerson Theatre donated its stage for our audition, where we performed *The Sorcerer's Apprentice*. The group sat in the empty auditorium, laughing and applauding as we unveiled our version of *The Sorcerer's Apprentice*. A few days later, we learned that we got the job. We would be performing for six weeks at the famous Radio City Music Hall during Easter in New York. What a gig!

"New York, New York—what a wonderful town," we all sang, celebrating over Chinese food.

Mom and I flew to New York at Bob's request to see Radio City's massive stage and make the necessary adjustments to our show. "Radio City is not your normal theatre," Bob Jani warned us before we made the flight. "You're in for a big surprise." He wasn't kidding. We were terrified at the thought of entertaining 6,000 people at a time.

"All of your props need to be bigger so that the audience members who are sitting way up there—" he pointed to the balcony, "—can see your show."

As I looked around that huge theatre, I thought to myself, *everything needs to be restaged*, and I swallowed hard. "We need to rent a *huge* space to rehearse in. There is no way this show is going to fit into our small warehouse space," I said to Mom as we fastened our seatbelts on the plane going home.

"I need to design a set—like a cave—that will embody the story," my mother muttered to herself. "But where to build such an enormous drop like that?" she wondered aloud.

"The brooms are going to have to be three times their size," I said. "How are the performers going to manipulate them?"

I was really worried. I suddenly realized that to pull off this performance we needed to increase our staff. Ida Colallilo came for an interview and Frances and I interrogated her. We went on about integration, working with the players—being their friend, helping with personal hygiene and table manners.

"So you think you can handle all this?" I asked her.

"Well, I *do* know that the fork goes on the left, the knife on the right, and which dessert fork to use," she joked.

We laughed. "Okay, then do you mind taking the broom? We need to audition you."

"You want me to sweep the floor?"

"No, for *The Sorcerer's Apprentice.*"

Ida wasn't prepared for her physical tasks in her tight skirt, yet she auditioned for us, bending down, crawling on the floor and taking my direction.

I liked Ida instantly—she had spunk. "Anyone that would audition in a tight skirt, with a broom, in front of strangers, has to get the job," I said to Frances.

Ida became invaluable. She helped in the office, volunteered to work in props with Mom, and even trained the performers to run errands.

"They called," Ida found me one lunch hour downing a grilled cheese sandwich at the Greasy Spoon.

"Who?"

"The Ice House in downtown Toronto. It's a huge warehouse—apparently the opera builds sets there. We can rehearse there for Radio City."

We arrived early one morning at the Ice House and unloaded the props from our truck. The size of a gymnasium, it was exactly the space we needed to get us ready for the Big Apple. With a stopwatch in hand, we timed each of our transitions. It was going to be demanding—running from the vulture to the broom to the stars to the swordfish. It would especially be hard on the performers who were on stage for most of the performance. Cathy Camp, one of the new girls in our company, was tall, strong and not afraid of hard work, but she did have her reservations on how we'd all pull it off. "I'm the apprentice—

I'm on stage for every scene!" she shrieked when she saw the stage.

"Me too," Ida said.

We got busy testing the performers' physical endurance. "Brenda—go! One, two, three, four, five, six, seven… twenty." She was out of breath by the time she got to the other side.

Warren, who would disappear and reappear in his sorcerer's costume as he ran backstage to grab the comet that flew from left to right, was exhausted. On top of the physical challenge, we had to work with larger props that weren't as easy to handle. For example, it was harder to get the cute animation with the large brooms, but slowly, they started to get their own personalities.

For one month, we ran, jumped, crawled and skipped to each part. Then I started to switch everyone around on different parts. "If someone gets sick, then we need to double up." Days before our departure, we were ready to go.

When we left for New York in March 1980, the anticipation was enough to give us our own wings to fly to New York. As soon as we got off the plane, we could feel the rhythm of the Big Apple and we were ready to take a big bite out of it. As we checked into the Mayflower hotel everyone was jumping with excitement.

"Calm down—let's get our focus. We're here to work and if rehearsals don't go well, we're out!" I did my impersonation of Ray Arnett, "OUT!" I said, waving my arms the way he did.

We were scheduled for technical rehearsals at 8 a.m. sharp, but just to be sure, we arrived at Radio City at 7:30.

We would be sharing the bill with the Rockettes, the Vienna Boys Choir and a singing group called the New Yorkers. Radio City's stage manager came to greet us.

"Welcome. Now be careful, this is a dangerous stage; stage elevators are going up and down all the time. I'd hate for your foot to get caught in the door, so follow me this way." He took us around the backstage area until we reached the elevator on the ground level. "You'll be on the fifth floor," he said as he pushed the button. Every act had its own dressing room on each floor. The Rockettes—stage right elevator, basement level. New Yorkers—stage right, second floor. Vienna Boys Choir—stage left, fifth floor—opposite end of the corridor from Famous PEOPLE Players.

He watched us get settled in our dressing rooms, hanging up our jumpsuits, and then asked us to follow him back down the elevator to the main stage.

"Turn to your right," he said, as he opened a door that took us to the front of house.

"Oh, my God!" Ida screamed. "It's Radio City—I can't believe it!"

"Me feel so small," Greg smiled.

Everyone sat and waited until we were ready to go. In the meantime, we watched the orchestra tune their instruments and the dancers tape their feet.

The choreographer was yelling, "Lift your legs—smile—sing into the microphone!"

The whole scene was starting to terrify us. "Oh my, what if we make a mistake?" Brenda started to shake.

Cathy immediately calmed her down,

"Don't worry. We'll be all right."

We sat and sat while hours went by.

10 a.m.

11 a.m.

12 p.m.

1 p.m. "You can go for lunch—just be back in an hour," we were told. But we were too afraid we'd miss our call, so Warren went and got sandwiches for everyone.

2 p.m.

3 p.m. The Vienna Boys started to take their positions.

4 p.m.

5 p.m.

6 p.m. Warren went and got dinner.

7 p.m.

8 p.m.

9 p.m.

10 p.m. "Famous PEOPLE Players—you're on!" the stage manager yelled. Most of us had fallen asleep.

"Wake up, Greg. Come on, Brenda. Let's show our stuff," Mom encouraged.

We took our places on stage. The stage hands brought in Mom's backdrop: the cave she had envisioned when she first visited Radio City with me. It was the first time we'd seen it, since it was always on the floor in pieces being painted. The stagehands started to applaud.

"We love it," the choreographer hugged my mother.

"You did it, Mom, you actually did it."

She was so proud.

The orchestra played the music for *The Sorcerer's Apprentice* and my heart started thumping fast…mistake after mistake. "The brooms—lift them up!" I shouted. "The bucket is upside down!"

At the end of our run I asked if we could rehearse it again—to get used to the stage. "Okay," said the stage manager, "you have five minutes to re-set."

"Five minutes? Oh my God—RUN!" I screamed.

My hands were waving in the air like a maniac. "You'd think she was the conductor," I heard Elman Anderson, the musical director, say to a musician.

The music started again and we ran, jumped and lifted the props. "Higher for the comets!" I shouted. "Broom— listen to the music! Energy!"

A hand rested on my shoulder, "They will be fine if you stop shouting," my mother assured me.

At the end of our second run-through, the stage manager gathered our group. *We're fired*, I thought. But I was prepared with my answers: *I'll say that we sat from 8 a.m. to 10 p.m.—we were tired—couldn't concentrate, need more rehearsal.*

"You sat there all day and never complained and you performed like a true group of professionals," said Elman Anderson. "Don't worry about the mistakes, Dora."

"Dora? How do you know my nickname?" I asked.

"Your reputation precedes you," he laughed.

The next day, I rallied my group. We were ready. Again, the intercom became our friend. "ATTENTION ALL COMPANY, this is your stage manager speaking. I want a good show—we have a full house—no slips. Famous

PEOPLE Players, please take your places on stage. We'll be ready to go in five minutes."

I ran out to the front of the house to watch. Something I hadn't noticed in rehearsal was the way the orchestra came up the elevator and then slid back 70 feet on stage to thunderous applause. Famous PEOPLE Players was opening at Radio City Music Hall and I couldn't believe it!

When the curtain went up to reveal the sorcerer at his table, I was dumfounded. I couldn't get over seeing my company at Radio City Music Hall. The cave, the bats moving—it looked like a painting coming to life. I watched as if I'd never seen the show before. The vulture was leaning on his perch, hovering near the magic table and observing what was going to appear—a butterfly! The little apprentice ran around chasing it until the sorcerer made it disappear.

Oops. I held my breath. *The bucket is upside down... Phew, Brenda is turning it right side up.* The music built. *Where's the star? Come on, Greg, appear, appear. Oops, too late. It's time to disappear now. Greg, get off the stage! Here comes the fish, good John. Wait, slow down, Cathy has to take the sword.*

I was pleased with the overall performance. But I couldn't wait to get to the fifth floor dressing room and tell the players about the slip-ups. "Stop, Dora," my mother's hand barred the way.

"On a scale of one to 10, it's an eight,"

"An EIGHT?" my mom said.

"Well, there were some mistakes," I pushed past her to give all the performers my notes. "We can't leave until the audience has left the theatre and the stage manager has given us his notes." (Notes were the stage manager's remarks on how to improve the show.) "Did he notice the mistakes?" Ida asked.

"I'm sure he did, Ida," I answered.

"ATTENTION, COMPANY, you can leave now. See you back for the evening show—not one minute late."

"He didn't say anything, so I guess it's okay," I said.

"I'm scared of him," Sandra said.

"We'd better be perfect tonight. No mistakes," I warned.

"John, stop looking at the Rockettes," Warren pulled him by the turtleneck.

"There's a magician," the stage manager was saying as he approached me on our way out, "who will be in the show starting next week. I thought he did a god-awful rehearsal. I didn't let him open—his tricks didn't work. I told him to fix the act and open in three days."

I must have slept through that rehearsal, I thought to myself.

"Too bad he'll miss the reviews," he added.

After the first show, we had two hours off before our next call time. The rhythm of New York was at its best—everyone walked with upbeat, long strides. The only long strides in our company came from John, who was always ahead of everyone—he walked faster, ate faster and talked faster than anyone else. We went to grab a bite to eat, then came right back and hung out in the dressing room.

The evening show went smoothly. Still, there were a few mistakes. "I saw your props peeking behind the curtain," I said to Greg and Sandra.

We were just relieved to have completed our first day at the Music Hall. Exhausted, we changed our clothes and waited for the stage manager's voice to come through the intercom to tell us when we could leave.

"ATTENTION COMPANY. ATTENTION COMPANY." We froze and listened. "I'm glad I got your attention. You saw what happened to the magician yesterday. The same thing is going to happen to you if you don't clean up your act. New Yorkers, I told you before, don't expose your microphone to the audience. Sing like you mean it. Rockettes, kick higher. There's a little weight showing. I'd hate to send you back to the fat farm," he laughed. "Okay, company, see you tomorrow."

He didn't mention us. A big sigh of relief. Thank God. Now, we could relax, at least until the next day.

We waited anxiously for the reviews the next morning. Here's what a few of them read:

The New York Times called us: "*a nice little novelty act that features black-light and giant puppets... the inspiration, of course, is Walt Disney's 'Fantasia.'*" *The New York Daily News* said we were: "*...an inventive set of puppeteers who do a delightful animation of 'The Sorcerer's Apprentice.'*"

We were on a high! Proudly, we walked past the stage manager's office to get to take the elevator to the fifth floor.

Each day we listened to the intercom for our notes, but each day there were none. One night, after the show, the intercom came on. "ATTENTION ALL COMPANY, ATTENTION ALL COMPANY. Rockettes, New Yorkers, please report to the stage immediately. There is a lot of fixing we have to do with your performance."

As we walked past the stage, we saw the stage manager and the choreographers giving the groups some tough notes. "Just like Diane," Sandra whispered.

Mondays were our day off, and we enjoyed our downtime. The guys usually went to Yankee Stadium and the girls went window-shopping at Sak's Fifth Avenue. We had no money, but we could dream about buying designer clothes and shoes.

Before we left, Seymour called to remind me to buy a hat and walk in the Easter parade, which has been a tradition among New Yorkers for years. Jeannine and Joanne were the first to lead the parade in our group wearing their hats, looking like fashion models in their new dresses. It was a parade of hats and each hat was original in design. "Look mommy, that man is wearing a hat that looks like the Statue of Liberty," Jeannine noticed.

One day, during our run in New York, I got a call from ABC television's *Good Morning America*. "We read the reviews—congratulations," said the producer. "We want to do a special feature on Famous PEOPLE Players." They had hoped to get into Radio City to film us, but because of union rules it was too expensive. Instead, they agreed to fly to Toronto and film us when our run was over.

Each day over the six weeks we watched the Rockettes, the singers, and the magician (who was now in the show) get their notes. I finally mustered up the courage to ask the stage manager how we were doing.

"Great," he said.

"Do you think our show is good?"

"Listen," he said, "you'd know about it soon enough if it wasn't. I have a tough job here; this is a big stage, lots to oversee. In fact," he took me around the place, "there are several stage managers in addition to myself." He started to introduce me to the others. "This is Harry. He is responsible for the orchestra. John, the Rockettes. Tim, the sets. Each manager has his own walkie-talkie and has to be accurate and ready, or the whole stage can get thrown off." I was impressed.

One day, sitting in the empty theatre before our performance, I received a tape of Nikolai Rimsky-Korsakov's "*Scheherazade*" from Marc Daniels. I sat, listened, and fell in love with the deep, rich melodic music. Images filled my mind:

In a palace, the princess Scheherazade lies sleeping. The great sultan enters, dragging her from her bed and throwing her to the floor: her execution is at hand! But as the gleaming sword descends, Scheherazade cries: "Wait!" She grabs her storybook and entices the sultan to listen to her tale.

There is a magnificent palace where she tells her story and as she speaks, the palace soars upward and her story magically comes to life.

Camels appear, snake charmers crouch over their baskets, and Sinbad is holding a lamp that releases a genie and a dazzling array of jewels and gold treasure. When the treasure lies gleaming on the ground, Sinbad fights off dragon snakes that try to claim the treasure.

Sinbad's voyage begins as he travels across a turbulent sea—where lightning and thunder appear in the form of a

*purple wind god that blows against the ship until it sinks,
only to be saved by the white god of the sea.*

*Sinbad is carried away to the heavens by the carved
angel that is torn from the stern of his ship. The palace
reappears. Scheherazade has saved her life for tonight
and for 1001 nights to come.*

I envisioned all the scenes taking place on the empty
Radio City stage. When the set designer for the music hall
was setting the stage one day, I became Scheherazade and
enticed him to play the sultan in my story. He loved it. On
the last day, he gave me a gift of beautiful drawings of
"Scheherazade" that captured the visions of my wild
imagination.

For our last show at Radio City, the Vienna Boys Choir
came to our dressing room and sang, "Auld Lang Syne."
We all hugged, cried and promised that we'd see each other
again. Then the stage manager came into the dressing
room to thank us. "I just wanted to tell you that you must
come back and perform on Broadway. I think you guys are
good enough."

"You've got to be kidding," I said.

"No, I really mean it—you should do it."

I was proud of my performers on and off the stage.
Renato had walked through Times Square, Fifth Avenue,
Yankee Stadium and even around the Statue of Liberty
while people stared at him. Brenda only lost her temper
once. As for the rest of the group, they were growing into
solid professionals.

As we walked along Avenue of the Americas, I glanced back at the bright lights on a marquee that was advertising the latest Broadway shows. "Look up there, guys. See those lights?" I told my troupe as I pointed in the horizon. "Picture our top hat, cane and shoes lit up for all of New York to see! We're gonna be up there some day—you wait and see. And that's a *promise*."

CHAPTER NINE

Ouch, My Heart Hurts

T here is never an end to dreaming. When one dream ends, another unfolds.

Scheherazade became our new project. It lifted everyone's spirits and filled the emptiness of leaving New York behind.

Scheherazade was a more ambitious undertaking than any performance we had done to date. I decided that Cathy would be Sinbad. Her magnificent performance as the apprentice at Radio City had proved that she was ready for the challenging Sinbad role. Like the Apprentice, Sinbad would be transformed from a one-person character to a more complicated character that had to be operated by three people.

"The audience will be astonished when Sinbad, in the blink of an eye, goes from fighting off the giant dragon snakes to flying through the air," I said to Cathy.

But to get to that point, it was going to take a lot of practice and coordination. Brenda was assigned to Sinbad's feet. She was one of my better performers who caught on quickly. Cathy was on the hands, while Warren operated the puppet's head. There were many, many days like this one:

"One, two, three—go!" I instructed the players who played Sinbad. Carefully, the players had to perform a sequence of actions in perfect rhythm in the dark in order for Sinbad to woo the audience. *SNAP* went the legs.

"Ouch," Cathy fell.

"Brenda, careful, she can't see in the dark," I reminded her.

"I'm trying," she grumbled.

"That's okay, let's do it again."

"One, two, three—" and they both fell, tripping over each other.

"Remember, Cathy moves first—then you follow her."

"Don't you step on me," screamed Brenda as she hit Cathy in the foot. "Ouch!" Cathy jumped up.

"Brenda, stop right now. Do some deep breathing exercises in the corner over there—nice and quiet. Think to yourself about what you did and then come back and apologize to Cathy. We don't hit you when you make a mistake," I said.

"I'm getting tired of being on feet." She got up in a huff and stormed off to her corner.

"The dragons—let's see. Warren, you be the lead dragon. John and Benny, you're on the other dragon, and Sandra and Ida are on the last dragon."

"Hey, wouldn't it be neat," Ida suggested, "if when Sinbad pulls out his sword, he cuts the head off the dragon and it goes flying away?"

"Yeah!" everyone whistled and applauded, including me.

Albert started to cry…because he was happy.

"Stop crying, Albert," I glared at him.

"Okay, okay, Diane, promise."

This was just the beginning of months of gruelling rehearsals. It was about the same time James MacDonald took some time from his busy schedule at Disney to come and see us. "You've been home only a couple of months and already you're at work on a new production," he said, playing with his handlebar mustache.

"I can't sit still one moment—you know that," I danced around my living room. Playing the music of *Scheherazade*, I acted out every part for him while Jeannine and Joanne ran back and forth using pretend props. Jeannine held out a toy box for the treasure chest that Sinbad would find. "The tea kettle, Mommy," Joanne said as she ran into the room to use it as a magic lamp.

Scheherazade was our new inspiration, even for my daughters. After Mass one Sunday, Bernard and I took the girls for a walk in the park. Jeannine stopped us and pointed. "Look, they're making magic under the tree."

I looked over and saw two men in turbans, smoking a big pipe. "Jeannine, you've just given me an idea for Grandma! Let's run home and tell her to make a puppet that looks like that man for *Scheherazade*."

James, or Jimmy as we now called him, later spent a week with us to help us with sound effects before our next opening at the St. Lawrence Centre. To help Brenda control her outbursts of temper, we put her in charge of making Jimmy feel important. "Be nice, smiling, happy around him and he won't go home," Ida reinforced.

Our gig at the St. Lawrence Centre had become an annual event. In addition to performing our new production, it became a tradition to also celebrate our achievements, present the Liberace awards to the Most Improved Performer, and thank our special patrons. Our award for Outstanding Support went to Imperial Oil and Xerox Canada for their sponsorship. We even presented an award to our dear friend Marion Patterson. She had continued to sell poetry books over the years and give us all of the proceeds. It didn't matter that her donations were smaller than the corporate ones because she gave them with her whole heart and really believed in us.

We also wanted to take the opportunity to tell the audience how hard we'd been working over the last year. So Ida and I selected the best pictures taken of our company in New York and, at the end of the show, we dropped a projection screen and shared memories of our six weeks at Radio City Music Hall. There were slides of John wearing his T-shirt, I took a bite out of N.Y.; another of Cathy, Ida, Brenda and Sandra dancing in the dressing room with the Rockettes; and one of Benny waving from Yankee Stadium. During our presentation, we even performed our latest character puppet, Liza Minelli, who sang her version of "New York, New York."

At the end of the slide show, Ken Bell superimposed a Famous PEOPLE Players T-shirt onto the Statue of Liberty. It was a fantastic crowd pleaser. To top it off, Cathy performed our last number—a takeoff on a takeoff—"The Stripper"! Cathy was dancing to David Rose's bump-and-grind music. She peeled off layers of an ornate fluorescent costume, until she completely disappeared. The stage was left black. Even her legs, arms and head vanished.

"The Stripper" was even a favourite among media, especially the *Globe and Mail* film critic, Rick Groen, who called it:

Charmingly risqué...a bump and grind routine, featuring a heart-pounding, realistic stripper. The dancer tosses off her flowing attire with the élan of a nubile burlesque queen until, after a final flick of her subtle wrist, she bares all and reveals nothing—having shrunk discreetly into the black light.

At the reception following the performance, Jimmy MacDonald cut through the crowd, holding the hand of a young girl. "Excuse me," he pushed his way through. "Diane, meet my friend, Debbie Lim."

"Your friend?" I looked at him.

"Yes, we've just met. She came up to me and asked me to introduce her to you. You be nice to her because she wants to join the Famous PEOPLE Players."

"How wonderful," I smiled.

"I wanted to meet you really badly," she said to me. "So I went to Mickey Mouse to get introduced."

We laughed. "Go to Mickey Mouse if you want to meet Diane Dupuy," Jimmy said.

I noticed that she had trouble smiling. She was blind in one eye, with weak vision in the other, but she was well mannered and articulate. "I'd love you to meet Ed Kozak, one of our parents. He can arrange an appointment for you and your mom, and tell you all about Famous PEOPLE Players."

"I know all about Famous PEOPLE Players. I've watched you many times on TV..." Debbie kept talking as I waved my hand to get Ed's attention. He came over to meet Debbie.

"How about tomorrow—can you start tomorrow?" I asked.

Her face looked as if she had just won the lottery. "Wait till my mom hears I got the job without her help!"

Ed Kozak laughed, "I'd love to meet her, if you can arrange it, and get her involved in our Parent Volunteer program."

Debbie grabbed Ed's hand and pulled him through the crowd to meet her mother.

Shortly after Debbie Lim started, we were on our way to Nova Scotia and Prince Edward Island by coach. It was the first time we were performing in the East Coast and I was thrilled. I felt almost like I was revisiting a favourite children's book, filled with colourful characters and beautiful scenery. Our narrator for the East Coast tour—thanks to Marc Daniels—was the Canadian actor Lloyd Bochner. He lived in L.A. and earned his living playing every villain on television, including many guest appearances on *Columbo*. I'd met other movie stars, but I was nervous meeting this great talent because he was always so convincing as a murderer or some kind of bad guy.

We were fortunate to have other star talent join our tour, including our man Jimmy with his wonderful sound effects. He was now a regular member of Famous PEOPLE Players when we toured. He joined us when we went to meet Lloyd Bochner in the dining room of the Prince

Edward Island Hotel. There, Lloyd was sitting with his wife, Ruth, my mom, Jeannine and Joanne. They were all laughing.

"He can *laugh*?" I murmured.

"He's not a psychopath. It's just a character he plays in the movies," Jimmy led the way.

Sure enough, Jimmy was right—Lloyd and I hit it off instantly. To top it off, he was quite a comedian who was never short on jokes. He had just the right character for his role in our performance. Lloyd knew how to make great facial expressions for the Ogden Nash verses of *Carnival*, raising one eyebrow and giving the audience a conspiratorial look.

By the time we got to Glace Bay in Cape Breton, we were beginning to learn something about Maritime-style life. Unlike the whirlwind pace of Toronto and New York, things in small-town Canada have a very different pace. During one show, for example, the show was supposed to start at 8 p.m. but five minutes before the show the stagehands hadn't even set up yet.

"Don't worry. No one is coming for eight," a stagehand informed me.

"The ticket says 8 p.m.," I insisted.

"No one will show up until eight-thirty or nine."

The audience didn't arrive until 9 p.m. When the crowd finally settled to enjoy our show, it went wild when the Anne Murray puppet appeared. A Maritimer herself, Anne was born and raised in Nova Scotia.

After the Maritimes, we toured Western Canada. In the small city of Lethbridge, Alberta, we witnessed the same type of small-town easiness as in Glace Bay. The audience went from three people just 15 minutes before curtain time to a full house half an hour later. But it was in smaller centres where we often found the cheering and applause to be more appreciative and enthusiastic compared to the reaction after a big-city performance.

Back home in Toronto, the props for *Scheherazade* had taken over the warehouse. With our repertoire growing from our original famous people show to *Carnival*, *The Sorcerer's Apprentice*, and now *Scheherazade*, there was hardly enough room left for the players.

"We're getting evicted by the puppets!" Warren said.

It was time to look for a new home. I hated moving but we had no option. We had to uproot all our props and ourselves and relocate to bigger quarters.

Warren found our next space, not far from our last home. It was the third floor of 301 Lansdowne Avenue and it was filthy and rundown. Before we moved in, it had to be fumigated for cockroaches and rats. This time, instead of painting the walls, we just scrubbed them down from top to bottom. Our new home had some wonderful benefits: it was twice the size of our previous space and finally, after seven years, I had my own office.

Once we were set up, two new performers came to join our troupe. One of them was Debbie Rossen. "First thing's first," Renato said to her proudly, "I will teach you how to do errands all over Toronto. This is a very important component of Famous PEOPLE Players. Before rehearsing, you learn the transit system—to think clearly, make decisions, and find your way around the city."

After a month of training, it was time for Renato to let Debbie manage her tasks. She was going to run an errand to the bank. "I can do it myself," Debbie asserted.

"You've been to the bank every day since you started," I encouraged her.

"Yes, ma'am," she would say to me.

"You know your way?" I continued.

"Yes, ma'am."

She left at 10 a.m. By noon there was no sign of Debbie. 1 p.m.—no Debbie. 2 p.m.—no Debbie. I called the bank. Debbie hadn't shown up. "Call her mother," I said to Ida. I was sweating by this time. At 5 p.m., Mrs. Rossen appeared. "I'll wait right here," she said, sitting on the doorstep.

"The police were notified at two o'clock," I said to her.

"I'll wait," she replied.

By 7 p.m. the Toronto Transit System called me to say that Debbie was found riding around and around on the subway and they were bringing her back to work. When she arrived, I made a beeline toward her.

"What were you doing on the subway all day?" I demanded.

"I was sitting."

"Why?"

"I got lost."

"No kidding, Debbie," I said sarcastically.

"What do you do when you're lost?" she asked.

"Ask for directions—why didn't you?"

"I don't know," she started to cry. "I forgot, okay?"

I was surprised that her mother didn't interrupt me. "Stop crying. Only babies cry," I continued. "What would you have done when it was midnight—call and ask for your pajamas to be sent to you, because you were going to sleep on the subway tonight?"

"No." She wiped her tears away with her hand.

Mrs. Rossen then asked me if we'd give Debbie another chance. "Yes, we will," I told her. "She'll start by going to the bank tomorrow by herself and *asking* for directions if she gets lost."

While Debbie Rossen grew more independent when running errands, Debbie Lim, who joined us before our East Coast tour, became my inspiration. Quiet and determined, she persevered to learn her parts in *Scheherazade* despite her impaired vision. Each day she became stronger than the day before.

Scheherazade was set to premiere in June 1981. It was the International Year of the Disabled, so it was an especially important performance for us. It was just as important for the Canadian organizing committee, which booked its premiere at the National Arts Centre in Ottawa and at the St. Lawrence Centre in Toronto. Boris Brott would conduct the Toronto Symphony at the St. Lawrence and the National Orchestra when we performed in Ottawa. It was important for us to make an even greater impression because there was an opportunity to get some corporate sponsors, since several businesses were interested in supporting the disabled.

"We have to look great when we take our bows," I said one day, eyeing everyone in the lineup. I noticed that Sandra Ciccone had swelled two dress sizes. "Give up the french fries," I told her. I even pleaded with her mother to help by serving her healthier meals.

"We do try," Mrs. Ciccone explained, "but she just refuses to listen."

"Okay Sandra," I said, "you're coming to live with me for three months—we're going to turn you into one of Charlie's Angels!" Sandra needed to lose weight so she could get up and down from the boxes without injuring herself. I also knew that losing weight would make her feel better and give her a confidence boost she needed.

"*Me?*" she looked surprised.

"Yeah, you're going to become Sexy Ciccone."

I joined in the program too—dieting, jogging, sit-ups and laps in the community swimming pool—to motivate Sandra. Even Jeannine and Joanne pitched in when they could to help Sandra stay on track. There were the times when we went for walks after dinner: Joanne and Jeannine would run ahead of us and hide in the bushes for Sandra to find them.

"You little rascals!" Sandra would run to keep up with them. In return, the girls were delighted to know they were doing something for someone who had changed their diapers for years, and whom they had come to love.

By the end of the three months, Sandra had lost two dress sizes. It was now time for the big reward. We each bought a new outfit and treated ourselves to a haircut, colour and manicure. "Wow, I'm beautiful," Sandra said in awe, as she gazed at herself in the mirror after her makeover. Now that Sandra was feeling really good about herself, she had more energy to do better during rehearsals, and her energy spread like wildfire.

"Everything Old Is New Again," we sang on our way to work. Back in rehearsal, we took a break from 12-foot camels, 16-foot palm trees, snake charmers, treasures and gargoyles that were part of the *Scheherazade* show. We started working on a Frank Sinatra puppet and—my favourite number—an outer space extravaganza with *Superman, Star Trek* and *Star Wars* all rolled into one. These numbers were going to be in the lineup when we premiered the *Scheherazade* show. In the middle of all this work, I got a call from Father Tom McKillop.

"Say yes," he said immediately.

"Say yes to *what*?"

"Just say yes, it's an emergency. Just say yes."

"Tell me first."

"No, just say yes to 7 a.m. on Saturday."

"Okay, yes."

"Great! You're doing a performance at a prison and the truck is coming to pick up the props. Be ready."

"You've got to be kidding. I can't."

"Ah, come on, this is Father Tom speaking. I need you to reach out to these people with your magic. They need it; they're counting on you. Be ready—Father Tom is coming with the truck."

There were smaller shows we did in between the larger ones. Many of them were payback for the support we'd received over the years. I wasn't comfortable with this one, but I did it for Father Tom, who continued to help. I never thought I'd ever be behind bars. But there we were, performing at a prison on a small stage surrounded by bars that served as the main curtain. It was the most intimidating place I'd ever visited—automatic gates closed behind us as we entered different areas of the prison. But there were ordinary men there, men who appreciated our talent and loved our show.

"You're a hit," Father Tom said as he congratulated us. "You've saved souls today," he sang. I didn't know what I was getting into when Father Tom called, but weeks later the experience spawned an act as part of the *Scheherazade* show.

One night, as I was working late, Stephen Sondheim's beautiful song "Send in the Clowns" came on the radio. Inspired by my recent prison visit, I started to plan out a scene in my mind. I envisioned a small, lonely clown sitting by himself but with lots of creativity he didn't know quite how to express.

When we incorporated the number into *Scheherazade*, we had the clown walk across a tightrope. But every time Albert brought the rope on stage, it had a knot in it. I was getting frustrated until finally Benny said to leave it.

I looked puzzled, "Leave it?"

"It looks sadder, like the clown is trying hard to be perfect but he gets all tangled up," he observed.

I was astounded by his insight. He was right, yet I hadn't seen the same symbolic connection until he pointed it out.

As many of the players made progress to reach their dreams, others had their own dreams to follow. Warren, who'd become invaluable to us since Ron's departure, was now chasing his own dream. "I'm leaving after we premiere *Scheherazade*," he said to me one morning. "I'm getting married and I have to get a job that doesn't require travel. I know you understand."

I understood perfectly, but I was heartbroken. Traveling took a toll on me too. Whenever I traveled away from Bernard, Jeannine and Joanne, I felt very lonely and I couldn't wait to come home.

Scheherazade was a huge hit at the St. Lawrence. I never thought it was possible. From the moment the camels entered the stage, the audience was gasping with oohs and ahhs, especially when Sinbad took his voyage on the 14-foot ship with a mast that stretched 10 feet into the air. We had succeeded in taking the audience through a voyage— a voyage with pure magic!

"What?" I looked up to see Victor Polley, the general manager of the St. Lawrence Centre. "The show—a long show," he said. "A show where the flats didn't fall down, or where a performer didn't jump off the stage to watch the show instead of performing!" We laughed recalling some of the disastrous performances early in the history of Famous PEOPLE Players.

Our next stop was a gala at the National Arts Centre in Ottawa and our host was Maureen McTeer, the wife of former Prime Minister Joe Clark. At the time, he was working as the opposition leader in the House of Commons, while Maureen was a confident and outspoken lawyer, a wife and a great mom. I first called Maureen at home to ask her about being my first chairperson at the gala. I was so relieved that she didn't say, "Why are you calling me at home instead of at the office?"

"Selling tickets, promoting us—has a great stress factor in itself," I started.

"I know you," she laughed, easing my tension. "I like your company—it's great. I'll do it, but I'll do it in my own way," she said, letting me know she was now fully in charge.

It was reassuring to know that preparations for *Scheherazade* at the National Arts Centre were being organized by a very efficient and competent person. I didn't have to worry about anything, except the show. Maureen was more than remarkable—she worked with members of all the political parties to sell tickets and make it a successful event.

When we arrived in Ottawa, Maureen took us on a private tour of the Parliament Buildings, including a visit to the House of Commons for Question Period. I was mesmerized seeing Joe Clark and Pierre Trudeau square off against each other. Later that evening, Maureen held a superb buffet dinner at Stornoway, the name of the official residence of the leader of the opposition. While Jeannine, Joanne and Catherine—Maureen and Joe's daughter—ran all over the grounds, playing tricks on the RCMP, the adults mingled in the dining room. I was astonished to see Liberals, Conservatives and NDPs all joking with each other. *If most Canadians could see this, they wouldn't believe it,* I thought. *A couple of hours ago, they were at each other's throats, but now they're enjoying each other's company.*

The gala went like clockwork and our performance went just as smoothly. I was especially impressed with the efficiency of volunteers on Maureen's committee and their support. They didn't try to upstage the performers or take any credit for the event's success.

After our performance, Maureen took me aside. "You know that trip you told me you wanted to take?"

"What trip?" I asked.

"China—remember? You said that you wanted Famous PEOPLE Players to go to China with *Scheherazade* and be the first group of your kind to perform in the People's Republic of China."

"Oh, *that* dream." My eyes lit up, never believing Maureen would ever bring it up again.

"Oh *that* dream?" she repeated, laughing. "The trouble with you, Diane, is you have too many dreams. Let's just concentrate on this one—going to China. I'm going to get the Chinese ambassador to write to the government of China about you." She was as good as her word, and the ambassador, who had seen our performance, agreed to write a letter.

When we got home, Ida collected the mail that had been sitting around for a week. One letter was from the B'nai Brith Women of Toronto. I tossed it over to Cathy, saying, "Think of someone to nominate for their Woman of the Year."

She read the letter as Greg brought me a cup of coffee. "Coffee, dearie."

"Ugh! Too much sugar, Greg. You know I don't take sugar."

"Me know," he admitted as he left, laughing.

"Diane," Cathy looked at me strangely.

"Uh-huh," I muttered, as I kept writing my letter of thanks to the Chinese ambassador.

"B'nai Brith," she continued.

"Yeah, did you come up with someone to nominate?"

"Well—" she hesitated.

"Well what?" I kept typing away.

"They've nominated *you*. You're going to be the B'nai Brith Woman of the Year."

"*What?*" I was floored. This honour was coming from a group of women who did wonderful work themselves. Each one of them deserved her own award for Woman of the Year.

Months later, on the day of the awards breakfast, I was as nervous as a cat about to have kittens. I had never made an acceptance speech in my life. How could I stand up and speak in public? To add to my nervousness, the audience was packed with Famous PEOPLE Players' corporate supporters. As I walked toward the podium, I was shaking inside, still not sure of how I was going to start off my speech. Then I saw my family and my mom, and I began speaking from the heart.

"Mom, you are like all of these wonderful ladies who have bestowed this award on me. You picked up the pieces quietly when I screwed up. You stood by me when no one else would.

"Greg, I want to thank you for teaching me the meaning of patience. Whenever you suffer from terrible migraines, you just smile and keep working.

"Brenda, thank you for having to bite your lip when controlling yourself. I know how hard it must be for you—not losing your temper—because I lose my temper too.

"Cathy and Ida, I want to thank you for something that is hard to do. When people say, 'Isn't she talented for a retarded girl?' you don't mind what people think. You both exemplify good human beings who work alongside us all equally and with love. It takes special people to work with special people and you are amazing.

"Renato, you of all people, were the one who gave me courage to face the world, look up at the sky and see the stars.

"Mom, thank you also for the lion, the hens, the musical notes, the oak trees, the Sorcerer, the cave, the brooms, the birds—all of it. I love you. We couldn't manage without you.

"To all you wonderful people—you show the world the meaning of taking the impossible and making it possible. This is an award I will treasure with my heart, reminding me to dream the impossible dream."

Today, that award has special significance. Of all the awards that I have received over the years, including the Order of Canada, this is the one I hold dear to my soul because it came from a group of people with a powerful commitment to helping others.

That personal achievement gave me another dose of encouragement to reach for bigger dreams. And China was one of them. I scheduled a meeting with Richard Liu, the vice-president of the Chinese-Canadian Friendship Association in Victoria. He was leaving for China, so I gave him a copy of the letter from the Chinese ambassador.

It was a great introduction to Famous PEOPLE Players and it was the best shot we had for getting to China.

When I returned from my meeting, I remember sitting on the ferry, which crossed the strait between Victoria and Vancouver, and in the distance I could see a rainbow. It seemed to be leading the way for the ferry. *This is it—God is speaking to me again*, I thought. I could almost hear his answer to me: "*Diane, I'm working for you. You are going to China, but be patient.*"

As I waited for word from China, another guardian angel appeared in our lives in Vancouver. His name was Jack Webster, a man with a rough, direct manner who spoke to the point, but had a heart of gold. He had seen Famous PEOPLE Players on TV, and was touched by our work, so he wanted to help promote us even further by putting us on his television show.

He plugged our company and show in Vancouver for weeks on his TV news show. He even raised money on our behalf and wouldn't take no for an answer until potential donors finally coughed up some funds.

"Show me the money!" he challenged his viewers. "I'm narrating *Carnival of the Animals*, *The Sorcerer's Apprentice* and *Les Patineurs*—a Christmas fantasy—and you'd better be there!" he'd say in his thick Scottish accent.

The lieutenant-governor of British Columbia attended the premiere of our *Les Patineurs* show, a light-hearted Christmas production inspired by the music of Meyerbeer's ballet of the same name. The children in the audience shrieked with laughter as Santa fell asleep and the elves took over his workshop. The model train went out of control, while a ballerina kept spinning around and around and a toy soldier fired his cannon over and over again. A nervous elf then awakened Santa to help him fix the toys so they could be delivered in time to the children.

In *Les Patineurs*, penguins skated by a big gorilla. *That's my Benny on that penguin*, I thought as I applauded. And I was so proud when I watched Renato on the gorilla, his first time taking part in a show. *If only the audience knew what a moment this is for you,*
I thought. For the climax of the evening, John placed a star on the Christmas tree, which meant he had to run in the dark, jump on the black boxes, and lift the star up on the tree. I was so moved by the flawless performance that I was in tears during my closing speech to the audience. The audience stood and joined in on the sobbing.

I was often emotional during my closing remarks. Only a few people could understand what an accomplishment it was to have a wonderful performance following relentless hours of practicing. On one night, prima ballerina Celia Franca had asked our photographer, Ken Bell, about my emotional reactions during my speeches. "Why does she always get so choked up?" she complained to Ken. "She loses her dignity when she cries on stage."

When Ken told me that, I went right over to Celia and said, "I hope I don't offend you, but I love what I do and I love these kids, and when they achieve something big on stage—it's a miracle. And when that miracle happens, I cry." I was upset about her remarks for days. Just the same, I knew I had to be careful because when I cried, Albert howled.

And when Albert cried, everyone stopped to deal with it. I knew I needed more performers that were already trained and ready to slip into a performance if there was a problem, like Albert's crying.

One night I called Ann, who was now married to Ron. "We need an understudy school, and you're the only one who can pull it off."

"I'd love to," she said. She agreed to take a group all day on Saturdays.

"If we can get them used to the black-light technique, with hoods on their faces, their bodies limbered up and work on their hygiene, it will be easier for us when they eventually join the performing troupe," I said, thrilled that Ann was involved with us again. "I'm going to call it the Famous PEOPLE Players Farm Team!"

We were at a point in our business where I needed to assess what we had done and where we were going. Audiences loved classical pieces like *The Sorcerer's Apprentice, Scheherazade* and *Les Patineurs*. While the classicals stirred imaginations, numbers like *Superman* and *Star Wars* were more appealing to the younger audience. I decided to choose theme songs from famous movies, such as James Bond's *For Your Eyes Only, Goldfinger, Live and Let Die* and *You Only Live Twice* to lengthen our shows.

As excited as we were about a new number, a sombre Cathy came into my office shortly after we started work on it. "Don't tell me," I said, "this is your last tour."

"How did you know?"

"I know. Believe me, I can read it now like a book." It seemed to be a continuing pattern: every time we had a new beginning, there was an unexpected ending, usually among personnel. But I accepted it as part of the company's growing pains.

Brenda began to have trouble coping again, and her temper kept flaring dangerously. There seemed to be problems almost every day, mostly because Brenda had become attached to Cathy and didn't want her to leave. I took her to her family doctor for guidance.

"You can't depend on pills. When you're on the pills, you're tired and you can't perform," I said. "You must use self-control. You've done it before, so you can do it again."

Cathy worked hard to help Brenda come to terms with her departure, but it was difficult. When Brenda wasn't yelling, we were all afraid to talk in case we triggered one of her tantrums.

Throughout the transition, I began to assign roles for the new numbers. Brenda manipulated a large voodoo mask that would suddenly appear in the darkness while drums were beating. For "Live and Let Die," we'll have a witch doctor dancing and magically playing the congas. "For Your Eyes Only"—an Atlantis underworld scene with a submarine and when the hatch opens, two skin divers come out. "Goldfinger"—Benny, you'll play the character Odd Job. You look like him." Mom made a fluorescent suit and a beaver hat for his role. Benny came out on stage in a gold car, and then took off his hat, threw it and the gold statues' heads flew off—just like in the movie.

"It's Richard Liu on the phone," Ida interrupted us breathlessly, running into rehearsal. "He just got back from China."

I picked up the phone as everyone huddled around to listen.

"You are officially invited to China," he said.

Everyone was excited. "China! China!" we yelled, as we jumped up and down in a huddle. Brenda wasn't celebrating.

"Brenda, come on," I said.

"Brenda, join in."

"I won't—I hate you!" She picked up a chair and smashed it against the wall. I wasn't sure if we could take Brenda on tour if her temper kept flaring out of control. I'd have to evaluate her behaviour on the next Canadian tour we took.

The next day, we started to fill out the long, complicated questionnaire Richard Liu had sent us. The Chinese Embassy wanted to know personal details about every performer in the group.

"Uh-oh," Ida said as she pointed to a line, "Look, John can't go—he has a criminal record."

I called our lawyer to see what he could do. Given the circumstances, I wasn't sure John Vass's assault record would hold him back. "Diane, John Vass will not be able to travel to any foreign countries. You can't take him on tour."

"He was great on the Canadian tour."

"Yes, because he was confined. How long has he been home?"

"One week," I said softly.

"Wait—just wait. Time will tell."

I was determined to see John healthy, so I insisted he resume his therapy now that we were home. He agreed that I'd accompany him to his doctor's office the next day. When he came over the next morning, I opened the door to let him in. I was walking around in my bare feet. He got an erection and started to chase me. "I want your feet," he cried. "Give me your feet!"

As I ran around the living room, I yelled back, "John, follow me and I'll let you have my feet." I ran to the front door and opened it. "Look who's there," I pointed outside. He stepped out to see and I slammed the door behind him. I could hear him screaming outside, "I want your feet!"

When I called Bernard, he insisted I fire him. I did. Then I called John's psychiatrist to tell her that I couldn't keep him. John was placed in a group home, where he continued to chase women's feet.

I always thought John would do well on a farm. It was the perfect environment for him—there were no distractions and lots of work to use up his energy, just like the schedule for most of our tours. That's why he usually behaved so well when we were on tour. Ironically, when I saw his mom one day, she told me they had sold the house and bought a farm. She had remarried and was looking forward to her new life. God works in mysterious ways, I thought.

Months later, I had lunch with John's social worker, who sadly told me that John had burned down the barn and his stepfather had had a heart attack and died. His mother tried desperately to place her son in a confined institution, but no one wanted him. He was too much trouble.

"What about a 24-hour supervised group home?" I asked the social worker.

"The waiting list is too long."

"Let me help. I know the new lieutenant-governor of Ontario, John Aird. With his help, maybe we can get John moved up the waiting list."

I made an appointment to see John Aird. It took a month to move John up the waiting list—with John Aird's assistance. John Vass was placed in a 24-hour supervised home. It was a special place that offered a gymnasium, a school and a worship service. He would be kept busy.

I often get discouraged when I hear about people like John because I see how well they could potentially do in Famous PEOPLE Players. I see how some of them can learn to focus on certain tasks, run personal errands and lead an active lifestyle, which all helps them become more independent. They grow as their minds are being exercised. And by keeping busy, they lead normal lives. But I've also seen how people like John can regress if they're not kept busy when they leave us, like Dustin Hoffman's character in the movie *Rain Man*. It's the ultimate heartbreak to see performers succeed and turn their lives around, only to wind up deteriorating beyond any assistance.

Day in and day out, I tried to focus on the upcoming stars. And one of them was rising from our understudy school—Darlene Arsenault, a tall blonde who loved music. We gave her the part of a statue in the *Goldfinger* number.

Like Benny, she had problems remembering her cues. But touring gave Darlene an opportunity to learn on the road. She would get lots of experience trying out new numbers during our next tour, beginning in Ontario and extending to the West Coast.

Our bus driver, Dave Balinsky, became a member of the Famous PEOPLE Players' family. Wearing our company T-shirt, he helped unload and set up the stage. Nothing would make him happier than to get some homemade pie at the end of shift. "Pie? Did you say pie?" he asked as he pulled into the theatre's driveway in Petrolia, Ontario. Dave was the first to reach the theatre's green room, where a volunteer had made pies for everyone. Someone had told her how much Dave loved pie.

"No one gets a piece until Dave has one," she said.

"Watch it guys. Only take one piece—you have to perform," Ida squawked.

When it came to show time, everybody took their places on stage and the curtain rose to our James Bond medley. By the time we got to the *Goldfinger* number, I could already hear the whispers from stage right to stage left.

"Pssst, where's Darlene?" someone in black whispered.

Darlene was a no-show. And the head of the statue did not come off like we had rehearsed so many times before.

"What happened?" I asked Darlene in the dressing room.

"I don't know," she scratched her head.

"Where were you during *Goldfinger*?"

"I don't know."

"What do you mean *you don't know?*"

"I can't remember," she looked at me.

Here we go again! I thought to myself, anticipating the months of work ahead of me. Tour stop after tour stop, *Goldfinger* came and went without the statue's head coming off because Darlene never showed up for her part.

"I don't get this," I said in exasperation to Ida one day. "She's always there for her parts in rehearsal. I'm going to stand backstage to watch and see what happens."

During the show, I snuck up behind Darlene. I watched her holding on to her statue. The minute the music started for *Goldfinger*, she suddenly broke into song.

"Goldfinger…" she sang.

She missed her cue because she was performing in the wings off stage! The problem wasn't that she couldn't do the part, but that she didn't have enough parts to keep her busy. So, we gave her more parts to help her keep focused.

"No dancing or singing in the wings. On stage—that's where you perform," I reminded her.

"Okay, okay, I got it," she said.

Debbie Rossen also gave us some interesting moments on this tour. In Winnipeg, she forgot her coat at the hotel. Dave turned the bus around and went back to retrieve it. In Calgary, she forgot her purse. Dave turned the bus around to get it. In Vancouver, we forgot her! Well, only for 15 minutes, while Ida watched her hiding behind a plant in the lobby. "I won't forget again," Ida said as she boarded the bus.

It wasn't until I put her in charge of me—my coat, my purse, my suitcase—that she felt responsible. "I'm in charge of Diane," she would boast. Looking after me taught her to look after herself.

When we got back home, I had to deal with the problems Brenda was having after returning from our tour. "I don't like you," she said to Debbie. "You too," she looked at Greg.

This went on for weeks, even though she didn't act out while we toured. "It's because we're not on tour," Ida said. "They need touring to fill the time."

"Yes, but she also needs to develop self-control. She's upsetting everyone." I was determined to push her as far as I could. I did later one morning.

We were rehearsing the James Bond sequence when I said to her, "Lift up the butterfly prop with both of your hands."

"No, I won't," she replied.

"Yes, you will."

"No I won't—make me," she challenged me.

For a moment no one said anything. Then she began mumbling under her breath.

"Stop mumbling, none of us can take it."

"Shut up," she said, throwing the butterfly on the floor and stepping on it. "So there," she looked at me.

"So there, too," I said. "Here's your coat," I walked over to take it off the hook. "Goodbye—you're fired."

Brenda stared at me for a moment, looked at her coat and then went screaming into the bathroom. I saw Sandra make a mad dash toward her.

"No, leave her. She's really out this time. I mean it," I told the group.

We went back to rehearsing. An hour later, when Brenda realized that no one was coming to comfort her, she came out of the washroom and walked over to see me. "You're right," she said. "I'm tired." She took her coat and left.

I continued to support Brenda in her therapy. Eventually she found a good job at a candle factory, where the people she worked with didn't speak English. It was great because when she mumbled insults no one knew what she was saying—and that was half the battle!

We stayed in touch and Brenda still comes to some of our performances to cheer us on. And yes…to offer us her criticisms too. Ouch!

CHAPTER TEN

Start Digging

China was our dream come true, but we had to work hard to get there. We often joked that we were digging our way to China as we got planning. We started fundraising for the tour and were fortunate to get Xerox and Imperial Oil on board, as well as Canadian Pacific Air, which covered the cost of shipping the props overseas. With the help of John Aird, who was still the lieutenant-governor of Ontario, we raised most of the remaining money. Beyond corporate sponsorship, little things like T-shirt sales also brought in some funds.

Once we secured our travel plans for our May 1982 debut, we worked on tweaking our performances to connect with Chinese audiences. For example, Richard Liu translated a sign that Mom made for Greg and Benny to carry across the stage. It read: CANADA AND CHINA: FRIENDSHIP FOREVER GREEN. He also translated (and then narrated) the Ogden Nash verses into Chinese for our *Carnival of the Animals* performance.

On this trip, we'd have more company than usual. The mayor of Victoria was accompanying us throughout the tour, since Victoria was the sister city to Suzhou—the first city we would visit in China. A film crew, who were making a documentary of our visit, would also be joining us. My dear friend Judi Brake of CBC-TV was working as an assistant to the crew so that I didn't have to worry about anything except the show. It would be a demanding tour with a big show at each city, featuring mostly instrumental numbers like *Carnival of the Animals, Scheherazade* and *The Sorcerer's Apprentice* that had no language barrier, as well as a number with the Anne Murray and Liberace puppets. It took rehearsal after rehearsal for the performers to build up their stamina in order to be able to complete the show.

Just as we were about to leave, Anne Murray came to visit us at our rehearsal hall to say goodbye and wish us good luck. "The puppet gets to go to China, but what about me?" she joked as she autographed a washroom cubicle door at my request. "May I not be the last," she wrote.

We had a layover in the Vancouver airport and were greeted by the lieutenant-governor of British Columbia. "You are representing Canada and you are our ambassadors of goodwill," he told us. We were feeling more and more like royalty as we neared our destination.

We continued on to Hong Kong, where we had a two-day layover. We made the best of our free time. There was the duty-free shop (one of the biggest markets in the world); afternoon tea at the famous Peninsula Hotel; and a boat tour of Hong Kong Harbour. When we got off the boat, Benny yelled, "Look at those men; they're sleeping by the…" he scratched his head. "The rickshaw!" I yelled.

We ran over and piled into two rickshaws while the elderly men, who looked terribly frail, jumped up with a lot of energy and carried us for an hour around Hong Kong. We sang, "Before the Parade Passes By," as we waved to onlookers. At the end of the ride, we opened our wallets to pay the men, but instead they reached inside our wallets, grabbed the loot and ran! We figured that we must have spent about $150 for that one-hour ride.

The next day, we boarded a tiny plane to mainland China. We were all amused to hear the sound system playing "Jingle Bells" and "Red River Valley" in Chinese over and over again until our landing.

Our interpreter greeted us at the airport and we climbed into a limousine that had doilies and frilly curtains that looked like my grandmother's tablecloth. China was nothing like Toronto. As we rode along a dirt road, we saw Chinese people working in the rice fields, with their straw hats— just as they did in the children's books that I had read. The only visible means of transportation, other than our limousine, was on bicycle. There were thousands of them everywhere we looked.

Outside the hotel, about 100 children stood outside waving banners, holding plastic flowers and chanting, "Welcome!" We thought the crowd was anticipating the arrival of Henry Kissinger, who we had heard was also visiting China. "No, it's for you," said Richard.

When we went inside to check in, Richard took Jeannine and Joanne aside. "Where are you going with my children?" I asked.

"They get their own room."

"Their own room? No, they stay with me," I said shocked.

"In China, we treat our children with respect—as adults—so they will behave accordingly," he explained.

I begged Dr. Liu to allow my children to stay with me, but he warmly assured me that there would be no problem. I took a leap of faith and the children stayed in the room next to mine. I soon discovered how responsible Jeannine and Joanne, who were 7 and 5 respectively, could be on their own. They learned to hang up their own clothes and line up their shoes at the foot of their beds. Jeannine proudly said to me the next morning, "Look Mommy, me and Joanne are living in our own house. This is my bed."

"And this is *my* bed," Joanne piped up as she did a somersault across her bed.

"Mommy," Jeannine looked at my feet, "please take your shoes off when you visit."

I had another cultural shock when I discovered there were no locks on the doors. "Anyone can walk into our room," I said nervously to our personal guide. But I was reassured again that I had no reason to worry. In fact, not a single thing was stolen from our rooms or storage. Two days after we had arrived, I took a train ride and lost a lovely silk scroll that I had purchased in Suzhou. Remarkably, it was returned to me in my hotel room in Waxi—the next city on our tour. To this day, I still don't know how it got there.

On the first night of our visit, we were treated like Henry Kissinger, with a 16-course banquet in our honour. Each plate was decorated like an artist's canvas with the food we were about to eat. And every course was designed in the shape of animals, like a rooster, fish, bird, etc.

The next morning, I panicked when I discovered that Joanne and Jeannine weren't in their room. Renato, Darlene and I ran out of the hotel and into the nearby village after we searched the hotel for them. As we ran down the cobbled roads, looking into houses, we found the girls sitting in an open doorway, playing with the children who lived there. The girls had left their room and wandered on their own, which freaked me out. "Mommy, fish eggs," Jeannine held her nose. "We were invited inside to sit down with them for breakfast." After the incident, I had the girls stay with me in my room.

"City of Flowers is what we are called," explained our interpreter as we gathered in the main lobby for a city tour that afternoon. The village of Suzhou was full of narrow lanes, cobbled roads and the sound of bicycle bells ringing. As we made our way through streets lined with lush foliage and cherry blossoms, the people of Suzhou seemed to stop dead in their tracks.

"Why do they stare at us?" I asked our interpreter, as we walked past the trees that hung over each other.

"You all look alike," he said.

"Look alike? I don't think so. Renato is different from Benny. He has glasses and Benny has a mustache. Debbie is skinny; Darlene is blonde and tall. How can you say we look alike?"

"Well, you do," he laughed.

As we continued to walk, we crossed a pretty foot-bridge. "This is called the Watergate Bridge," he said very seriously.

"Watergate? There's a Watergate in Washington."

"Yes, we know—why did you make such a big deal out of it?" he smiled.

I often thought about that myself as I gazed over the Watergate Bridge. We had so many other causes that could occupy our minds, yet Watergate took up all the airwaves, time, financial and emotional energy.

We started setting up our stage the next day at a little theatre not far from the hotel. Factory workers were hired to assist us. To our surprise, the stage was set before we could say, one, two, three! But there was a problem.

"The bottom of Liberace's piano is missing!" Mom screeched.

"Don't worry," Richard said.

The next thing we knew, after a series of translations, the factory workers made a replacement under Mom's direction as quickly as they set up the stage.

"They should work for us," Benny laughed. "They're fast."

Before our opening, which was seen by about 300 people, mostly factory or field workers, I gathered the players together in the dressing room. There I read out congratulatory telegrams from Pierre Trudeau, Anne Murray and Liberace. Then I spoke to them with tears in my eyes.

"Look how far you've come," I said, as Renato stood by proudly. "From your four walls to the Great Wall of China."

Richard ran in, "Let's go!"

"But I'm not finished," I answered.

"In China, the curtain goes at 7:30 sharp." (It was a big difference from Glace Bay, Nova Scotia!)

It was a unique spectacle—like no other we'd ever been a part of throughout our history. In addition to our performances, the event was interspersed with customary traditions, fine acts and many proud moments. As we walked to take our places on stage, I noticed someone had put a table covered in a lace tablecloth with a spread of teacups right in the middle of our stage. Richard and the dignitaries took their places at the table, facing the audience, and started to drink their tea.

"What is this?" Renato laughed. "The Mad Hatter's tea party?"

As a special tribute, we were instructed by Richard to line up and take a cup of tea from the table. After our little tea party, they moved the table, with its tablecloth and teacups, off stage and the show began.

The one-hour show surprised the audience, especially the Anne Murray puppet. Her blonde hair, blue eyes, and deep voice intrigued them. They sat quietly at the beginning of *The Sorcerer's Apprentice*, but they laughed hysterically when the little apprentice got smacked in the bum.

Carnival of the Animals, which followed after a brief intermission, was the next act we'd be performing. Judi,

Mom and I were sitting in the audience, laughing as we watched Richard Liu enter the stage, very dignified with his black tuxedo, to take on his role as narrator. He took his seat at a table with a little red lamp and he'd pull the chain and, click, he turned it on as he read the verse of the lion. Click. He pulled the chain and the little light went off. Click—light on. He'd read the next verse. Click—light off.

During intermission, 15 children from a school for the deaf entertained the audience with dancing, while we prepared the stage for the second act. They were fabulous and we were proud to share our stage with them. I was especially impressed with their performance because they had spent part of their morning meditating instead of rehearsing.

We received an amazing response from the audience for our flawless performances, but we never expected the reaction we received. We were like rock stars whose fans kept wanting more. With one curtain call after another, the audience just wouldn't let us leave the stage! In every city where we performed, the reaction was the same.

The next day, slightly down from our high of the night before, we were taken on a tour of some of the inspiring programs developed by the government to help disabled individuals make use of their skills. Our first stop was a factory where the deaf worked. We were surrounded by machinery that made such an excruciatingly loud noise that I thought I was going to pop an eardrum.

I couldn't bear the sound any longer when Mom shouted, as she held her hands up to her ears, "Why on earth are they smiling?"

"They are deaf," Richard answered. "Everybody's disability is put to good use."

I was glad to see these individuals working. However, I was saddened that they didn't have the same choices disabled people have in our country, where we can be whoever and whatever we want to be.

Later, Jeannine and Joanne joined the children in a series of eye exercises that help prevent nearsightedness. We joined them in their playground and danced with them while Benny and Sandra taught the children how to manipulate the fish in our show. I was inspired watching the performers play with the children. No one spoke or understood each other and they suffered from various handicaps, yet they all came together at that moment.

Our next stop for the day was a silk factory in the city of Nanking. There, we watched blind people hold silk pods to their ears to determine if the pods would produce good silk. It was amazing, something I'd never witnessed before. We were later led into a room to listen to the same factory workers play for us as an orchestra. Wherever we went, we saw people with disabilities working in jobs that used their talents—just like Famous PEOPLE Players.

Our last stop was Beijing, the Forbidden City. Its architecture symbolized and seemed to sum up Chinese history. I was taken by the grandeur of our surroundings and imagined what it would have been like 4,000 years ago under the Ming Destiny, when battles were fought for control of the city.

Before we said goodbye to China, we took one last sightseeing trip—the Great Wall of China, an enormous stone wonder, which spans across east to west China. It was the perfect destination to symbolize our journey. As we continued to walk upward, pulling ourselves along as if we were climbing a mountain, we stopped and looked out. Benny sang and Renato pretended he was an emperor who once ruled China. We saw a train in the distance with tiny puffs of smoke billowing from its engines. It reminded me of the little engine that could. *I think I can, I think I can, I think I can.* As I looked in awe at the wonder before us, all I could think of was the many, many mountains we had climbed to get to this point.

We had little rest when we returned home to Canada. We had another performance coming up in just 10 days and we needed to rehearse for it. The show, which was a benefit (organized by Father Tom) for the Pelletier Home—a residence that works with adolescent girls who have personal, social or family difficulties—was our way of extending our gratitude for our great trip to China to everyone who helped make it possible.

The night before our performance, Father Tom invited Famous PEOPLE Players to visit the girls at Pelletier. We squeezed into the small living room to meet the residents. Father Tom started asking us questions as we gathered together.

"If you could change anything about yourself, what would it be?"

"I'd get a new brain," Benny answered promptly.

"I'd find somebody who loved me," Debbie Lim said. "And the whole world would share in my love."

I started to cry. I was so overcome by the courage and strength of each player—who, for me, showed that he or she was comfortable in his or her own skin. In a room of strangers, they said exactly what they felt. It was like a scene from *The Wizard of Oz,* and Father Tom was the wizard. He told them that they already had what they wished for, just by doing what they do.

This was the start of a three-year relationship. For years, Famous PEOPLE Players did benefit performances for the Pelletier Home. In return, we were proud to be affiliated with a worthwhile cause. The staff once told us with great warmth: "You give with love till it hurts. God bless you all—we can now keep our doors open."

"We bought a house!" I bounced into work one day. "No more apartment. We will have lots of room. Jeannine and Joanne are getting their own rooms and a backyard."

The backyard was also a bonus for Bernard, who loves to garden. In fact, all those years of living in an apartment, I never knew what talent he had for colour or design in landscaping our garden!

Our first houseguest was Harold, who came to live with us for six months. He had a serious drinking problem and I wanted to help.

"I thought we had it under control," his mother said to me. "But it's when he's kept busy that he doesn't drink."

I thought if I had my eye on him and kept him busy, I could help him overcome his addiction. But I wasn't sure if he had an addiction or if drinking was just something he did when he had nothing else to do. While he lived with us, he practiced to become a performer and Bernard helped him with his personal hygiene. He helped around the house by cleaning and we discovered his remarkable talent for cooking.

"What's in the potatoes?" Jeannine asked one night.

"Cheese, with salt and pepper."

"They're great—I want more."

"Harold, we should send you to cooking school," Bernard smacked his lips as he tasted the cuisine before him.

Our house was now becoming a real home; a home that was making its own history as we settled in. We began recording Jeannine and Joanne's heights with pencil marks on a wall in the kitchen, making note of the day, month and year of their growth. Bernard was planting peonies to celebrate our personal and family achievements, like the time Jeannine got an A+ for a story she had written at school or for Joanne's first Holy Communion.

We were also noting our own achievements at Famous PEOPLE Players. Besides Harold, Debbie Lim also had a gift. She could play the piano, and I enrolled her in private piano lessons. I encouraged the other performers' talents, including Harold, whom I convinced to take cooking classes.

Just as the players were expanding their portfolio, so too was Famous PEOPLE Players. This time it was completely new territory for us. "We've got a deal," Marc Daniels said on the phone one day. "Thank goodness you performed at Radio City because my dear friend and promoter/producer Joe Cates saw your show and sold the story of Famous PEOPLE Players. We're going to make a movie! I'll be directing and the award-winning screen-writer Corey Bleckman is writing the story."

The next month, Corey toured with us while we were in Glace Bay, Nova Scotia, get a 'feel' for Famous PEOPLE Players and learn more about the characters he would be writing about. We were excited at first, but when months went by without a word, we didn't think a movie would ever get made. We found out that there were rewrites after rewrites and Marc and Joe Cates were having trouble finding an actress to play me.

Without any warning, Marc called one day to tell us they were shooting in Toronto in May. "That's next month." I choked on my sandwich.

"Brooke Adams is you."

"Me? I don't know her."

"She was in *Invasion of the Body Snatchers* with Donald Sutherland. An excellent actress."

Making a movie taught me a lot about how to tell a story. The script not only had to be interesting to viewers, but it had to deliver on many fronts. It had to include information on how the company was formed, develop individual characters and lead up to a climax—which, of course, was our performance with Liberace in Las Vegas.

Rehearsals for the movie began on schedule in May. And we had a chance to be a part of them. "I want to see your eyes roll," Benny said to Brooke.

"Her eyes roll?" I asked him. "Why?"

Brooke laughed. "In the movie *Invasion of the Body Snatchers* I roll my pupils—actually, I spin them."

"That's a special effect," I mumbled. Then she started spinning her pupils.

"How on earth do you do that?" I asked, wanting to learn.

"I've been doing that exercise for years—that's why I don't wear glasses."

"They did that in China," I told her, recalling how the children in the school for the deaf did their eye exercises.

Brooke was dedicated to learning about the *real* me. One week before the shoot, she followed me around, watching us rehearse and learning my body movements. I felt uncomfortable being watched all the time. Now the tables were turned, and being me made me feel uncomfortable. It made me act differently—I felt I couldn't completely be myself. I was acting being me instead.

There was a lineup of professional actors playing various roles in the movie *Special People*. Ron James was cast as a fictitious character who combined the qualities of several different performers. Lesleh Donaldson played a character based on Alice, the girl who left our company to become a prostitute. Susan Roman played Ann. Benny, Renato, Sandra, Greg, Harold and Brenda were all invited to play themselves. Unfortunately, nobody played my mom because she wasn't included in this story, a hole I wasn't happy about, because her talent for prop creation had been an important part of our success. "We can't do everyone," Marc said, when I questioned him about it.

I was also annoyed that some events Corey had written about weren't based on the truth. I called Liberace to complain about it. "The script from Corey has me lying down in front of your limo to entice you to watch my show. I know I did some pretty bold things, but I never did that."

"Now, now, Dora," Lee said. "When I read the script, I felt that it was something you were capable of doing."

"Gee, thanks. Now everyone will think I'm a nutcase."

The script took another artistic liberty. In the movie, my character gives up on Famous PEOPLE Players following one of our earlier disastrous performances and doesn't give it another chance until the performers—led by Ron James—come banging on my door to show me a news clipping about Liberace coming to town. That really irked me, but Marc, in his experienced way, said, "We only have an hour and 30 minutes—the rest is commercials. The story must go smoothly and quickly."

But the making of this movie also taught me a lot about me. Part of making a movie was having an actress like Brooke truly understand my character, and the only way she could do that was to rehearse and train the performers for a show. Marc and Brooke decided that I should vacate the premises for a day so she could be alone with the performers. That way, she could bond and get to know them without my influence.

When I returned to work the next morning, I could hear the yelling coming from the rehearsal hall. When I entered, I saw Brooke waving her arms with great determination.

"We're rehearsing the piano sequence," Brooke was gasping for breath. "Busy, busy, busy," she smiled. "Okay Greg, bring the piano bench on!" she yelled. "No, wrong," she stopped the music as she watched him.

"Wrong, me? Me not wrong—me do it right," Greg said confused.

"No, I want you to do it wrong. I want you to do it upside down."

"Upside down," he grinned.

"In the movie, it's supposed to be like the first rehearsal with Diane where everything is wrong. Remember, Greg?"

"No. Me do it this way," he said.

"That's right, Greg, but for the movie it's supposed to be *wrong*." Then Brooke moved over to the people on the musical notes. "Bump into everyone, like you did on the first day. Lots of blackouts, hear me?"

I watched and listened. "Don't do it that way," Brooke's arms were waving in the air.

"One, two, three—go!"

They went. "Stop! Not right," she said. "Sandra, come here, please. Your hair, it must be clean."

"Marc told me to be dirty."

"Yes, oops, he's right. We want it dirty for this movie so that in the end we'll see how lovely you look now."

"Okay, okay," Sandra said.

Then Marc turned to me for assistance. "Diane, we're having trouble getting the group to be like they were."

"It's hard to reverse years of hard work," I said.

"We're making a movie. Make it happen, please." I took in his words and sat back.

As I watched Brooke play me, I asked myself, *Why didn't I just give up? She's trying so hard, going over and over the show. Why doesn't she give up?*

Suddenly Brooke let out a shriek. Everyone froze. "The show—the show is tomorrow and the piano just broke!" she said, reciting her lines from the script.

Why is she so rough on them? I wondered. Then it hit me. *Wait, stop, Diane*, I thought, *you're looking at yourself from a distance.* I was watching my life flash before my eyes, as if I had arrived at the Pearly Gates and Saint Peter was taking me through key moments of my life. Then I realized, as each day was progressing forward and as each scene was being played out, the performers had become my guides. I had learned more from them about life. Silently, they had been speaking to me through their actions, teaching me more about patience, love, empathy, compassion, diversity and honesty than I had realized.

"Quiet on the set!" Marc yelled.

The performers were silent. "Take one," Marc said. "Aruba Liberace" began to play.

"Cut!" He sounded mad. "Diane, get over here." I walked over to him. "You have not been paying attention," he complained. "Throughout the movie, our character, Diane, is trying to get the performers to make the musical notes come out of the piano. Now, in this scene, they finally get it right, except that you haven't taught them how to do it."

"Marc, I changed it because everything was getting so confusing—right—wrong—right."

"I'm very disappointed in you, Diane."

He was right. I had been too focused on watching Brooke play me—how she looked, what she was wearing, her hair, her make-up, her motivation that I hadn't focused on anything else in the movie.

"I'm so sorry, Marc," I said. I called the group together and became Diane again. Just like a patient whose heart starts beating after being deemed clinically dead, I was brought back to life. We sorted out the problems with the musical notes and filming went on.

The last scene was shot in Las Vegas at the Hilton Hotel, the appropriate setting to highlight our performances with Liberace. I was glad to be joining the cast and players throughout the filming of this scene. And it felt great to be back with our extended family.

"Hey Dora," Lee walked up to me, smiling, with open arms as we entered the Hilton showroom, where the filming was taking place. We embraced.

"I love your outfit," I said as I started polishing his diamond buttons.

"Oh, there's Ketchup!" he said as Sandra came up to him, followed by Jeannine and Joanne.

"Small Bird," Ralph, Lee's bass player, waved to Greg.

"Dora, get the children please," I turned to find Ray Arnett.

"You still look the same," I smiled. "And they still aren't children."

"Success, success, Hollywood—Hollywood is calling. I couldn't be in the movie. There's only one star and that's Lee," Ray joked. "Autographs, anyone for autographs?" he looked around the stage.

"Places," Marc called out and Ray stepped aside. "Company, I want you to stand on this mark. You're taking your final curtain call with Liberace. The audience will clap, you'll bow, and then Lee will enter to join you. Got it?"

Everyone nodded. "Quiet on the set! Action!"

The actors and players walked forward, holding each other's hands, stepped into the spotlight and bowed. Lee joined them to thunderous applause—and then came the close-up.

"Come here, kids," Lee said as he got them in a huddle. Diane—the character—joined Lee as he spoke to the performers. "It's not because of who you are that makes people laugh and cry. It's because you're good! Real good." 'Diane' hugged Lee and the lights went to black.

"Cut! It's a wrap," Marc called.

I ran on stage and hugged Brooke and Lee, "Diane, I mean Brooke, you were great!" Now we all had tears in our eyes as we stood on the Hilton stage. I only wished Bernard and Mom were there to see and feel this experience, especially after all their help and support to make it happen.

"It's a miracle, Dora, a real miracle," Seymour said. "To think, it seems like yesterday that we first saw you at Hamilton Place...and now it's Hollywood. Remember, Our Father now art in Hollywood!" Seymour laughed.

"Here's your soul back," Brooke touched her heart and put her hand on mine. "I've got to go on to a new role, as a seductress in a CBS mini-series with Phoebe Cates and Kevin Kline."

The next morning, after a night out on the town, we headed down to the lobby to check out. It was the same lobby where the players had learned to write their names back in 1975. As I approached the checkout desk, I saw the performers in tears.

"I hate to go home," said Greg.

"You'd better believe it," replied Sandra.

"What the heck—what's one more day?" I thought. I treated the performers to another day in Vegas. That day saved our lives.

When we boarded the plane the next day and fastened our seatbelts, I picked up the newspaper and saw the headline: "PLANE CRASH."

"That was our flight," Ann leaned over to show me the newspaper.

"We were supposed to be on that flight yesterday," Ron James said quietly.

Then, as I turned to the last page, I saw Dr. Allan Roeher's picture staring back at me. He had died on that flight. He never got to see the actor who had portrayed him so beautifully in the movie. I was heartbroken. My mentor, my friend, the man who gave me my first chance, was gone. I couldn't take it in. Dr. Roeher had boarded the flight in Dallas, where he had attended a conference, fighting for the rights of the disabled. *Why him?* I kept asking God. *Of all people, why him?*

CHAPTER ELEVEN

Famous People Disappear

Touring is like a scene out of *The Adventures of Tom Sawyer.* Anything and everything can go wrong. We wanted to see the premiere of the movie, *Special People*, in our motel room while we toured a small town in northern Ontario. Then we discovered that our TV didn't carry CBS.

"Find someone who has it!" demanded Renato. "I'm not missing the drum roll."

Our bus driver, Dave, drove us through the northern wilderness in search of a set with American TV feed. It was pitch black, except for the occasional headlights as a car passed.

"Watch for moose." Benny was on guard at the front of the bus.

"There!" He pointed at a satellite dish outside a restaurant. "Stop the bus!" Renato ran down the aisle, announcing, "I'm going in to ask."

"It says Italian Night," Debbie Rossen looked up at the lights.

"Your reading is getting better," I told her proudly.

We watched Renato walk through the deep snow, leaving a path behind him. He disappeared into the doorway.

"Please, I want to see the movie," Debbie said, as she looked out the window for Renato to return.

When Renato came back, kicking the snow off his boots before entering the bus, he didn't have good news. "I spoke Italian to the owner, but he said he has an Italian wedding and he's too busy to take us in the back room."

I had a plan. "Dave, drive down the road. We have to find a payphone." I jotted down the name of the restaurant and directed Dave to pull up next to a payphone a few kilometres away.

"Tony's Place," the man answered.

"Hi, my name is Mrs. Richards with CBC *National News*. We have a group that is traveling in the area. We need them to watch a movie that has been made about them called *Special People*. It's important we interview them afterward and, naturally, we will mention your establishment on-air."

"No problem," he said. "Tell them to come back and see Tony."

That's how we watched ourselves on the small screen that night. We applauded as Renato, Sandra and Greg made their acting debuts. It was funny to watch the guests at the wedding reception wander over and watch the movie with us.

"Buy these stars a drink," one of the customers said.

After the debut, *Special People* brought us instant recognition. *People* magazine, for example, wrote about the performers who played themselves as being: "*more appealing than the professional actors hired to play the mentally handicapped people.*"

"Boy, you'd better be great—no mistakes!" screamed Renato as he came into the rehearsal hall. "I was just recognized by the bus driver as that famous Renato. He said he saw the movie and he's coming to our show. I'm a celebrity!" he yelled. "Not one screw up."

Debbie Lim joined in. "Me too. I was at the mall— they saw my Famous PEOPLE Players T-shirt. The lady said she loved Famous PEOPLE Players. No mistakes." She glared at the new players to make her point.

(There have been many instances over the past few years when I would go backstage to give notes and find Debbie Lim giving them out herself. I'd hear her say, "You missed your part, Harold. Lift the note this way," she'd say, then she'd show him. "Listen to the beat of the music." When she was done with the performers, she'd turn to me standing next to her, and tell me, "Oh yes, Ms. Dupuy, don't wear your shoes on the velvet floor.")

Benny got into the action too. "Diane, you'd better start thinking up new numbers for the show. We'll take care of the rest," he said, brushing the black boxes.

There were many tours that followed. They took us everywhere from sunny Hollywood, to sub-zero Winnipeg. That was the time the heater broke on the bus.

"How much further do we have to go before we get to a gas station to fix the heat?" I pleaded with Dave.

"We're five minutes closer that the last time you asked me. Now shut up and let me drive." He had had enough of my nagging.

Finally, with our ears and noses nearly frostbitten, we made it to Winnipeg. "Don't you dare come back till you fix the bus," I told Dave as he left to find a repair shop and dropped us off at a mall.

"Yeah, yeah, you sound like my ex-wife," he said.

We'd bought blankets and sleeping bags to keep us warm, just in case something like this were to happen. But we needed to check in somewhere for the night until the bus was repaired. We hadn't done a show in 48 hours— my bones ached and my hair was a mess.

When we spotted a hotel, we pulled up and I ran inside to beg the desk clerk to rent us a room in exchange for a show. "We don't do that here," he said.

"What do you mean *you don't do that here*?" I demanded. I made such a fuss that he donated the room to shut me up. I have no idea what I was thinking—I would never donate a show. But I was desperate to get the crew out of the extreme cold.

"No one is coming," I told the group about our upcoming performance at the Centennial Theatre. "Mark my words. It's 42 below zero—who in their right minds would ever come to a show?"

We prepared the stage just the same. While we were unloading the props from the truck (which accompanied our bus) to the stage, I felt like I was driving a team of huskies with a blizzard in my face.

"Are you Diane?" asked a tall, tobacco-chewing stage-hand with a hooded coat that covered his face.

"Yes."

"You're wanted on the phone." He turned for me to follow him.

"I can't believe how cold it is," I said as the two of us left snow tracks across the huge Winnipeg stage in the Centennial Theatre. "I feel like we're in the Arctic setting up for an outdoor concert."

"We're used to it," he laughed.

I went into a small cubbyhole backstage to pick up the dangling receiver. The call was from a dedicated doctor in Portage la Prairie, Manitoba, an hour-and-a-half drive from Winnipeg. He knew we were in town from a story on the CBC evening news. "There's a young man here that I'd really like you to see. Could you come up and visit him?"

"Why?" I sounded curious.

"His name is Clarence Asham. He's in his late twenties, retarded and blind. He's been institutionalized since he was a toddler. He can't learn Braille and just lives in a world of his own."

I gulped, remembering the world I lived in for years as a child who had trouble in school.

"Music—he loves music and he's a wonderful musician." The doctor sounded anxious. "He can play anything the first time he hears it."

How could I say no? I thought the doctor was going to cry. He reminded me of the time I pleaded with Seymour to get Liberace to come see Famous PEOPLE Players. I had to go.

"You're what?" Debbie Rossen questioned when I told the performers.

"We're going to take a short trip after the show to see Clarence."

"Clarence?" she responded. "Who's he?"

"We'll see when we get there," I said.

After the show, we drove to a large institutional building in Portage la Prairie. After a long walk down the corridor, we met Clarence, who was sitting at an upright piano. We listened to him play his repertoire of pop tunes, jazz and classical music—perfectly, and all by ear.

"He can play anything the first time he hears it," the doctor repeated. "And he can do the same thing on the accordion, guitar and xylophone."

"Diane, let him hear the music to our show," Debbie pushed a cassette recorder near him. We played him our Broadway songs. Clarence listened, then put his hands on the keys—and played. I could hardly believe my ears. Note for note, not one mistake. I knew at that moment that I wanted to do something for Clarence.

"I want to bring him to Toronto," I said.

In spring 1984, Debbie Rossen and I met Clarence and his nurse at the Toronto airport. It was the first time he had ever been outside of the institution.

Thanks to my dear friend Doug Riley, who had done many of our musical arrangements, Clarence got a job playing at his restaurant, Jingles, for his week-long stay. In addition to this engagement, Imperial Oil allowed us to feature Clarence at one of its private corporate events being held at the Sheraton Hotel, and the Sheraton donated the accommodation for Clarence and his companion for their stay. Imperial Oil also generously donated $2,000 to the institution to help Clarence study at the Winnipeg School of Music.

Clarence was also featured on many TV programs, where he got national exposure. And it was making an incredible impact on his life. By the end of the week, he was starting to talk and he began eating with a knife and fork—instead of eating by putting his head in his plate like a dog. There were no knives or forks allowed at the institution in order to protect the other residents. I was shocked to find out how he had been living there.

"He must learn to eat like a human," I told the nurse.

"I know, Diane," he said. "I want him to too, but the institution is so big. There is no time to give him the support he needs."

When the week was over, Clarence boarded a plane back to Winnipeg. "Goodbye Diane," he said slowly. With his head up, he took his seat on the plane. I was torn about him returning to the only life he knew—behind the four walls of an institution. I didn't think he should have been there in the first place.

"There must be a loving and dedicated family somewhere that would adopt him," I cried to the doctor on the phone.

"It's difficult, Diane, and it breaks my heart too. Thank you for giving all of us a week of hope." I kept in touch with the institution to check up on Clarence throughout the years. He never lived outside the institution, but continued to make astonishing connections with his musical gift.

Not long after that event we were on the road again, this time back out West. And, again while on tour, we faced another crisis. Just as weather can take you by surprise, so can touring—taking you from calm sunny days to tornadoes and lightning-packed nights. When situations arise, I always remember the Alcoholics Anonymous motto: I didn't cause it and I can't cure it—but I certainly can cope with it. It's what Famous PEOPLE Players learned to do best.

One of my performers, Cathy Camp, once wrote a poem about life on the road. I still have it hanging on my office wall. The last verse reads:

The night is cold and airless
as the troupe rolls down the road.
The players share a laugh or two
to ease some of the load.
And down below and silent
'neath the chatter, warmth and glow,
The magic waits for morning
and another town and show.

Another tour, another city. In Victoria, a frightening hate letter was delivered to me at the theatre. "Burn her at the stake," it said. Inside the letter was the company photograph—all of us standing on the Great Wall of China. The sender included another photo from our program, one of *The Sorcerer's Apprentice* that he said implied that I was a witch and the puppets, just like the dragons in *Scheherazade*, were demons. The letter read: "As a Christian, I am required to destroy witches."

I was frightened and didn't want to put anyone in jeopardy. Thankfully, the police stepped in and offered their protection for the rest of our B.C. tour.

With every tour, we seemed to learn something about each other and ourselves. There were many lessons, such as take one day at a time. Or, we can never rest on our laurels—a movie, Vegas, Radio City, China…none of that matters after it's over and done. It's this performance that counts—whether it's opening night in Moose Jaw, Saskatchewan, or the Special Olympics in Baton Rouge, Louisiana. But sometimes the obstacles to a good performance seem to get bigger and bigger. This time it was when we were invited to Baton Rouge to perform at the Special Olympics. I sent Ida and Renato down a day early to set up before me and the players arrived. I got a call the night before our arrival.

"You'd better get down here in a hurry," said a frazzled Ida on the phone to me from Baton Rouge, "because I don't think this is what you had in mind."

"What's happened?" I asked.

"First, the accommodation—and we'll just leave the cockroaches out of this for a moment, even though they're the size of baby alligators. Let's just talk about the sheets—there are none. So do we have a budget you'd like us to work with?"

"Budget?" At first I was confused, then I realized she was looking for 'upgraded' accommodations.

"Look, I don't mind all this, but when I'm forced to share a bathroom with 40 other people, that's where I have to draw the line."

"I gather you're trying to tell me that the accommodation is not so good."

"You got it, Pontiac. Book us into a hotel. We'll tell the organizer that university dorms are *not* acceptable."

No sooner had I arrived in Baton Rouge than Fast Eddie, an organizer for the Special Olympics, was at the airport to defend himself. "There is nothing wrong with the accommodation we provided," he said firmly.

"Eddie, let me explain something to you," I said even more firmly. "We are a professional company and my performers need proper accommodation. If they walk into a place where they do not have their privacy, they become very unhappy. Unhappy performers do not do well on stage—and I'm sure you want a good show, right?"

"If you move them to a hotel, we are not paying for it," he said.

"I have news for you, Eddie. They are going to a hotel and you are paying for it."

Eddie arranged for us to check into a more suitable hotel, but in the end, we got stuck with the bill. The main thing at the time was that all of us slept soundly that night. Early the next morning, Ida tiptoed into my room and woke me up.

"What are you doing, sneaking in at this hour?" I asked.

"Stay calm," she had tears in her eyes. "Please Diane, I need you to stay calm."

I thought my mother had died. After a long, nervous pause, Ida broke into tears, "Liberace, Streisand, Elvis, Kenny Rogers, Rod Stewart, Liza Minelli, Dolly Parton— are gone." She was referring to the puppet heads that were professionally made by Bob Baker in Hollywood.

"What do you mean *gone?*"

"They've been stolen."

"STOLEN!"

"I went back to the theatre last night because I was worried about the props," she said. "I thought I'd bring the heads back here, so I put them with my suitcase and some other stuff in the truck. I drove back to the hotel and unloaded the suitcase. I was only gone two minutes— and when I came back they were gone. I just…" she began to hyperventilate, "…I'm—so—ah, ah, ah—don't stare at me, Diane. Hug me or something."

We took turns crying and yelling. Finally, I tried to pull myself together. "Call Eddie, Ida. Get him on the phone. Now."

Ida, who was shaking, dialed the phone. "He's not there," she said. "They left a message and he will meet us in the lobby."

"Did you call the police?" I asked.

"Yes, I called everyone—the hotel clerk, concierge, general manager."

I met Eddie in the lobby. "Why are you so upset?" he asked. "They're just puppets."

"*Puppets!* They are our livelihood!" I was flooded with tears. But Eddie didn't understand me and stormed off.

Ida was distraught with guilt. The performers wouldn't speak to her. And I was heartbroken—we could never replace what we had. I called a staff meeting.

"When things get tough, the tough get going," I said. "Benny, Renato, if you're going to cry like that, don't sit on the couch—set the stage. Debbie, Darlene, look after everyone. I'm going to see Eddie."

"The company is finished," cried Greg. "No show."

"Do as I say."

I went hunting for Eddie. "Did you call the police?" I said when I found him.

"They're not going to look for puppets," he smirked.

"You'd better call and use whatever influence you have and find our heads. Post a $5,000 reward."

Two hours later, I noticed the performers walking with flats across the campus.

"What are you doing?" I ran over.

"Eddie said to tear down the stage and set it again in another theatre," they told me.

"Another theatre!" I screamed. "Eddie!"

Now I was really going to hunt him down. Eddie calmly informed me that the Special Olympics Committee wanted the show to move to another location. In the same breath, he informed me that the committee had no money to pay for our accommodation, so we'd be covering our own expenses.

I was angry and fired up. But I wasn't going to be any less than professional because we had a job to do. I gathered the performers. "I know we've only got half of our numbers," I told them, "but we're professional—so let's do a professional show."

The players were ready to go. Now I had to come up with a plan to allow for less material and new transitions between numbers. I decided to stretch out the show by narrating the Ogden Nash verses and sharing anecdotes about the company with the audience. The performance went as well as it could have under the circumstances.

As devastating as this trip was for the company, we discovered that Famous PEOPLE Players was not only a professional theatre company in every sense of the word, but also that when push came to shove, we found creative solutions to every problem. I learned that there is nothing worse for a group of people giving it their all to hear, "It can't be done" or "It won't work." So it became natural for me to emphasize, "How can we make this work?" "How do we find a solution to the problem?" For me, when a company and its people follow this approach, it's a sign of a strong leader, a great company and outstanding team players who will be closer to fulfilling their dreams.

When we returned to Canada from Baton Rouge, we felt as if we had been through a war—a war that we had fought with dignity and made us stronger. Even more importantly, we became a better company than when we had left.

We soon heard that the puppet heads were found in a swamp outside New Orleans—damaged beyond repair. The *Toronto Star* newspaper, which had heard about our loss, launched a campaign to raise money to replace our expensive puppets. Thanks to the paper, we raised enough money to have Bob Baker make all new puppet heads.

It was spring 1984—always a great time for Famous PEOPLE Players. Although Ida had left Famous PEOPLE Players to do some special work in Africa, new people were joining our company. New numbers, new people, a new mission and a new outlook on life—that was our motto.

We had already reached incredible goals as a company. But there was one place we hadn't been to that could offer even more opportunities. *Why not go to Broadway?* I mulled the thought over in my mind. *If that stage manager at Radio City thought we could definitely make it...then I know we can.* I started to put more Broadway tunes together and incorporated them in our daily rehearsals. We worked with "That's Entertainment," "Oklahoma," "42nd Street," and *My Fair Lady's* "Get Me to the Church on Time." Then I came up with a montage of characters that represented many of the same Broadway shows—for example, to represent *Oklahoma*, we added a singing horse throwing horseshoes at a cowboy, large white tap shoes for *42nd Street* and bells ringing for "Get Me to the Church on Time." This show, entitled *A Little Like Magic*, was a visually stunning, fast-moving tribute to the old and new Broadway.

Michael Jackson and Cyndi Lauper also joined our cast of characters. 'Michael' would perform his loose-limbed moonwalk and 'Cyndi' would sing her hit, "Girls Just Want to Have Fun."

Once we had the numbers in place, we needed a plan to get to Broadway. My plan began with trying to get more exposure in the United States. We decided to form an American board of directors—Seymour, Marc, Jimmy, Joe Cates, Robert Jani and Tom Sullivan, who had hosted our special on the ABC network. My American board had just the right mix of people—those individuals who had been with us through our most difficult times and our greatest triumphs.

I knew that getting to Broadway wasn't going to be easy. We needed to test the waters; get booked for one night and measure the response. Seymour suggested we approach Arthur Katz, who was a major investor in Broadway shows. Arthur came to see our show in Toronto and booked us at the Beacon Theater immediately, a stunning building with breathtaking Art Deco architecture and sculptures. Many famous Broadway shows and artists had performed at the Beacon stage and we were honoured to be sharing a place in history with them. He also booked the Shubert Theater, considered an historic jewel in the downtown core of New Haven, Connecticut, for a tryout.

"We need to raise money if we're going to Broadway," said an energetic Seymour. So fundraising began and thanks to Gino Empry, our publicist, the wonderful Tony Bennett held a benefit concert for us at Toronto's Royal York Hotel. Our dear friend, Brenda Woods, the same Brenda who had exploded all over the stage, became the fundraising chairwoman. She sent out many letters with her signature on them to hundreds of corporations that read:

I am a graduate of Famous PEOPLE Players. This company helped me become a strong, self-sufficient member of society. Help me to help others by buying a ticket for $100.00 for a dinner show.

Past and present performers, like Ron and Ann, pitched in to help us. Renato became chairman of a T-shirt drive. We even set up fundraising tables at Swiss Chalet, thanks to Greg's father, who worked there.

T-shirts sold like hot cakes. The dinner tickets were gone in a month. Everyone was working together like a team. It was all going smoothly until one day, when I walked into work and discovered several hundred dollars missing from the filing cabinet that we used as a safe.

The police arrived within 15 minutes to make a report.

"It's impossible," they said. "No one broke in here. This is an inside job."

"An inside job!" I gasped. "I can't believe it."

"Someone had a key to get in here," the officer said.

Slowly, one by one, the players came in to work. "What happened?" Greg looked up at the officer.

"We had a break-in."

Everyone ran toward the filing cabinet. "Oh no," Renato cried.

"I don't believe it," said Benny, throwing his bag down.

"Who—who did this?" Sandra started to cry.

"I don't know," I sobbed. "But we're missing over $200. I'm the only one who has the key—except for Mom."

"Well not anymore," my mother stormed in. "Mine's missing from my key ring."

I looked around and saw Harold, who was turning away because he couldn't look us in the eye. He was still living with us and was the only person who couldn't be accounted for at the time of the break-in.

"Officer, may I be left alone with my players?" I asked.

The officer realized that I had my suspicions about who had done this. "Here's my phone number," he said, handing me a card. "Call me. I want to know if you're pressing charges."

Silence engulfed the room. "Harold," I addressed him. Everyone stared directly at him. "You did this, didn't you?"

Silence.

"Speak up!" barked Renato.

"I did it," he admitted at once.

"You stole my key?" Mom stepped in to speak.

"Where's the money?" I demanded.

"I lost it."

"LOST IT!" Everyone screamed at the same time.

"I was on Yonge Street at the pinball machine."

"Stupid!" Renato screamed. "Let me take him outside—I'll kick his head in, then hand him over to the police." Renato grabbed Harold by the shoulders.

"Stop it! Nothing gets solved by violence!" I pushed Renato away.

I never did press charges. How could I, even though we had been betrayed by one of our very own for something so frivolous? I had no choice but to fire Harold from Famous PEOPLE Players. But I couldn't turn away a broken soul. It was my downfall too. With help from a director on my board, we found Harold a job in a restaurant kitchen.

"There's not going to be a Diane Dupuy there to bail you out," I told him as he started his new job. "You have to make it on your own."

Our Broadway tour began and the reviews from New Haven were glowing! One of them read: *"The dazzling puppetry that has* The Sorcerer's Apprentice *clashing swords on horseback with an army of magical brooms is worth a few thousand ooh's and ahh's."*

The Beacon Theater in New York was even more exciting. While we were setting up the stage, I walked out into the lobby to check out the crowd. As I looked around, I noticed the beautiful walls and old Art Deco mirrors. Then my eyes moved slowly toward the bar, where I saw a man who looked familiar to me.

Is that...? I wondered. *No, it can't be.* I stared and stared. *If it was, the people would be asking for his autograph.* I kept staring as he moved to pour a Budweiser into a tall glass. The bartender smiled and leaned over to whisper something to him.

It is him! I can't believe it! Why isn't anyone bothering him? I decided I would make a move. *If it's not him, then whoever it is will be thrilled that I mistook him for a famous actor. If it is him, I hope I can speak without stuttering. Hmmm, what should I say?*

I finally got the nerve to approach him. "Hi, Mr. Newman."

Paul Newman's blue eyes looked up at me, "Yes?"

I sighed with relief. "I'm Diane Dupuy from Famous PEOPLE Players. I'm honoured that you've come to see our show."

"I am too." He smiled that same gorgeous smile that has lit up movie screens for decades all over the world. "Have you seen my friend, Hotchner?"

"Um, no, I haven't," I said, slightly off-guard because I hadn't expected A.E. Hotchner to be there either. Hotchner was Newman's business partner and the author of Ernest Hemingway's biography, *Papa Hemingway.*

"There he is." He waved at another man who was entering the doorway.

"Did you get your cheque?" Hotchner asked me.

"Cheque?" I questioned him.

"From Newman's Own—$10,000." (When we got home, I received the cheque he was referring to and put it in a trust account for our future.)

Before I could respond, the lights were blinking. It was five minutes until curtain. "Quick, follow me," I said.

I took Paul Newman and Hotchner backstage. *The company is going to die*, I thought. When Paul walked across the stage under the black light his teeth and hair glowed. The performers appeared from the darkness and came over to meet him.

"Oh my God!" Benny yelled. "It's alive! It's not a puppet!"

"I came by tonight to congratulate all of you on your success. I'm very proud of you," Paul Newman said. "Unfortunately, I can't stay for the show."

"Aw," everyone said at the same time.

After he shook hands with the performers, I started to escort him out front. As I opened the door I mouthed to the stage manager, "Hit the tape."

The music started and the curtain went up. As Paul was walking up the aisle to leave the theatre, I asked him to just turn around and look for a second.

The music of "A Little Like Magic" played and our logo—complete with top hat, cane and gloves—glowed and danced across our velvety black stage. Paul Newman was transfixed. He took an empty seat at the back of the theatre and didn't move for the entire show. I watched him as he focused on the stage, laughing and applauding, especially when the Liberace puppet performed.

"It's as if it's really him," he turned to me during the show.

After the show, Paul, Hotchner and his wife made a mad dash backstage, almost tripping over the props in the dark. When they reached the performers, they were cheering, pleased with themselves for doing a great show and that Newman was backstage to congratulate them.

"We've got to thank you," Paul said, referring to the players "I've got the easy job—I just sign the cheques. You've got to do all the work and it's wonderful!"

"Mr. Newman," Benny said.

"Yes."

"Did you know your eyes are purple under black light?"

CHAPTER TWELVE

Buttons to Broadway

It was winter 1985. I could see the snow falling heavily outside my office window. One by one, I could hear the sound of the performers kicking the snow off their boots before they came through the door. As I walked past the row of coats to join my troupe in the lunchroom, I could tell which of my players had been in a snowball fight.

"Mrs. Dupuy," Renato had a coffee ready for me. "Greggie and I miss New York. We want to know when we're going back."

"Next year—around this time. It's going to be the biggest challenge we've ever faced—but nothing has stopped us before." I poured cream into my coffee. "What do you think Broadway will mean to us?" I asked, taking my first sip and leaning against the fridge, facing the performers.

"We'll be so good that I'll never have to work in a sheltered workshop or live in a group home," Debbie Lim said, exciting the rest of the group.

"Broadway isn't like all our other shows because you can't get any higher than Broadway. It means you're really a success and nobody can say otherwise."

"We'll be great," said Debbie Rossen. "We can show them what we can do."

"A star," said Greg. "We will be *stars*."

"Nobody can put us down anymore," added Renato.

"I'd love to be on Broadway because it will mean that eventually I could be on *The Young and The Restless*," said Darlene.

"*The Young and the Restless?*" we all laughed.

Famous PEOPLE Players has always been a company about helping individuals try out new challenges, giving members the tools to meet those challenges and encouraging them to feel proud when they succeed. I knew Broadway was going to give us a great sense of accomplishment. But, our American tour promoters, whom we hired to book various venues for us, were skeptical about us reaching our goals. We were entering unknown territory by touring the United States and the cost would be enormous. "It's going to cost a lot of money," they said. "It will be hard to raise it."

"*We'll* raise the money," I assured them.

Just the same, I worried: *How are we ever going to raise a million dollars?* My stomach started to churn. It didn't make things easier to know my own mother wasn't so sure about our possibilities to reach Broadway either. "If someone hired us…then, yes for sure. But to raise the money ourselves and go…I don't think so."

I needed some kind of guarantee from someone else, besides myself, for the times when I wasn't sure. So, I called a trusted friend, Seymour.

Seymour was enthusiastic. "That's great," he said, "but to raise a million, where do you get that kind of money?"

I started to test the waters. Actor Tom Sullivan advised me to call one of the top Broadway advertising agencies in New York. He told me to call a well-known New York art director by the name of Frank Verlizzo. "See if he can design your Broadway poster. Look at it, see how it feels. Besides, you need a good sales package if you do decide to take on the Great White Way."

I called the agency right away and asked for Frank. "I know you," he said right away. "I just watched you on CBS last night. There was a show called *A Little Like Magic*, narrated by Ann-Margret—you guys are great!"

What fate, I thought. *I can't believe it.*

He continued, "I was sitting with my friend Joe, watching the Famous PEOPLE Players on TV, and we discussed coming to Toronto to see you."

"You're kidding," I said. "I'm exploring the possibilities of bringing the group to Broadway..."

He interjected before I could finish, "We do 90 percent of all the Broadway shows, and if anyone knows what will work, we do. I'll help you get organized. First, you'll need a good general manager. All Broadway shows have general managers. Second, the budget—that's what the general manager will help you with. Third, select a theatre."

I didn't waste any time and hopped on a plane to New York. I met, for the first time, the man who would become my closest and dearest friend.

I went with Frank and his partner, Joe Logimari, to see the Lyceum Theater. As soon as we walked into the famous historical theatre, I knew. It had to be ours. I looked around at the empty stage. I was standing on the same stage where another one of my favourite actresses, Judy Holliday, once stood.

"Charles Laughton played here, along with Leslie Howard and Maurice Chevalier," Joe interrupted my thoughts.

My eyes kept scanning the theatre. I admired the rich purple seats, the crystal chandelier and the dark brown wood that lined the walls.

"Hey, Diane," I heard as an echo in the distance.

I looked out into the empty theatre. It was dark. Only the ghost lights were on, casting a dim glow throughout the theatre. I could see the outline of Emmy award-winning documentary producer Peter Rosen, who was standing at the very back of the theatre. He had stopped by to take us for lunch.

"He's the man who made the documentary that you saw on Famous PEOPLE Players," I told Frank as I waved to Peter from the stage. "We're coming down."

"Phil Donohue's office called," Peter told me. "They saw the special—loved it—and want you and the Famous PEOPLE Players on the show."

"Phil Donohue!" I screamed. "That's wonderful!"

Within a month, Famous PEOPLE Players was back in New York and getting ready to perform on Donohue. It would be the perfect time to share our big news, but I wanted the group to decide. "So, what do ya think, guys? Do we or don't we make the announcement?"

"Yes!" Everyone yelled at the same time.

Before we took the stage on *The Phil Donohue Show*, we put our heads together like a football team. "One, two, three, good show, GOOD SHOW—WE'RE GOING TO BROADWAY!"

As I sat on my stool, in front of a live audience, the handsome, silver-haired Phil Donohue entered to enthusiastic applause. All I remember about the show was the announcement we made that Famous PEOPLE Players would be coming to Broadway in 1986. I can't even remember what else we talked about. The hour went by so fast.

With Frank Verlizzo's help and advice, I knew what I had to do. I called every friend I knew in the business—I even got telephone tendinitis. Weeks into my campaign, friends of mine in television agreed to help me make a TV commercial. With the luck of the Irish (on my dad's side), Paul Newman, Jack Lemmon and Liberace agreed to make individual commercials to help us encourage people to come and see the show in Toronto. Each of them was dressed in a black turtleneck, and looking into the camera said, "Do you want to see something wonderful? Something so wonderful that you have to see it to understand it?" Then a two-second flash of black-light artistry was shown, followed by them saying, "*A Little Like Magic*—the Famous PEOPLE Players—like nothing you've ever seen before."

We had to start planning south of the border too. So, on Frank's and Joe's recommendation, we hired Maria DiDia as our company manager for Broadway. "You have eight months to raise $1 million," she said firmly.

389

The race was on and all of us searched for creative ways to meet our target. Our friends Maureen McTeer and Joe Clark agreed to help. "We'll do another gala in Ottawa and one in Toronto to help raise the money, perhaps as much as $50,000 to help you go to Broadway."

Even the players were prepared to sacrifice a little to reach our goal. "I'm giving up cigarettes and putting my smoke money in this empty paint can," said Renato. "Anyone who touches it is dead." Other players joined in by throwing in their loose change.

The rest of the funds would come from what we did best—performing. We booked a special Canadian tour to start in Newfoundland and work its way right across Canada. The money we raised from the performances would go directly toward our Broadway campaign. What was just as important about this tour was that it would also give us a chance to work out the kinks before our Broadway appearance. The show had to be DYNAMIC!

I started shaping it by getting the very best numbers from our performances over the years. I knew I was going to include *The Sorcerer's Apprentice*. The critics who reviewed our Radio City gig loved it.

My mind was in full gear. The program would also feature our trademark numbers—Liberace, Elvis, Streisand, Stevie Wonder and Michael Jackson. To close off the show, we'd use a medley of famous Broadway tunes, opening with "That's Entertainment." We'd follow with numbers like "42nd Street," "The Night They Invented Champagne" from *Gigi* and the Can-can. And we'd wow the audience by recreating Streisand in *Funny Girl* when she entered the scene on a tugboat and passed the Statue of Liberty. The show was going to close with a white-light number, using the life-size character of James Cagney, who would sing "Give My Regards to Broadway." The great Cal Dodd volunteered his time and talent to record the song.

Mom got her team designing and building the sets. The Statue of Liberty would be 18 feet tall with a torch that would light up. The props were going to take on a life of their own. In fact, they would look so real that the audience would think we had uprooted them from their original spot to bring them on stage.

I put my best friend, Judi Schwartz, in charge of the Broadway funds. She was just the right person to handle this vital role—she was continually reminding me that we had operational costs to cover. So we now had to think of another fundraising project to achieve our goal.

"I've got a great idea," Benny said. "See this button I'm wearing of the Maple Leafs? Let's get buttons with a picture of our logo on it and sell them for a dollar."

I liked the idea and ordered one million buttons. I had no idea what a million buttons looked like until I saw the boxes coming off a delivery truck.

To get us motivated about our new fundraising project, Mom made a giant thermometer and Sandra coloured it as the money came in. "How much today?" Greggie said as he waited for the mail to be opened days into our campaign.

"Twenty-five dollars," I said.

Sandra took her red magic marker and coloured another notch in the thermometer. "I do it myself," she said.

We took our boxes of buttons with us to the airport to check in with our luggage while touring. Before our flight to Newfoundland, as one of the performers reached out toward the conveyor belt to grab a box of buttons, it sparked the curiosity of a woman in line behind him.

"What's that?" she asked.

"They're buttons for us to go to Broadway," Benny said. "Do you want to buy one?" He walked toward her.

She reached in her purse and gave two dollars for two buttons.

"Way to go!" Renato screamed.

Other passengers started to join in the excitement. Even the ticket agent pulled out a dollar and pinned on a button. At the gate, we were notified that our flight was delayed, so we continued our button sale. One passenger stood on a chair and shouted, "Hey everyone, do you know who these people are?! They're the Famous PEOPLE Players and they're one hell of a good group who deserves our support!"

"Don't be shy, Diane, go sell those buttons!" the passenger told me.

Even the flight attendant sold 60 buttons on the plane. And during our layover in Halifax, we sold hundreds more, especially to those guys who were drinking in the bar.

Newfoundland got the ball and cash rolling. When we got there, we met a truck driver who took a box of 1,500 buttons and sold them across the province. By the time we arrived in St. John's, he already had $1,500 cash. A 12-year-old boy took a bag of buttons, came back a day later —in time for our second show—and gave us $100. We were overwhelmed by the honesty and commitment. And there were other moving moments—one lady during our tour stood in the bitter cold outside the theatre and sold 150 buttons. "I didn't mind the cold," she wrote in the letter accompanying the cash she collected, "because it made me feel warm just to think how wonderful your company is. I wish you the best of luck on Broadway."

The support across the rest of Canada was the same. Everywhere—and I mean *everywhere* we went—people gave a dollar for a button.

"How many people live in Canada?" Greg asked.

"I don't know, about 21 million."

"Let's sell everyone a button—we'll make a fortune."

Even our celebrity fans took part in the button drive. Don Harron, famous for writing the musical *Anne of Green Gables* and for his Charlie Farquharson comedy routine, drafted a letter to about 5,000 people on our mailing list asking them to sell buttons. We even offered a free trip to New York as an incentive for anyone selling a box of 1,500 buttons or more.

One of our largest contributions came from the funds raised by Maureen McTeer's Ottawa gala—a whopping $50,000. Despite their former prestigious roles as the prime minister of Canada and first lady, Joe Clark and Maureen McTeer continued to be the most wonderful, unpretentious couple I had ever met, always lending a hand to our company. During the gala, for example, Maureen said to me: "Forget the big shots, the VIPs in the audience. The focus is Famous PEOPLE Players. We'll sit in the balcony." Another time during a ride in a limousine with

Joe Clark, my daughter Joanne stuck her foot in front of his face and asked, "How do you like my new shoes?" He wasn't fazed in the least.

The months flew by, the colour on the thermometer was rising, but we still had a long way to go and many tasks to complete. There were many times when I wanted to reach up and hold back the hands of the clock. Before we knew it, Dave Balinsky was shouting, "On the buses! We're on our way to the Big Apple!"

On arrival day, Maria DiDia gave each player a warm welcome as the doors to the bus opened. A wonderful woman, who had been the captain of the Rockettes at one time, threw her arms around the performers and checked us into the Wellington Hotel—our home for the next eight weeks while we performed our show, *A Little Like Magic*.

That same day, Sam Ellis introduced himself as our production manager during our performance run. Doug Gray, who had a stellar reputation as Twyla Tharp's and Harry Belafonte's stage manager, was going to assist Sam. He had a smile that would make anyone melt. "We're going to make this work," he said.

"It's raining," I said the day we moved into the Lyceum Theater.

"Oh, don't worry about the rain," Sam said. "Rain means you're gonna have a big hit."

We were already hitting some stumbling blocks and we had barely settled in. For one, the unloading of props and puppets didn't go so smoothly. Initially, the props sat in the theatre seats—waiting to be called up on stage as we worked to finish our set design.

"That looks weird," one of the New York stagehands said, referring to the seated puppets. "Like a sci-fi movie."

There were also sets to be hung, technical rehearsals to conduct and run-throughs to organize. Not to mention some tweaking here and there. "The backdrop—it needs something. It's too dull," said Maria.

Mom wasn't impressed. "Bring that set down now," she ordered. The fly bar came down and she took off the backdrop and bundled it up. "I'm out of here," she said in a huff. We watched her exit out the stage door and slam it behind her. There was a deafening silence in the theatre.

The next day, Mom returned to the theatre armed with a new backdrop. "Bring in that fly bar and hang this up now," she demanded. When the black lights came on, Mom looked at Maria and said, "There, is *that* bright enough for you?"

"It's wonderful," Maria congratulated her.

"Should be," Mom said, "I flew back to Toronto, re-painted it, and flew back today."

"Previews in two days," Greg reminded me.

I was scared. It seemed like we were off to a bad start and nothing was working quite the way I had envisioned. But I didn't let my performers see my anxiety.

Still, it was getting more difficult to contain my emotions. With each day and event, the stress was growing. As we positioned the props, for example, Mom shrieked when we placed the Statue of Liberty on stage. It was too big and wouldn't fit in the wings. Another time, during a run-through of our Broadway show, Seymour and Peter Rosen popped by, only to see mistake after mistake. Dora Doom was slowly coming out from hiding.

But if I was Dora Doom, the box office manager at the Lyceum Theater was Dick Depressed. "Tickets ain't movin'. There's a big ballgame happening—World Series —and lady, this show is no *Cats*." He was referring to the fact that the Mets had made the World Series. *Great*, I thought, *there goes the box office*. New York had baseball fever and nobody was buying tickets to our show. I can't tell you how much I hated the Mets at that moment.

I couldn't help but think that maybe I should've listened to my mother. *Maybe it wasn't a good idea to come to Broadway after all*. I was losing my enthusiasm.

It didn't help that it rained and rained and rained over the next few days. I cried and cried and cried.

"Stop it." I turned and saw Catherine McKinnon, the famous Canadian songbird, and Dorothy Spencer standing in the wings. "It doesn't matter about the tickets," Catherine said. "The important thing is that you brought the company to Broadway."

She was right—I had to regain my focus. We went into overtime and I went into overkill.

The day before the opening, Mark Goldstaub, our Broadway press agent (who also represented Shirley MacLaine), came running down the aisle. "Grab the Famous PEOPLE puppets! *The New York Times* wants a shot of them walking across Times Square!" I was hoping this was the break we needed.

Renato held Stevie. Benny—Elvis. Sandra—Liberace. We even did a double-dutch skipping act with Stevie Wonder jumping rope while a huge crowd watched. In the meantime, Maria arranged to have the exterior of the Lyceum look more appealing since it was being renovated.

But the press gig didn't have the kick I was hoping for. My heart sank when the first preview, which was by special invitation only, just managed to pull in about 75 percent capacity. "What are you complaining about?" Sam asked. "There's a World Series going on." Although the show was great, I was focused on numbers.

On October 26, opening night, it was still raining. The company was opening on Broadway, but I was ready for a psychiatric exam at Bellevue Hospital. As we all walked to the theatre hours before our performance, Benny stopped to buy an umbrella.

"Look," he pointed, "it's us—up there."

I looked up and through the rain I saw our huge poster sandwiched between *42nd Street* and *La Cage Aux Folles.*

"You know something, Diane?" said Benny. "If we bomb, it doesn't matter, because look at us—we're right up there!"

"That's us Diane," echoed Debbie.

We squeezed each other hard and the tears flowed faster and harder than the rain that drenched me to the bone. "Don't cry, Diane," Debbie Rossen put her arm in mine. "We're going to do a really great show for you tonight."

"For you, Debbie. Do it for you too," I told her.

Thanks to the World Series, the curtain rose on opening night to rows and rows of empty seats. But it didn't make a difference to the performance we were about to see. In fact, in all my years at Famous PEOPLE Players, I have never enjoyed a show so much as the one I saw that night. I laughed and I cried and I was moved. For two hours, I forgot about the empty seats and fell in love with the light.

That night, my players astounded me. And they did the same for the crowd, who gave them a standing ovation for a long 10 minutes. The house that I first saw as being half empty was now half full. And that thunderous rain outside was drowned out by the roaring applause. I raced backstage—my hands sore from clapping. "You did it! You did it!" We were jumping around like crazy people.

Liberace, who was in the crowd that night, came rushing over with tears in his eyes. "I wouldn't have missed this show for the world. I'm so proud of you!" he said, beaming. "Of all the people I've introduced over the years, you are the first who have really made a name for yourselves on your own—except for Barbra Streisand, that is." He looked at me. "Dora, there is one thing I want to say to you." Suddenly he looked very serious. "Don't tamper with success. Don't let people tell you to jazz up the show or change it. Because people will tell you that."

"Liberace," Darlene stepped forward. "We have something for Diane." She pulled a crumpled paper out of her purse. "Sandra and I wrote this together," she said. "This is our review of you, Diane." She began to read their scribbled letter:

Dear Diane,

Things are great here on Broadway. I really are having a wonderful time. So much things to do and see. Thank you for bringing me here. You are a good director. You make us learn wonderful parts and you put a great show together for Broadway. It's not black light or puppets that's important, it's everything you taught us that's important. You are a good friend. If I have a problem, you would be there when I need you. And Diane you are the nicest sweetest friend that I could ever ask for...

"My turn," Sandra took the paper from Darlene excitedly.

...But as the old saying goes, if you can't stand the heat, get out of the kitchen. Because you have given me a new life and I am not lazy any more and I don't watch soaps any more and that's what I think of you and Diane thanks for all the consideration but when the going gets tough the tough get going.

"So what do ya think about that?" Sandra laughed.

I was deeply moved. "It doesn't matter what the critics say," I told them. "It's what you've said that is the most important—and if they don't like us, we will still be a smash!"

"Uh-oh, she's crying again!" the performers all shouted.

"And another thing, kids," Lee moved in closer. "Never forget your roots—and all the people who have helped you along the way."

"We won't—I promise you that," I said, all choked up.

"Let's party!" yelled Sam.

Everyone ran to the dressing room to change. I pulled Sam into a corner, "I don't have money for a party," I told him. "I spent the money on sterling silver bookmarks from Tiffany's for the performers. I wanted them to have something they would always remember. So, I engraved the words Fighting the Odds to the End on them."

"Don't worry," he reassured me. "People owe me favours. I booked the party at a nearby restaurant and the food's on me," he smiled.

While the company went to their celebratory dinner, Maria came and took me to Frank Verlizzo's ad agency. There, Maria, Mark and I would wait for the media reviews in the evening papers, a long-standing tradition after performing on Broadway. I took a seat beside Joe Logimari and we all waited anxiously until midnight.

"Don't open any of the papers until we've got them all first," said Frank and Joe to me. They wouldn't let me in the room. I paced, scared. I prayed, "Dear God, please, I know I've asked for a lot over the years…"

"*I'll say you have,*" I could hear Him answering.

"…do it for the company," I pleaded. "It would mean so much to them."

"*And what would you do to give thanks?*"

I thought about what God was 'saying' and told him: "I promise I will never forget my roots—and when I wake up in the morning—I will thank you for letting me be me, and have this day to learn from."

"*Every single day?*"

"Every day," I promised with my hand over my heart.

"*One more thing, Diane.*"

"What's that, God?"

"*Be nice to your mother.*"

The next thing I knew, I was back in the room with Frank, Joe, Maria and Mark.

"You're a hit!" they shouted.

The *New York Times* stared me in the face. "You're a hit!" Joe hugged me.

We grabbed a cab and raced to the party across town. We walked in the door and saw the company sitting around, waiting anxiously.

I stood on a chair and held the newspapers in my hands: "WE'RE A HIT!"

I honestly don't know how the walls didn't cave in from all the jumping and screaming that seemed to last for an eternity. Renato danced all over the restaurant as Sandra danced on a table. Debbie Rossen, Greg, Debbie Lim and my mother were cheering wildly. Jeannine and Joanne were wearing New Year's Eve hats and blowing horns. I first started to read from the legendary the *New York Times*:

Here are a pair of dancing feet, a hat and hands—identifiably human but disembodied. Now the insistently pervasive music shifts to Liberace, and a very large Liberace—a caricature—pounds a piano that is also a caricature. It all emerges from the dark. There are mammoth chickens sawing fiddles to a Celtic tune, and a scenery of a desolate sort floats in as the backdrop for the enactment of The Sorcerer's Apprentice. *Now our attention is riveted by country singers and rock stars as well as animals struggling to the death to the strains of Mussorgsky.*

"Go on, go on!" everyone screamed. I caught my breath and began to read again:

Black light is the secret of this viewer-friendly, iridescent spectacle that drenches the senses in sight and sound for almost two hours...

'Magic' is clever, colourful and cute. The colours are loud and so is the music. Sometimes it feels as though you are sitting through some gigantic rock video, with the selections ranging from Saint-Saëns to Kenny Rogers by way of Cole Porter, Rodgers and Hammerstein, George M. Cohan and Stevie Wonder...Everything had a kind of Technicolor brightness...

There are times that A Little Like Magic *does seem like magic: the magic of theatre, the magic of diversion, the magic that impels one to say, "That's entertainment."*

I started to cry. "Come on, Diane, read it! Finish them!"

"Okay, okay—this one is from the *New York Daily News.*"

Watching the Famous PEOPLE Players in A Little Like Magic *at the Lyceum Theater is rather like being Alice in her first few minutes in Wonderland, when everything before her eyes seemed a hallucination.*

...the best moments are those when the black stage is filled with floating apparitions—mammoth goldfish, an ungainly, spindly-legged ballerina, a clown who ends his tightrope act wafted into space by a balloon, a stripper whose body literally disappears with every article of clothing she removes from it.

...the stage is like an artist's canvas, every corner of which tingles with delight.

"Oh wait, here's what the *Newsday* guy said," I interrupted myself.

The arts of stagecraft and puppetry merge to create a delightfully innovative and cheerful theatre experience... a precisely coordinated ballet of intricate movements.

"I want you to read Clyde Barnes from the *New York Post*," shouted Sam.

Life-size celebrity puppets are worked with uncanny skill. No praise is too high for the visual art effects of Mary C. Thornton, the lighting by Ken Billington and the dazzling expertise of the unseen performers.

"Yeah, Mary!" everyone cheered.

Mom broke down and cried. Then my voice broke. I stepped down from the chair and hugged her tight while Maria and Sam took turns reading the remaining reviews.

With these rave reviews, the box office started to pick up as the rain suddenly stopped. There were even celebrity sightings during many shows. One night, Judi and I were standing outside the theatre when a long white stretch limousine pulled up to the curb. The door opened and out came six children—and behind them, the Bee Gees! I snuck up to the balcony where they were seated in the front row seats to catch a glance at their reaction. Naturally, I was thrilled to see them laughing, applauding and whistling throughout the show—they even jumped to their feet at one point. And at the end of the show, they all came backstage to meet the performers.

Paul Newman and his lovely wife, Joanne Woodward, who were now fans, also came to the show. "You have all grown so much since the last time I saw you at the Beacon Theater," he said. The next seven weeks became the highest point of our careers.

When the run came to an end, Dick Depressed told us that although the box office had picked up because of the reviews, it wasn't enough to cover our losses. Yes, we had lost money, but really, we won because we made it that far on talent alone. And our run on Broadway helped the company in other ways too. The media attention helped to rekindle interest in our touring, even though it took two years before we made it back into the black.

In December 1986, we said goodbye to the Great White Way. As we were leaving the stage door entrance, Dick Depressed came running up to me. "I didn't want you to leave without telling you…this was the greatest show I've ever seen!" he said.

"Dick, you're slow, but you're worth waiting for," I smiled at him.

He handed me a telegram that read: "For people who move around in the dark, you turn lights on in our heads." Alan Alda.

As the bus pulled away from the theatre, the rain started up again. *This is where we came in*, I thought. We were all quiet as we drove toward 42nd Street, until Benny broke the silence.

"The stagehands, Diane, were crying," he said.

"So were Maria and Sam," Darlene added.

"I'm crying too," said Debbie Rossen.

"Me too," Debbie Lim was wiping the tears from her eyes. "But we have to leave," she continued. "Because we have to start it all over again tomorrow."

"Paging Diane Dupuy. You're wanted on the telephone." The announcement came blaring over the speaker while we were setting up the stage in the Vancouver theatre.

I raced backstage. Nearly out of breath as I ran to the front of the building, I picked up the telephone receiver that was dangling from the wall.

"Diane here."

"Hi Diane, this is the *Toronto Star* calling and I wanted to get some comments from you on Liberace's passing."

I was in shock and speechless.

"Are you there? Hello?" The reporter sounded concerned.

"Yes, I'm here," I tried to hold myself together.

"He died of AIDS," the reporter said. "What is your comment on him being gay?"

I didn't answer. Liberace had always claimed he wasn't gay—in fact, he won a libel suit against a London paper for printing he was gay. I didn't know what to say.

"Hello, are you there?" He started to sound exasperated.

"Liberace was a great artist, a great human being, a great friend. I will, as the company will, miss him dearly."

"I want to know if you knew he was gay."

"I don't concern myself with people's personal lives," I asserted. "I knew Lee as a great artist, a great entertainer —the best in the world—as a dear and loving man who gave so much to all of us at the Famous PEOPLE Players," I started to cry into the receiver.

"But Diane, he was gay. He worked with you and your company for years—surely you have something to say about all this."

"Yes I do. Lee is going to be missed. I remember the time when I got into serious trouble in Oklahoma and I didn't know what I was going to do with this particular situation. And I called him on the phone at four o'clock in the morning and he got on the next flight from Vegas and he was there for me."

"That's nice, but is there anything else?"

"Yes. I remember when he took the performers out shopping for Christmas presents for their families and I also remember how hard he worked. He worked us just as hard as he worked himself," I stopped to think for a moment. "And I remember how great he played the piano —he was a true showman. The best in the business."

"You said that."

"Sir, you have it. We loved him," I told the reporter. I hung up and cried, standing in the empty corridor with my head pressed against the telephone.

"Diane," I looked up and there stood Renato, "What's wrong?"

"I'll tell you after we finish setting up." I walked away.

As we continued to set up the stage, no one said anything. I knew the performers knew about Liberace. When they were done, I gathered them quietly in the dressing room to confirm their suspicions.

"He died, didn't he?" Renato said.

"Yes," I nodded.

Everyone began to cry, holding onto each other.

Then there was a knock on the dressing room door. Sandra opened it to reveal the security man for the theatre. "Sorry to interrupt, but the press is waiting in the Green Room. They need to see you. I can't tell them to leave. I'm sorry, but they won't go."

As soon as we walked out of the dressing room, reporters ran up to the players. "What do you think of Liberace being gay?"

The players were in shock. Before the situation got out of hand, I quickly told everyone to go back into the dressing room. Then I faced the reporters alone. "Just report that Liberace was the greatest entertainer in the world—with a heart of gold—who dedicated his life to helping others. End of story."

The hardest part of that day was convincing the players that the show must go on; that Lee would have wanted them to perform. His puppet would carry that message for him on stage that night. We decided to announce to the audience that our best friend, teacher and mentor, Liberace, had passed away.

"Ladies and gentlemen, tonight we offer our tribute to one of the greatest entertainers and finest human beings we have been honoured to know. Liberace."

The music started for the "Aruba Liberace" number. The ultraviolet light came on to reveal Liberace, sitting frozen at his piano. All of the musical notes, the candelabra and everything moved and danced around him, while Liberace sat still for the entire time and smiled at the audience. After the Liberace number, the entire show moved and flowed beautifully. Lee would have been proud.

The year is 1994 in Toronto. There's excitement filling the room as we are just a day away from fulfilling another one of our 'unreachable' dreams: the opening of the Famous PEOPLE Players Dine and Dream Theatre. Months earlier, we had toiled to turn an old dilapidated, rat-infested warehouse into a state-of-the-art theatre with a dining room that we could finally call home.

The following night, at the opening, we'd be greeting a roster of celebrities, including the Governor General of Canada, Ray Hnatyshyn, will be here tomorrow night. We were also expecting Paul Newman's representative from Newman's Own, his food products company, Phil Collins' personal assistant, and, yes, Seymour Heller.

In the midst of organizing all the last-minute preparations, I was busy meeting with a new possible member of our troupe, a young man by the name of Sean. After introductions, I took Sean around the building to meet the performers while I conducted an informal interview. "Why do you want to join the company, Sean?" I asked.

"I graduated from theatre school and I'm interested in theatre and performing," he said confidently.

"The Famous PEOPLE Players is more than just somewhere to perform—we're family here. For us, this is a real commitment," I told him firmly. "The best way to describe the Famous PEOPLE Players is like running away from home and joining the circus," I explained. "It's hard work; we set up the tent, perform, cry, laugh, tear down the tent and even clean up the elephant mess left behind."

"I don't quite follow what you mean," he looked me right in the eyes.

"Sean," I stopped him in his tracks, "if you're looking to be a star, this isn't the place for you. If you're looking for fulfillment, a place to learn life lessons, to grow, to explore the universe inside you—this is it. You'll learn a lot from all these wonderful performers who make up the Famous PEOPLE Players."

I could tell he was nervous. I kept on talking. "The position you are replacing is one of my most dedicated and trusted staff performers who also trains the performers in the company. It takes special people to work with special people. We all have a handicap, Sean, and the worst handicap is a bad attitude."

We kept walking, but we were both silent now. *I need Sean, I thought to myself. We're short-handed and it's hard to find people to work with the Famous PEOPLE Players.* I was hoping in my heart that he wouldn't walk away from this opportunity. He stopped to look at the Liberace picture hanging on the wall, taken on our opening night on Broadway—the last time we ever saw Liberace.

"He must have been someone very special," he smiled at me.

Before I could answer, Debbie Lim came running up and interrupted, "Oh hi, I'm Debbie Lim. I'll show you where to put your coat and where your locker is."

Sean started to follow her, while I watched them walk away. "That was a nice picture of Liberace," he said to her.

"Yes," she said, "he was our friend and when he died we continued to do what we do every day."

"What's that?" he asked.

"Start all over again," she said, "'cause Liberace taught us the show must go on."

As I watched Debbie introduce Sean to the other members of the company, I couldn't help but feel very proud of how much each performer had grown over time.

"These are the rules," she continued. "You can't be late for work and when we get into rehearsal you must never walk in front of a prop or you'll cause a big blackout. Got it?"

Tears started to well in my eyes. I knew Sean was in good hands, so I turned away to walk down Memory Lane, a corridor between our dining room and theatre where we hang photos of our triumphs. On the walls were my teachers, the professors who guided me during the years while I 'attended' the training camp we've come to know as Famous PEOPLE Players—the place where I learned how to forget about myself and become myself. All my life I felt like I couldn't succeed, that I was a failure. Early on, I had defeated myself by saying, "Don't bother trying— you can't do it," yet somehow I had been given some special friends throughout life to help me get through those difficult times.

"Wait, don't go!" I turned around to see Sean running toward me, almost out of breath. "Debbie is awesome and I just met Benny. Wow, we have something in common— we both love the Toronto Maple Leafs. I think I can learn a lot here," he smiled. "Look, I want to give this a shot in the dark, if you know what I mean."

I knew exactly what he meant. Besides, I grew up in the dark and my dreams came true. I became the Lone Ranger, jumping over hurdles and now ready to take another jump of faith to show Sean how dreams can come true.

ABOUT THE AUTHOR

DIANE DUPUY is founder of the Famous PEOPLE Players, which celebrated its 30-year anniversary on June 1, 2004.

Diane is also a renowned motivational speaker who has traveled the world inspiring individuals and corporations. Her extraordinary work on both artistic and humanitarian levels has garnered her many prestigious awards, including the Order of Canada. She has also received honorary degrees from several universities, including University of Toronto and University of Calgary.

Diane has recently returned from the Alliance for New Humanity conference in Puerto Rico, where her friend Dr. Deepak Chopra invited her to speak as a panellist alongside former U.S. vice-president Al Gore. Her personal story of struggle and success was featured on CBC television and made into a CBS movie of the week called *Special People*. She is the author of two best-selling books, *Dare to Dream* and *Throw Your Heart Over the Fence*. Diane has also recently published her first children's book, *The Little Girl Who Did What?!!!*

Diane is married to Bernard Dupuy and currently resides in Toronto, Ontario. They have two daughters.